Marsha Norman
A Casebook

edited by
Linda Ginter Brown

GARLAND PUBLISHING, INC.
New York & London
1996

812.54
N843Zb

Copyright © 1996 by Linda Ginter Brown
All rights reserved

Library of Congress Cataloging-in-Publication Data

Marsha Norman : a casebook / edited by Linda Ginter Brown.
        p.   cm. — (Garland reference library of the
humanities ; vol. 1750. Casebooks on modern dramatists ; vol. 19)
        Includes bibliographical references (p.   ) and index.
        ISBN 0-8153-1352-7 (acid-free paper)
        1. Norman, Marsha—Criticism and interpretation.   2. Women
and literature—United States—History—20th century.   I. Brown,
Linda Ginter.   II. Series: Garland reference library of the
humanities ; v. 1750.   III. Series: Garland reference library of the
humanities.   Casebooks on modern dramatists ; vol. 19.
PS3564.0623Z78   1996
812'.54—dc20   95–52416
                                                                CIP

Printed on acid-free, 250-year-life paper
Manufactured in the United States of America

To Kathy,
the ultimate mirror
1996

METHODIST COLLEGE LIBRARY
Fayetteville, N.C.

Contents

General Editor's Note

Marsha Norman, originally from Louisville, Kentucky, gained recognition as a playwright when in 1977 she won the American Theater Critics Association award, and later in 1983 earned the Pulitzer Prize for drama with *'night, Mother*. While these two plays have to date garnered the most attention, literary scholars and drama critics alike have come to recognize Norman as a major voice on the American stage. This collection of critical essays has been written by established critics, as well as by younger scholars, who focus on the entire range of Norman's works rather than on just the better-known plays.

The editor of this volume is Linda Ginter Brown, who is a professor in the Humanities Department at the University of Cincinnati. She received her Ph.D. from Ohio State University, where Katherine Burkman, Professor Emeritus of Drama, directed her dissertation, "Toward a More Cohesive Self: Women in the Works of Lillian Hellman and Marsha Norman." (Burkman, herself, edited a Garland Casebook on Simon Gray.) Professor Brown teaches courses in literature, professional writing, and ethics in the workplace. Her research interests include women in drama, women playwrights, and gender issues in the workplace. She is currently collaborating with a Finnish colleague to study issues of male/female communication in the workplace. Her friendship with Norman and her interviews with the playwright add a special authority to this book.

Kimball King

Preface

I well remember the first time I was introduced to Marsha Norman's
work. Approximately eleven years ago in a graduate seminar in modern drama, a fellow student suggested I read a play by a new playwright, Marsha Norman. The play was 'night, Mother, and I can still
feel the anger it evoked in me. As a mother I was outraged that
Norman's character, Jessie Cates, would consider suicide, let alone
explain her decision to Thelma, her mother. Upon a second reading,
however, I understood that the play was about triumph rather than
despair. I knew I had experienced an extraordinary work by an extraordinary playwright. Eleven years later, my view remains the same.
My classmate's prophetic pronouncement, "You just watch; someday they'll be teaching her works in the classroom," was borne out.

Norman, originally from Louisville, Kentucky, burst on the scene
in 1977 with *Getting Out*, which won the American Theater Critics
Association award, and later with the stunning success of *'night,
Mother*, for which she was awarded the Pulitzer Prize for drama in
1983. These two plays have garnered much attention. Even so, contemporary critics give Norman less attention and acclaim than she
rightly deserves. As one of America's foremost contemporary playwrights, she merits more. Unjustly criticized by some for not being
enough of a feminist, Norman plows on unwavering in her purpose:
to give everyday people, in many instances women, voices to make
sure someone, somewhere, is listening. Esteemed drama critic Robert Brustein was (and still is) so enthusiastic about her work that he
declared it difficult to remain objective in his review of *'night, Mother*
in 1983. Still, neither Norman nor her plays, with the exceptions of
Getting Out and *'night, Mother*, are enough well known. This collection, I hope, will correct this situation. Written by established critics

as well as younger scholars, these essays focus on the entire range of Norman's works rather than just the more well-known plays.

The book, for the most part, follows the chronology of Norman's career. The first essay, "The Impossibility of Getting Out: The Psychopolitics of the Family in Marsha Norman's *Getting Out*," synthesizes psychoanalytic, feminist, and existential critical frameworks to show how Norman creates a psychodrama, using both realistic and expressionistic scenes to dramatize Arlene Holsclaw's oppression within a family that parallels the institutions that bind her. In the second essay, Grace Epstein examines *Third and Oak: The Laundromat* within the context of the current debate in feminism—how to reconceptualize women's reality as diverse and multiplistic. She demonstrates that Norman has always been aware of the differences between women and has sought to articulate those differences as well as the similarities.

The next three essays focus on Norman's most well-known work, for which she won the Pulitzer Prize for drama in 1983, *'night, Mother*. One essay compares *'night, Mother* to Samuel Beckett's *Footfalls*, and the other to Lillian Hellman's *Days to Come*. John Kundert-Gibbs investigates the intimate ways in which both plays are connected by virtue of the mother/daughter relationship. Each mother/daughter pair is drawn, both physically and emotionally, to a pivotal space on stage. In *'night, Mother*, it is the door leading to Jessie's room; in *Footfalls*, it is the central connecting point on the crossing loop that May paces out in her prison-strip of light. In my essay, I compare Jessie Cates to Lillian Hellman's Cora Rodman in *Days to Come*. Fragmented and confused, both these characters search for a "missing piece." Psychically, they long for a cohesive self; food metaphors in both plays reflect that psychic search. Anne Marie Drew examines the construct of time as a motivating action of the play and concludes that Jessie cannot look forward with hope. The future holds no benevolence for her; time will not improve her situation. Thus, she embraces suicide as her way of triumphing over time.

The last group of essays examines Norman's lesser-known works (with the exception of *The Secret Garden*, an adaptation). Robert Cooperman's essay, "'I Don't Know What's Going to Happen in the Morning': Visions of the Past, Present, and Future in *The Holdup*," explores this atypical play from an evolutionary and historical perspective and focuses on a number of myths peculiar to American culture. In his essay on *Traveler in the Dark*, Scott Hinson takes current critics who point out the play's weaknesses to task. He points out that Norman's greatest achievement here is the depiction of the psychology of the narcissist and the character Sam's struggle to come to terms with his grief and guilt over his dead mother.

The remaining three essays are concerned with more recent works. Katherine H. Burkman and Claire R. Fried show how Norman reinterprets the drama of the biblical story of Sarah and Abraham through the lives of the contemporary characters. They assert that what could become a very mundane marital domestic drama becomes, instead, a play loaded with issues of the survival of the Jewish people, the nature of sacrifice, and moon worship versus sun worship. Gender and power issues are also involved. Lisa Tyler's essay on *The Secret Garden*, Norman's adaptation of Frances Hodgson Burnett's children's novel, examines the departures Norman makes from the book. The net effect of those changes focuses the plot on a man exorcising the ghost of his dead wife, rather than on the children who have been damaged by emotional neglect and who resurrect themselves and each other through their nurturing of an apparently dead garden. The final essay, "Writing the Other," looks at *Loving Daniel Boone* (first titled *D. Boone*). Marya Bednerik asserts that Norman accomplishes a number of things in this play: She reclaims history for herself and other women; she transmits her culture and its energy through reforming the oral tradition of the folktale; she heals a breach between the theater and herself and the theater and its audience; and she explicates and critiques the historic gender categories that have been produced traditionally by the binary thinking that separates the "manly man" and the "womanly woman."

In addition to the essays, the book also contains Robert Brustein's 1983 review of *'night, Mother* and my interview conducted with Ms. Norman at the Gershwin Theater in October 1993 and at Actor's Theater in Louisville, Kentucky, in March 1995 as well as my interview conducted in March 1995 after the *Trudy Blue* production.

The book concludes with an annotated bibliography that includes works up until June 1, 1993. Readers may also be interested in Stephanie Coen's article, "Marsha Norman's Triple Play," in *American Theater* 12 (92), 23–26, and Jill Dolan's article, "Personal, Political, Polemical: Feminist Approaches to Politics and Theatre," in Graham Holderness' *The Politics of Theatre and Drama* (New York: St. Martin's,

1992). Linda Kintz's work, *The Subject's Tragedy*, published by the University of Michigan Press (1992), contains an insightful chapter: "In the Shadow of the Polis: Mothers, Daughters, Marsha Norman."

In that graduate seminar so long ago, I had no inkling that I would one day write a dissertation on Norman's works, nor could I know that I would meet her or later interview her for this casebook. All of those experiences have served to solidify my view that Marsha Norman rightfully deserves a place at the forefront of contemporary American drama.

In addition to each contributor to the book, I must thank my mentor and friend, Katherine Burkman, for her encouragement and, yes, prodding when it was necessary. I must also acknowledge my debt to Kimball King, the general editor of the Garland series, for agreeing that it was time for a casebook on Norman's works, and to Phyllis Korper, senior editor at Garland, whose understanding and encouragement during some very trying personal times meant so much. The Tantleff Agency in New York City was quite helpful, furnishing scripts and other information when necessary. Jimmy Seacats, of Actors Theatre in Louisville, was especially helpful in obtaining photos for the book. Linda Buturian was an enormous help to me, contributing computer expertise, for which I am most grateful. I must also thank Richard Trigg, David Talbott, Susan Mahann, and Actor's Reportory Theater for permission to use their photos. Finally, I wish to thank Alexander Metro, production editor at Garland's Connecticut office, for his considerable assistance. I must also thank the following publishers for permission to quote from their texts: Theater Communication Group, Dramatists Play Service, Hill and Wang, and Little, Brown. I very much appreciate their help. My husband, Don, also deserves thanks for his unflagging encouragement at times when I particularly needed it. Most of all, however, I wish to thank Marsha Norman; first, for writing these plays, and second, for granting me two personal interviews at exceedingly busy times in her life. It is my fervent hope that she will continue her work in the American theater for many years to come.

Linda Ginter Brown

Chronology
Marsha Norman

1947 Born on September 21 in Louisville, Kentucky. Daughter of Billie Williams, an insurance salesman, and Bertha Williams.

1965 Graduated from Durret High School, Louisville, Kentucky. Won first prize in local literary contest for her essay "Why Do Good Men Suffer?"

1969 Received a B.A. degree in philosophy from Agnes Scott College in Decatur, Georgia. Returned to Louisville and married Michael Norman, her former English teacher.

1971 Received an M.A. degree from the University of Louisville. Took a job teaching disturbed adolescents at the Kentucky Central State Hospital.

1973 Joined the staff of the Brown School for gifted children.

1974 Divorced Michael Norman.

1976 Wrote for the *Louisville Times*, for which she created the children's supplement "The Jelly Bean Journal."

1977 *Getting Out* produced in Louisville.

1978 Received the American Theater Critics Association Prize for *Getting Out*. Recipient of the National Endowment for Arts playwright-in-residence grant at the Actors Theatre, Louisville. *Getting Out* produced in New York. *Third and Oak: The Laundromat* and *Third and Oak: The Pool Hall* produced in Louisville. *It's the Willingness* (*Visions* series) written for television. Married Dann C. Byck, Jr.

1979 Received the John Gassner New Playwrights Medallion and George Oppenheimer-Newsday Award, both for *Getting Out*. Recipient of the Rockefeller playwright-in-residence grant at the Mark Taper Forum, Los Angeles. *Third and Oak: The Laundromat* produced in New York. *Circus Valentine* and

Merry Christmas in *Holidays* produced in Louisville.

1980 Directed *Semi-Precious Things* by Terri Wagner in Louisville. *In Trouble at Fifteen* (*Skag* series) written for television. *Getting Out* published by Avon. *Third and Oak: The Laundromat* published by Dramatists Play Service.

1982 *'night, Mother* produced in Cambridge, Massachusetts.

1983 Awarded the Pulitzer Prize for drama for *'night, Mother*. *'night, Mother* produced in New York and published by Hill and Wang. *The Holdup* produced in San Francisco.

1984 *Traveler in the Dark* produced in Cambridge, Massachusetts. *'night, Mother* published by Faber.

1985 *Third and Oak: The Pool Hall* published by Dramatists Play Service. *'night, Mother* produced in London. Revised version of *Traveler in the Dark* produced in Los Angeles.

1986 Received the American Academy Award. Divorced Dann C. Byck, Jr.

1987 The novel *The Fortune Teller* published by Random House. *The Holdup* published by Dramatists Play Service. Married Tim Dykma.

1988 *Four Plays* published by Theatre Communications Group. *Sarah and Abraham* produced in Louisville. The novel *The Fortune Teller* published by Collins. *Getting Out* produced in London.

1990 *The Secret Garden,* an adaptation of the novel by Frances Hodgson Burnett, produced in Norfolk, Virginia. *Traveler in the Dark* produced in New York.

1991 *The Secret Garden* produced in New York. Received the Tony Award for best book of a musical for *The Secret Garden.*

1992 *D. Boone* produced in Louisville.

1993 Wrote the book and lyrics for the musical *The Red Shoes. The Red Shoes* produced in New York.

1995 *Trudy Blue* produced in Louisville.

Marsha Norman

The Impossibility of Getting Out

The Psychopolitics of the Family in
Marsha Norman's *Getting Out*

Gretchen Cline

Dramatizing that the personal is indeed political, Marsha Norman's play, *Getting Out*, depicts a social world that justifies the systematic violation and oppression of human beings through its most "moral" institutions: religion, medicine, education, correctional rehabilitation, and the family. Through the protagonist, Arlene Holsclaw, and her younger counterpart, Arlie, Norman presents a psychodrama that explores the complex psychological process of female socialization. While the striking contrast of young Arlie's presence on stage to the "rehabilitated" Arlene may suggest that Arlene has "settled down" and is better off, I contend, instead, that the two characters on stage must be read as two dramatic moments within one person's psychological process. Together Arlie and Arlene create a psychological continuity that reveals the horrendous price Arlene as ex-convict pays for her successful socialization: her inwardness. The psychological continuity between the staged Arlie and Arlene scenes reveals first, that the process of internalizing social norms grips the very depth of Arlene's relationship to her self and others, and second, that the family is the first and most vicious site wherein certain "emotional restrictions"[1] become instituted and regulated.

In order to reveal the psychological complexity of Arlene's socialization, I focus on Arlene's struggle to confront her past—specifically, the abuses she suffered as a child within a dysfunctional family and as a young woman in a male-dominated society. Walter Davis' groundbreaking theory of the "crypt,"[2] a term used to designate the internal structure of the unconscious, provides the basis for my analysis of Arlene's familial and subsequent social scapegoating. His model is particularly appropriate not only for reading the Arlie and Arlene scenes as a psychological continuity, but also for reading

Arlene's shame and delinquency as her psychic struggle with her own "crypt."

The crypt suggests ways in which individuals and families bracket volatile core family issues. The crypt refers to one's deep defensive response to past desires that relate to the pain, shame, and loss involved in the early process of differentiation of the self from the other. In Arlene's case, her shame and pain are extremely volatile because of the abuses she suffered during her childhood. Arlene's psychological crypt manifests itself in her outward delinquent behaviors. Her juvenile and adult delinquency can be understood as her struggle not only with her past abuse, but also—and more importantly—her attempt to come up against the familial conflicts and desires underlying her abuse in order to work through it. Thus, Arlene's delinquent behaviors (as manifested in Arlie on stage) represent her authentic struggle with the crypts of her past that contain the possibility for her "active reversal"[3] of her familial conflicts. Her process of regression, as a constitutive part of her coming to terms with her past familial abuses, involves her psychic relationship to desires and emotions surrounding the humiliation and shame she suffered as a young girl. Arlene begins the process of active reversal, leaving the audience with the possibility that she has begun an authentic process of coming to terms with her past. However, although Arlene might well be on her way to active reversal within her process of regression, Marsha Norman's insistence on symbolically portraying an integrated Arlie/Arlene at the close of the play short-circuits the expression and experience involved in Arlene's psychodrama. I ultimately argue that Norman's closure presents an idealized notion of self-overcoming through Arlene's acknowledgment of Arlie.

I interpret the juxtaposition of the concurrent Arlie and Arlene scenes as the necessary dramatic structure for Arlene's process of repression and subsequent regression. As Arlene must come to grips with her past, Norman uses Arlie's staged appearance to suggest Arlene's past desires that have played an important role in her psyche but of which she is not aware at the outset of the play. In this way we might understand Arlie as Arlene's unconscious desires. Thus, Norman creates a psychodrama, using both realistic and expressionistic scenes to dramatize Arlene's increasing movement toward confronting the desires that have shaped her past and present. Arlene's present scenes with Bennie, her mother, Carl, and Ruby inaugurate her trauma and regression. These scenes are juxtaposed with Arlie's enactment of key scenes in her past—creating a psychological continuity—that dramatize her struggle and oppression within a family that parallels the institutions that bind her. Arlene's present encounters in her new apartment create anxiety related to her internal struggle with core emotional issues of abandonment and shame.

The Arlene and Arlie scenes comment on one another and provide a multidimensional psychodrama of the expressionism of Arlene's desires and past conflicts. In this way, the audience views the key psychological events that surround her primary deprivation when she was a young girl. The staged Arlie scenes are meant to embody the psychological phenomena of Arlene's past—whether they enact defense, repression, projection, or conflicted desire. Together the scenes make up the "crypt" of Arlene's relationship to her desires. Thus, the dramatic structure of the play creates an interior dialogue through Arlene's progression into her regression. The Arlie scenes create the possibility for her regression, for they represent her unconscious awareness of the desires of her past. And in fact, repression doesn't ultimately deny desire, but exacerbates its frustrated presence within the psyche. Herein lies the double movement of repression: While initially it denies desire, ultimately it creates the possibility for a regressive impasse that can eventually free one's frustrated relationship to desire. While initially Arlene's will to "get out," to adjust to the outside world, reflects her repression of Arlie's desires and aggression, eventually it reflects her complicated process of regression. Through her regression, Arlene frees "Arlie," a symbolic representation of her frustrated anger and mourning. In this way, Arlie's and Arlene's stage presences are inextricably intertwined.

The stage directions describe Arlie as "unpredictable and incorrigible" and Arlene as "suspicious and guarded." Arlene embodies a relationship to the self that has been largely determined and restricted by social and institutionalized norms. Therefore, we might understand Arlene as an expression of subjectivity coopted and created by a social unconscious that erects institutions that deny desire, and that turn the self into a thing, an object. Arlene represents a self committed to defending against itself, forever denying a part of itself, a self free of the tension and conflicts of desire. On the other hand, Arlie embodies a relationship to the self that has been restricted and abused by familial and social relationships, a self focused on its relationship to internal conflicts and desires, of emotions underlying defenses.

Indeed, Arlene's social and familial contexts deny her delinquency as a sign both of her psychological process and of its own nihilistic operations to frustrate and deny desire. In their deliberate misreading of Arlie's delinquency, the representatives of the social institutions within which she resides circumvent the possibility of understanding Arlie's behavior as a projection of that system. Thus, rather than understand Arlie's behavior as a measure of a social system's connection and response to desire, the social institutions represented in the play instead attempt to use her as a scapegoat.

In fact, in *Getting Out,* Arlie becomes Arlene through the process of her social scapegoating. And in order for Arlene to begin to confront her familial abuse she must also confront her past social scapegoating through her conscious acknowledgment of her attempted suicide, her act of initiation into the culture: Arlene's active remembrance of Arlie's attempted suicide represents her present trauma of her denial of desires through her psychic alignment with the sexist social order. Her trauma inaugurates her "active reversal" within her process of regression. Thus, the play not only dramatizes Arlene's struggle with her "familial impasse," but also how that process is always complicated by social order committed to regulating, controlling, and preventing desire. And the most intense and invisible way the *socius* regulates desire is through sexuality.

Recognizing that most of the ruling concepts within psychoanalysis today are in need of revision, Walter Davis investigates what he believes has been overlooked as "the core disorder" of the psyche. His new theory of the psyche rests on the assumption that "we 'begin' in spontaneous vitality," an experience he calls the "*elan conatus*":

It is that original, primary affirmation and thrust toward life, the energeia of Blake's eternal delight, our joyful, sensuous, and erotic response to those bodily experiences in which our being is ecstatically affirmed by the (M)Other. Subjectivity (and/as sexuality) arises from intersubjective recognition by the (M)Other with whom we find ourselves in ecstatic communication.

The Psyche is born proper, however, when the Other assaults or rejects this vitality because it re-awakens a conflict in their Unconscious. This is the doubleness of the (M)Other: the (deliberate) frustration of what they previously encouraged. After projecting their (unconscious) desire into the relationship the Other now denies the projection.[4]

Arlie's experience with the Other, her mother and father who make her watch, supports Davis' claim that one's primary experience of humiliation is a "primary regulator of the psyche." Davis writes:

We offer ourselves fully openly to the other and it is precisely our being so extended that is found wanting. (We aren't humiliated in this or that quality or context of activity but in our pour soi.) We can only experience such a humiliation when we are fully open to the other and they seize that moment as the long-awaited chance to laugh at us. Humiliation begets two emotions: one dominant, the other a-tonal. Shame is that state of mind in which we try to bury/crypt our humiliation by changing ourselves, an activity that makes unconscious ENVY the primary regulator of the false-self system. Shame resents and envies the other's apparent superiority/solidarity.[5]

Davis theorizes that the other and the projection of the other's unconscious is the foundation of the psyche, and that the dialectical relationship between cruelty, humiliation, and envy provides the first representation of the crypt. He reads humiliation also as the source of the possibility of a dialectic present in the psyche. Arlie's extreme abuse from her parents manifests the cruelty of her primary experience of the Other. This passage also introduces the term "crypt," our defensive process of internalizing the familial and social unconscious.[6]

The crypt is paramount to the threefold connection between the individual and the familial and social unconscious, for we invent it to ensure that our desires comply—at any cost—to the "consensual validation" of the *socius*. Underlying the experience of shame (involved in the creation of the crypt) is envy. "Envy provid[es] the (unlimited) fuel that drives the engine of adaptation to the *socius*."[7]

Arlene's experience furthers Davis' theory, and implies that we need the family and social order to witness our "crypting," because the process of crypting entails our psychic investment in recreating the cruelty the Other inflicts on us. She illustrates that we need to continually recreate our initial experience of shame in order to "crypt" our way to social and familial conformity. Arlie's story about the mutilation of the frogs[8] represents the process of her early experience of separation and humiliation from an Other, and her early crypting. Her process of separation involved a structuring of her psyche around humiliation, shame, and envy. The symbolic act both of the little boy watching the fragmented frogs from the window and Arlie's participation in the destruction of the frogs reveals her own psychic split—and subsequent struggle to assert herself: On the one hand, she watches herself much like Arlene watches herself carefully while inside her apartment—she feels shame and believes that Jesus is watching her. On the other hand, she envies the Other for inflicting such cruelty and humiliation and rebels against it by a symbolic act of inflicting cruelty on the Other. Thus, her delinquency reflects her genuine struggle with her humiliation. And as a result, the delinquency is a sign of her psycho-existential relationship to her psyche; in other words, her delinquency, in the form of her aggression, is her attempt to affirm her "self," her existence in a hostile world that will not recognize her.

As the dramatic structure reveals, Arlene's struggle with familial and social crypts is complex. While Arlie's relationship to the crypt underlies her early experience of envy through her attempt to deny her familial abuse, Arlene's present relationship to the crypt underlies her experience of shame through her attempt to comply with the social unconscious. Arlene's "decrypting" is complicated: She must confront two crypts. One is represented in Arlie, wherein her defenses split her into a process of flight that at one point contains the possibility of reversal; however, the possibility of the Arlie delinquent crypt is stifled (and channeled into "rehabilitation" with the backing of religion) through her encounters with hostile and abusive "parents" everywhere, from the prison guards to the psychiatrist to priests to school principals. The second crypt she must break from is the split symbolized by Arlene, the one that aligns itself with and is perpetuated within the social institutions. Arlene exists in a world that operates on the basis of male domination, a culture that accepts and even perpetuates rape. This world, represented in microcosm in the play, complicates Arlene's trauma through social and moral institutions, specifically through her encounters with the guards of the prison. Arlie's relationship to Carl, Bennie, the priest, the principal, the doctor, and the psychiatrist, her significant contacts with the outside, ironically keep her tied to her "inner" crypt. The play dramatizes Arlene's trauma and regression precisely through her familial and social crypts that have imprisoned her psyche.

Arlene's crypting (and decrypting) is further convoluted by a world structured around "collective" social unconscious envy. All of its social prohibitions and morals focus on shame as a way of regulating both humiliation and envy. Arlene's desire for recognition in the form of her delinquency collides with a social order that uses social institutions—as crypts that deny humiliation—to give its members "parental" recognition. Arlie's envy and self-destruction are her ways of coming up against her initial experience of humiliation so that she can begin to mourn it. Yet what happens is that the world she resides in thwarts her process of regression—ironically, through the hypostatization of envy and resentment. Unfortunately, Arlie experiences a double dose of cruelty—first through her family, then through social institutions that become her "family." Although her delinquency moves her toward her crypt of the core conflicts, the prevailing social unconscious intervenes and halts the fruits of her regression. Thus, Arlie becomes a simultaneous familial and social scapegoat. Her aggression, as her struggle to overcome the humiliation and crypts of her family and *socius*, threatens the prevailing social and familial order. Arlie's crypt, as manifested in her delinquency, takes on the stakes of her world; however, her delinquency becomes an insidious repetition compulsion, a fixation that acts to cover and bury the humiliation in much the same way as the shame-producing social institutions.

We might understand Arlie's "hateful" behaviors and anger as her way of hanging onto a desire—in the form of a defense—that prevents her from "working through" her familial abuse. Yet, that "hateful" self that she develops as a defensive crypt also, concurrently, is her one possibility to confront the unfinished desires associated with it. In fact, "Arlie" saves Arlene: Arlie represents the aggression of life itself (the *elan conatus* channeled into a defensive crypt). However, Arlene denies Arlie for two reasons: (1) the social discourse within which she resides cannot acknowledge or recognize that Arlie represents Arlene's relationship to an existential awareness of life; and (2) the aggression of Arlie therefore no longer works to sustain life, but becomes diffused itself into a crystallized repetition of discharged emotion. In other words, Arlie's aggressive behavior is not recognized as her attempt to come to terms with her past; instead of representing the life of unfinished desires, Arlie's aggression operates as a moment within the oppressive institutionalized structures and discourse of which she is a part.

The creation of "Arlene" is the first step or moment of Arlene's subversion of (Arlie's) Arlene's coopted aggression. Thus, Arlene's attempt to rid herself of Arlie mirrors her motivation for creating her: It's an attempt to recapture desire and the process of becoming. But again, in her attempt to destroy Arlie, Arlene finds herself in the same bind. Arlene is merely the flip side of Arlie; rather than a manifestation of coopted desire and aggression as the site of rebellion against social institutions like Arlie, Arlene becomes a manifestation of co-opted desire and aggression as the site of conformity to social institutions. In fact, when denying her aggression repetition, Arlene denies the desires arrested in that process and, thus, the subsequent possibility for working through them. Both Arlie and Arlene align themselves with the social unconscious within their struggle with their desires. Arlene discovers that her denial of Arlie inaugurates a crisis within her, one that creates the necessary possibility of coming up against the desires that she has split from herself and denied through her murder of Arlie. Thus, her delinquency mirrors the very process it is designed to rebel against. What this implies is that a crypt embodies both the text and subtext of humiliation. Yet a crypt refers to a primary experience of humiliation and underlies a series of actions.

According to Davis, subjectivity is woven from the cloth of humiliation; thus Arlie's experience of humiliation eventually results in her attempt to change, especially through her relationship with the priest, an Other with whom Arlene tries to make good. However, her relationship to the priest merely replicates the (primary) shame of her parental relationship. In fact, I contend that the "social unconscious" becomes a crypt, the Other that regulates shame on a collective social level—and that women traditionally become the designated scapegoats of that shame. Shame and its subtext, envy, become split along gender lines within the world in which Arlie is situated: Males occupy domination, which is a manifestation of envy projected outward, while women occupy submission, which is shame. These gender polarities occupy the world both inside and outside the prison. And the priest represents the morality of this male-dominated world—the inside and outside, the manifestation of disguised resentment. In fact, the priest manifests the crypt designed to bury the resentment underlying the social unconscious—a defense created in response to a subtext. The priest must ensure the stability of the social order through pulling Arlie away from her only possibility for reparation. One of the key insights of the play (Arlie's experience) is that we project our crypts outward (as we deny and bury our desires related to shame). And the larger implication of *Getting Out* is that getting out is impossible (as Arlie tries to do through her relationship to the priest—her symbolic projection of her crypt of shame onto a social order).

Thus the play reveals that our acts of getting out represent our real neurosis, wherein we've regulated the psyche and desire by shame, envy, and religion, the crowning achievement. Arlene's picture of Jesus represents the collective social unconscious watching over her. So the social order perpetuates crypts for penance. The play reveals that "getting out" itself is false: it is our fantasy (1) that we are free from ourselves; (2) that we've successfully "crypted" our way out of despair; and (3) that morality, as an apolitical/ideological objective reality, can save us. Arlie's struggle to get out in her scene with the priest reflects her act of bad faith designed to bury her psychic relationship to herself. And, as she finds out, the guarantee she was promised, and with which deceived herself, is false.

When Arlie's weekly visits to the priest begin, so, too, does her symbolic institutionalized scapegoating. Her visits reveal the symbolic manifestation of the social unconscious; on the surface they illustrate the way that social institutions operate to ensure the psychic stability of individuals and therefore the "good" of everyone. Her scapegoating neutralizes the competing tension of desire within the *socius*; thus her scapegoating manifests part of the social unconscious' crypt that is designed to ensure gender polarities. What is particularly important about Arlie's relationship to the priest is the power it has over her "socialization" process. Norman suggests that the church is one of the most obvious yet insidious regulators of desire. Not only does religion augment the regulation of individual desire through the social discourse, it relates to the individual's deepest desire to be recognized.

Arlie's relationship to the priest operates on several levels. On the one hand, it illustrates her process of regression: He represents her attempt to make good the past by relating to a "father" that might possibly recognize her—this time. But she eventually discovers his recognition is not without a price. He ensures that she relates to herself through humiliation. Thus, Arlie can only get the recognition she craves if she buries her impetus for "active reversal"; in this case, her delinquency. Although it is true that her delinquency ultimately represents a crypt, a repetition compulsion that works against her active reversal, her further denial of it through the social unconscious via her relationship to the priest is not an authentic solution to her familial crypt either. In fact, her newly found "father" further denies her familial crypt, offering her a coopted "false self" that refuses desires altogether, especially those surrounding her past losses and core family issues. As a result, she literally tries to obliterate that part of herself.

Arlene's prostitution represents another manifestation of her crypt designed to deny her relationship to her parents. It underlies her father's abuse and her mother's subsequent neglect. The trauma was painful enough that she defends against it by taking the whole experience into herself in order to master it (the outside is too threatening and unsafe as the persecutory object attempts to invade her inner world). We might think of her incest as a fixed state of rape buried inside her. Therefore, she directs a large amount of psychic energy toward the control of the internalized bad relationship.[9] Her prostitution reflects the internalized bad relationship "possessing" her. Thus, she behaves as if possessed by the experience. But her prostitution represents a role reversal; this time she is in control, so to speak. Through her prostitution, Arlie takes charge of her body and, more importantly, the Others'. Her prostitution represents her attempt to reverse the power her "bad" relationship has over her. Hence, the crypt operates for a long time as her symbolic fixation on her incest—albeit a displaced fixation, an introjected experience. While her connection to Carl certainly reflects her abusive relationship to her real father, insofar as Carl's pimping manifests a confusing and abusive form of protection, it ultimately reflects her arrested attempt to confront the abuses of her past—in particular, the abuses she suffered from her father. Even though Arlie takes control of men through her prostitution, Carl dominates her through his role as a pseudoprotector. Thus her relationship to him actually parallels the submissive role she played earlier within her relationship to her father. Ultimately, Arlene vaguely senses that her prostitution becomes a repetition compulsion to deny what it initially contained the possibility for her to confront: the pain and subsequent mourning associated with her familial violence. Arlene's crypt is further complicated by the environment within which she is situated.

Arlene becomes a public scapegoat because her psychological crypts collide with the social order within which they reside. The social order of *Getting Out* operates on the basis of male domination. From her father to Carl to Bennie to the priest (and basically every male she meets), Arlene/Arlie is subjugated by men. And the politics of this subjugation is affirmed through the social and moral order, from correctional institutions to the church. Arlene enters a world not only built on denying desire and uplifting envy and shame, but also manifesting the subjugation of women through sexuality, specifically through rape.

As I mentioned above, for Davis, domination arises from a psyche whose structure is based on humiliation. From humiliation springs shame and envy; shame is the experience of burying the humiliation so that one can achieve at long last familial or social recognition. As a result of one's crypting, envy arises. The split of emotions often aroused by humiliation becomes polarized. Social institutions not only ensure the split, but also respond to the split; as institutions are originally created in the service of shame, they unconsciously work in the service of envy (precisely because shame is the outward manifestation of envy). The relationship between shame and envy mirrors the process of repression: Because one must deny and bury aggression in order to create shame, one produces envy, the subtext of shame that is based on a lack of recognition. Envy arises from one's innermost desire to possess the object that denies one's experience, but that is needed for a sense of recognition, a sense of self. Thus, one might understand social institutions as part of a collective process of repression.

The culture within which Arlie resides assigns envy and shame to social institutions often based on gender: Men most often represent domination, and women, submission. Male domination embodies envy, while female passivity embodies shame. And the phenomenon of rape that Arlie encounters in almost all of her male relationships is the crowning achievement of envy. The priest, therefore, commits a metaphorical rape, and more importantly, this rape is a reliving of the rape she suffered as a young child by her father. Arlene's psychological rape represents her symbolic scapegoating, which upholds male domination and resentment. The ultimate manifestation of this kind of psycho-social-sexual oppression occurs when the priest performs a symbolic psychological rape on Arlie. The social and moral significance of the scene lies in the way Arlie must internalize her oppression through a crypt of shame. Moreover, she must symbolically learn how to rape herself in order to adequately exorcise her "hateful" self. And her symbolic action that manifests her shame and internalized oppression (within the social order) is her self-mutilation, her stabbing of herself with the fork. *Getting Out* reveals that the key to scapegoating lies in the individual's internalizing of self-loathing and abnegation; scapegoating is not a matter of what the Other does to one, but rather how the self internalizes the need for recognition from the Other.

After Arlene kills her "hateful" self—further burying her crypt— her emotions and actions are controlled and depressed. She moves stiffly and slowly in her apartment when others come to see her. She develops a cool reserve. She becomes the kind of woman that the culture needs to ensure its values. Arlene's arrival at her new apartment with Bennie not only reveals her relationship to her family and her familial unconscious; it also reveals her relationship to another manifestation of her social unconscious: her interactions with and treatment by the prison guards. And Bennie, her escort to the outside, represents her most important connection to her institutionalized scapegoating: institutionalized rape. His presence is symbolic of the treatment she encounters by every guard during her prison sentence. At one point Warden Evans explains, "Most of these girls are mostly nice people, go along with things. She needs a cage"

(37). Evans refers to Arlene in this passage, suggesting that if a woman doesn't comply, she should be shut in a cage. Earlier, he himself has defined exactly what "going along with things" means: Do what he or any man says to do, and most importantly, be treated as an object of men's pleasure. Both he and Bennie reveal their sexist attitudes in response to Arlie (37). Both treat Arlie like an animal. Evans treats her with cruelty and Bennie treats her like his possession. Both exert their male power over her, placing her in a position so that their domination always plays a role in every interaction.

Evans' hostility and terrorism through his "mind rape" of Arlie (14) symbolically ensures gender polarities of male domination and female submission. Similarly, the doctor oppresses Arlie through his injections, meant to silence her. Verbal abuse and mental rape constitute her treatment by the guards. And they silence her through medicine: She is injected by the "correctional" doctor when she eventually lashes out. The significant point about male domination, then, is that its deep psychic payoff affects everyone, including women in a culture where envy and shame regulate psychic desire, subjectivity, and interaction.

Male domination thus hypostatizes envy at the same time it comes to represent independence, self-sufficiency, and control. And this is certainly true of both the correctional institution and the religion Arlie encounters. Arlene's prison sentence is symbolic of her position within the politics of a male-dominated culture. She must (1) split herself and become like a man, or (2) split herself so that she becomes the accepted woman in her social order. For a woman must become a man or she must in some way function domestically. She can cook or be raped; otherwise, she will be considered crazy if she attempts to reverse or break from her oppression.

Arlene's relationship to Bennie represents her connection to both the familial and social unconscious of her male-dominated world. Significantly, Bennie is the guard who drives Arlene home—to the outside. He continually reminds her that she was wild, that she needs his help (8). He refers to her as a girl, a helpless child, who when left to her own devices, will end up in trouble. Bennie's attitude toward Arlene represents her relationship to life "outside" prison, to a moral and properly rehabilitated life that assumes that women are either wild or helpless. Yet his treatment of Arlene characterizes the prevailing sexist attitudes of life on the outside. He assumes that just because he takes her home, he can exert his sexuality over her. In fact, he doesn't even bother asking her if he can stay with her. Nor does he tell her of his plans to take care of her.

Just prior to his getting food for them, he tells her that she needs to eat: "You'll feel better soon's you git somethin' on your stomach. Like I always said, 'Can't plow less'n you feed the mule'" (12). His lines reflect his sexist attitude toward women—they're yours if you feed 'em. They also foreshadow his attempted rape of Arlene after they eat—he feeds her and then demands that she give him something in return. Furthermore, his behavior represents the privilege given to men on the outside. When Arlene notices the bars on her apartment window, he reminds her that they are meant to keep burglars and other undesirables out. In contrast, Arlene feels that they bind her. Arlene poignantly responds to Bennie's exclamation that "You'll get to like me now we're out" with "You . . . was always out" (12).

Perhaps the most blatant connection to the sexism that exists on the outside is Bennie's treatment of her in prison. He treats her like an animal when he bribes her with the Juicy Fruit gum (37). Significantly, Bennie wants to run a hardware store where he deals in nails—a direct connection to the picture of Jesus and Arlene's relationship with the priest. Just as the priest regulates the law of the Lord, Bennie bears the tools connected to the process of regulating prohibition—the self-sacrifice of women.

Bennie's sexism also manifests itself in his attempted rape of Arlene. The significant point Bennie reveals when he almost rapes Arlene is that he is privileged not to know that, indeed, his actions constitute rape. His lack of awareness reflects Susan Griffin's insights about male privilege in a culture that fosters rape:

But though rape and the fear of rape are a daily part of every woman's consciousness, the subject is rarely discussed by an official staff of male intellectuals (who write books which study seemingly every other form of male activity) that one begins to suspect a conspiracy of silence. And indeed, the obscurity of rape in print exists in marked contrast to the frequency of rape in reality, for forcible rape is the most frequently committed violent crime in America today.[10]

This same lack of awareness is reflected in the warden's attitude to Arlie when she questions him about getting out of solitary confinement (p. 38). Neither Bennie nor the warden sees that women are already in lockup. Bennie doesn't question his actions because he holds the sexist belief that what he thinks is good for him is good for Arlene. In fact, the only reason he stops raping her is that he thinks about his own image. He's more worried about being called a rapist than he is about Arlene's needs or feelings. Believing in the myth of the rapist as a monstrous criminal, a myth that Griffin believes permeates this culture, Bennie does not see that his actions constitute rape.

The fact that Bennie gets "turned on" when Arlene threatens to kill him illustrates his double standard: It's OK to rape a bad girl (Arlie) because she deserves what she gets. And as he reveals in his brief interaction with Arlene, he regarded his wife, Dorrie, as a good girl:

Wish I had a kid. Life ain't, well, complete without no kids to play ball with an take fishin'. Dorrie, though, she has them backaches an that neuralgia, day I married her to the day she died. Good woman though. No drinkin', no card playin', real sweet voice . . . what was that song she used to sing? (29)

It is only when Arlene brings up Dorrie's name during the attempted rape that Bennie begins to listen. Ironically, his actions to protect Arlene—driving her home, getting her meals, worrying about her safety—reveal that his form of chivalry to protect her against other men also grants him the privilege to rape her. Griffin's passage suggests the double standard:

In the system of chivalry, men protect women against men. This is not unlike the protection relationship which the mafia established with small business in the early part of this century. Indeed, chivalry is an age-old protection racket which depends for its existence on rape.[11]

It's interesting that Arlene remembers Arlie, in this scene when she quietly says that "Arlie coulda killed you" (33). Her words reveal that Arlie is more in touch with her own aggression and past abuse and pain than Arlene. Arlene has "quieted down."

Similarly, Arlie's encounters with the doctor reveal the hostility and sexism of her world. Instead of consoling or comforting
her, the doctor treats her like she's a crazy criminal, accusing her
like the warden in her prison. He patronizes her when he tells her
that "you could learn if you wanted to" (22). At the end of one of
her sessions, he hostilely tells her to stand up straight and take off
her hat. Likewise, the principal at school reprimands her, telling
her that she's not normal: "You've worked hard for this, well they're
used to your type over there. They'll know exactly what to do with
you" (18). Everyone keeps telling her what she is like—from Bennie,
to the principal, to Carl, to the wardens, to the loudspeakers, to
her mother. Indeed, they have created an identity for her, an identity that leaves no room for threatening desires like aggression or
fear; instead, they use her to project and deny their own aggression
and fear. Arlene has not been given any space to even begin to
confront—let alone work through—the abuses she has suffered;
that is, until she comes home.

The social institutions that Arlene encounters ensure that hostility and violence stay in place. And as I mentioned above, the sexism of Arlene's world manifests itself in a necessary gender split that
secures the violence through male domination. The morality of the
rehabilitated and healthy person arrests successful working through
of aggressive impulses through structures that deny them. In fact,
the morality of Arlene's world operates to arrest subjectivity as a
"process of becoming" and instead institutes it as a static relationship between self-as-ego and Other. In this way it promotes a gender
split wherein women are always relegated to the status of Other.
When aggression is denied at the deepest psychological levels, it will
find its way in the familial and social unconscious environments
(crypts) that refused it. Thus, sexism in part arises from aggression
channelled in polarized relationships between a healthy ego and the
Other.

Sexism—as a reflection of the social unconscious to deny desire—reflects an arrested state of aggression and pain necessary for
creative working through and intersubjective relating. I'm not suggesting that sexism arises from a man's frustrated and/or repressed
sexual desires—that somehow society forces men to repress their

overly strong sexual instincts or that men's desires are greater than women's. This argument has been used to explain and justify rape, and the gender polarity and split, without also addressing the deeper psychological, political, and philosophical implications for a situated—interfamilial and social—subject. What I am suggesting is that when spontaneous aggression associated with the child's process of apprehending external reality is thwarted for some reason, by the familial or social unconscious, the child will inevitably project aggression outward and remain arrested in an angry repetition compulsion to discharge. This cycle will, in turn, find its way back into the *socius* and the family. Furthermore, when the frustrated aggression gets thrust back into intra/interfamilial and social relationships, projected aggression is managed through a gender split wherein men dominate, regulating the "healthy ego," and women become the "Other-prone-to-hysteria." Thus, the child's desires and aggressive impulses get channelled into "acceptable" and "unacceptable" outlets. In Arlene's world, aggression, specifically sexual aggression, is clearly reserved for men. Ironically, Arlie's hysteria—once when they took Joey away and again when she was forced to take her soul away—reflects the process of her frustrated and oppressed desires and aggression.

Although Arlene gets stuck in aggression for a while and although she complies with the social Unconscious through her denial, she eventually confronts the aggression she's tried to bury and deny. She does this through her reliving of her self-mutilating aggression—a form her idealization of the social defensive crypt internalized. She relives the memory of her self-mutilation, but this time for another purpose: Rather than further denying her desires through a social unconscious, she recovers Arlie and the aggression surrounding her deprivation. Thus, her current trauma reflects her attempt to recover and transform Arlie from both her familial and social unconscious.

Just after her mother leaves her apartment, as Arlene talks to herself about Arlie and her anger toward her mother, Arlie appears on stage chasing Ronnie, a fellow juvenile offender. The juxtaposing of the present and the past is significant here, for Arlene's conscious anger toward her mother parallels her anger toward Ronnie; both Ronnie and her mother harass her (p. 25). Together the two scenes suggest that Arlene feels that her mother's competitive comments just took something away from her. Arlie is angry at a boy; her anger at him parallels Arlene's immediate anger at her mother. During this scene, Ronnie drops the necklace down his pants and tells Arlie to "Jus' reach right in" (25). His proposition is reminiscent of Arlie's father raping her. Ronnie represents the surfacing of her enraged anger toward her father.

The two scenes—the present and the past—suggest the multi-layered dimension to her issues and desires, depicting Arlene's struggle between aggression and sexual domination. When Arlene is angry at her mother and feels aggression toward her, Arlie appears with Ronnie using his advantage over her (he knows the doctor will believe him) to overpower her with a sexual advance. When Ronnie tells Arlie that she's "gonna fall in love," Norman suggests the basis of Arlie's relationship to her father: The way she got his love was by her hand in his pants. Her father took sex from her as Ronnie takes the necklace, and thereby defines the terms of his love. Furthermore, Ronnie represents Arlene's relationship to all the men in her life. She learns that the way to get men's love—beginning with her father—is only on their exploitative terms. She has to be a player in their dominant-submissive game to get any shred of affection. While consciously Arlene is angry at her mother, unconsciously her anger toward her mother involves her father and the site of her early abuse and deprivation. Although her father never appears on stage, his presence looms in Arlene's psyche. Thus, Arlene's anger toward her mother and her mother's defensive accusations of her reveal not only her mother's hidden competition with her, but also Arlene's anger and pain over her abuse. The two scenes significantly suggest that our emotions always relate to the confused, convoluted, and conflicted desires that bracket our entire family crypt.

Arlene's interaction with her mother taps into buried issues about Arlene's past, and we see these issues surface primarily through the staged Arlie scenes. While her family and the outside world thrust their unconscious humiliation on her—that is, while they attempt to mold her psyche through cruelty, humiliation, and oppression—she struggles to free her desires from their stifling hold. Indeed, her aggression and delinquent behavior are a sign, however ultimately futile, of her movement toward active reversal. While her delinquency comes to represent one crypt or monstrous repetition compulsion, Arlene's homecoming and subsequent breakdown, in conjunction with her acknowledgment of Arlie and her symbolic burning of Carl's and Bennie's phone numbers, represent her process of "getting out" of at least one layer of the defensive crypt of her past. But her actions raise an unsettling question: Can one sustain "active reversal" in the midst of the hostile social and familial circumstances that have defined one's desires? Although Norman's last scene reflects her answer—a resounding "yes"—I find how she arrives at that "yes" problematic.

Although it is possible to see Arlene's homecoming as part of her psychological good faith, we must not be seduced by the last scene, the integration of the past Arlie scenes with the present Arlene scenes. In this scene, Arlene alone listens to and remembers with Arlie her past (p. 56). As Arlene puts away her food, Arlie appears on stage and directly addresses Arlene, illustrating the merging of Arlene and Arlie, the unconscious meeting the conscious for a moment. This is the first and only time we see Arlie smile and laugh about her past. Arlene acknowledges Arlie when she says, "Aw shoot," as if to suggest that she (Arlie) isn't so bad after all, endearing herself to her. This last passage also significantly connects Arlie and Arlene to her mother. The memory illustrates Arlene's acknowledgment that her mother has played a significant role in past abuse. It also suggests that Arlene realizes that we are locked into certain psychological issues all of our lives, much as we are locked into a social and ideological system that may or may not acknowledge us, and indeed may abuse us. Her acknowledgment of being locked in her mother's closet suggests how much her family will always be with her. The symbolic image of being locked in the closet also suggests her being locked in a culture, a world that will not recognize her.

However, I contend that this final scene ultimately defies the crucial connection between Arlene's relationships to her family and to society that the playwright has constructed via Arlene's psyche throughout. Although we witness Arlene's awareness of her hidden aggression, the last scene depicts an Arlene who is not much different from the Arlene the representatives of the institutions created and abused. Arlene seems satisfied with her new apartment and her new goals—a job that puts her below the poverty line and the remote possibility that she will obtain custody of Joey. She may get the dish-washing job if she's lucky and begin her new sentence on the outside—but this time she's not guaranteed her next meal.

I have argued that Arlene is on the way to active reversal primarily because she has broken down—undergoing the necessary trauma to inaugurate it—and in the process has confronted some of the pain associated with her past. In particular, she has faced the loss of her attachment to the priest (her symbolic father) who, as a representative of the male-dominated *socius*, has defined her and given her a strong model of ideal behavior to follow. Throughout her life she has been defined by and abused by men—the priest is no different. I have shown how her connection with him was also predicated upon a rape, a metaphorical rape that split her psyche when she stabbed herself with a fork to stamp out her "hateful" Arlie self. Norman suggests with these scenes that the male-dominated culture within which Arlene lives has not only defined Arlene, but also shaped her life in devastating ways. The men Arlene encounters (including the women who comply with them such as Doris or Ruby) attempt to define her and arrest her subjectivity in gender specific terms so that she will remain powerless, passive, and persecuted. The moment she relives her trauma at home, Arlene begins a process of coming to terms with, at least, what happened to her in prison when the priest left her. However much she may remember or acknowledge Arlie, Arlene's memory at the close of the play affirms not an act of complete reversal, but a split and compromised Arlene.

Indeed, Norman beautifully reveals all the ways that Arlie and Arlene have been mutilated by her family and *socius*. In her analysis she unleashes anger, horror, terror, pain, shame, humiliation, fear, and envy—mainly through Arlie, Arlene's unconscious. In this progression of the drama, Norman captures the dialectical movement of Arlene's psyche through the dramatic structure. Norman opens the dramatic possibility of delivering what drama is most capable of being: an expressive and emotional medium wherein the audience's unconscious may itself be tapped. Yet the audience in this drama parallels Ruby as she witnesses Arlene's breakdown: Just as the strong and stoic Ruby tells Arlene that she "can still love people that's gone" (54), the audience can rest assured that they won't be asked to be emotionally uncomfortable. Ruby's line is the point at which the drama halts the dialectical process that Norman has been able to sustain thus far. The drama is, perhaps, taken over by Norman's unconscious defenses. Through Ruby, Norman implies an idealized individualism. In fact, one could argue that Arlene's memory of her mother's closet is not only Arlene's defensive rationalization for her awful circumstances now out of prison, but also the playwright's defensive rationalization for a hopeful ending. It's easier to have the protagonist smile at her unconscious "demons" than leave her broken down as they surface. In order for the idealistic individualism to work, Norman must split the rich psychological and sociopolitical connections that she has developed throughout the course of the play. Norman does not sustain the dialectical dramatization of her protagonist at the close of the play. Her dialectical vision stops at the door of individualism, where she converts complex psychodrama to normative idealism.

In particular, this idealism manifests itself in two disguises: Ruby's assurance and Arlene's integrated psyche. The idealistic vision that informs the play's closure not only lets the audience off the hook, it also reinforces a psychology based on a reductive subjectivity that hypostatizes the individual and the group as discrete categories. An "ego" psychology that splits the psyche from the complex forces that have created it within the guise of individualism undermines the rich psycho-social-familial connections the drama has the power to express. Thus, Norman assures the audience that they can go home with an untouched unconscious, however touched they might be by Arlene's narrative.

Norman's approach to the closure of Arlene's predicament shifts from one that she has developed throughout her dramatization of Arlene's psychological processes and conflicts. Throughout most of the drama, Norman's dramatization of Arlene's psychological processes suggests that her subjectivity is neither wholly ideologically constituted nor biologically or familially determined; she explores the multilayered forces that create a psyche in process. In this sense, Norman has developed her own dialectical psychodramatic method, exploring Arlene's psyche dialectically and psychodynamically. Yet however much the play discloses the complex dialectical processes of the psyche, its ending reflects a reductive linear approach to Arlene's psyche. The closing scene reifies the individual against the outside institutional pressures that have defined her. We are asked in this scene to forget the richness and complexity dramatized throughout and be assured that Arlene is now "integrated." We are asked to forget the pain and horror of Arlie's and Arlene's compromised "self" and believe that Arlene-the-individual will be all right because her psychological awareness is immune from the outside. We are asked to trade in an experience of Arlene as painfully complex for the smile of an individual against all odds. But most insidious of all, we are asked to do what we desperately need to do to feed our defenses: simplify our awareness of the dialectical process of our desires and choose between a dualism: the psychology of the strong, adapted ego of the individual versus the power of the *socius*. Norman has chosen the adapted ego for us.

However much the playwright seems to have arrested the rich psychosocial connections for her protagonist with the ending, she has opened the issue of closure in general. The drama reveals that closure is antithetical to the dialectical approach I have used to analyze Arlene's psyche. However, a dialectical method allows one to keep the inquiry open. That is, one can read against Norman's closure and still raise the following questions: What does Arlene's memory of the young Arlie mean for a situated subject? Who is Arlene at the close of the play—and what does her attachment to Ruby suggest? How does one sustain or suggest the dialectical expression of desire, defenses, and regression without reducing it to a limited subjectivity? How does one dramatize a subjectivity that entails a process of becoming through the continual recognition of one's paradoxical relationship to desire? Dialectic thus helps us see the way in which, in spite of Norman's closure, *Getting Out* does suggest that we are defined by the losses of a past that was never fully ours and that we can never reclaim, but that we must somehow nevertheless reckon with. Thus, despite Norman's closure, Arlene's process suggests that we live a relationship to loss through our active recognition of the past within the social, political, and familial present.

Notes

1.   See Mark Poster, *Critical Theory of the Family* (New York: Continuum, 1978). Although Poster doesn't specifically define "emotional restrictions," he uses the phrase to suggest various ways that sociopolitical contexts restrict and condition individuals' emotional responses while instituting certain needs, behaviors, and values within the family.

2. See Walter Davis, *Get the Guests: The Play of Aggression in Modern American Drama* (Madison: U of Wisconsin P, 1994).

3. See Walter Davis, *Inwardness and Existence: Subjectivity in/and Hegel, Heidegger, Marx, and Freud* (Madison: U of Wisconsin P, 1989), 263. Davis defines active reversal thus: "Active reversal is not an Umkehre or an unraveling of the psyche, but the process of trying to liberate something that has been consistently at work throughout our life. While the 'developed' forms desire takes assume from one perspective the monstrous proportions of a repetition compulsion, from another angle they reveal a flawed history of attempted mediations that contain, even if under the sign of defeat, the scars of possibilities well worth recovering. Each episode in which the psyche suffered genuine defeat was necessarily one in which it was also engaged in some significant effort to emerge from its prison." Although we might allude to Arlie's delinquency as a sign of her psyche suffering defeat insofar as it attains the "monstrous proportions of a repetition compulsion," it nevertheless also is a sign that she was genuinely struggling with the desires produced within her familial abuse.

4. Walter Davis, "Beyond Reparation: Art's Continuing Challenge to Psychoanalytic Theory" (paper presented at the American Psychological Association convention, Division 39, Chicago, April 1991), 5.

5. Davis, "Beyond Reparation," 6–7.

6. I use the terms "familial unconscious" and "social unconscious," respectively, to suggest the forces inherent in collective familial and institutional repression. Reinforcing one another, they prevent certain emotions, interactions, and desires from being realized within the individual or family.

7. Davis, "Beyond Reparation," 8.

8. Marsha Norman, *Getting Out,* in *Four Plays* (New York: Theatre Communications Group, 1988), 7. All subsequent passages are taken from this edition and are cited parenthetically in the text.

9. See "Mourning and Its Relation to Manic-Depressive States" and "Notes on Some Schizoid Mechanisms" in *The Selected Melanie Klein,* ed. Juliet Mitchell (New York: Free Press, 1986), 146–175 and 175–200, respectively.

10. Susan Griffin, *Rape: The Politics of Consciousness* (New York: Harper & Row, 1978), 4.

11. Griffin, *Rape,* 11.

Works Cited

Davis, Walter. "Beyond Reparation: Art's Continuing Challenge to Psychoanalytic Theory." Paper presented at the American Psychological Association convention, Division 39, Chicago, April 1991.

_____. *Get the Guests: The Play of Aggression in Modern American Drama.* Madison: U of Wisconsin P, 1994.

_____. *Inwardness and Existence: Subjectivity in/and Hegel, Heidegger, Marx, and Freud.* Madison: U of Wisconsin P, 1989.

Griffin, Susan. *Rape: The Politics of Consciousness.* New York: Harper & Row, 1978.

Mitchell, Juliet, ed. *The Selected Melanie Klein.* New York: Free Press, 1986.

Norman, Marsha. *Getting Out* in *Four Plays: Marsha Norman.* New York: Theatre Communications Group, 1988.

Poster, Mark. *Critical Theory of the Family.* New York: Continuum, 1978.

At the Intersection
Configuring Women's Differences through Narrative in Norman's *Third and Oak: The Laundromat*

Grace Epstein

> *Everything will be changed once woman gives woman to the other woman. There is hidden and always ready in woman the source; the locus for the other. The mother, too, is a metaphor. It is necessary and sufficient that the best of herself be given to woman by another woman for her to be able to love herself and return in love the body that was "born" to her.*
> —*Helene Cixous, "The Laugh of the Medusa"*

In a recent article reconsidering the viability of French feminism in the face of the larger problematic of differences—postcolonial and otherwise—among the variable groups of women worldwide, Gayatri Spivak reinterprets Helene Cixous' classic, "The Laugh of the Medusa," as an intertextual response to Beauvoir's concern for feminist ethical action in *The Second Sex*. By urging all women to become nurturing and supporting "mothers" to other women, Cixous, according to Spivak, depicts mothering in "a general sense. . . as selfless love, re-inscribed in Beauvoir as the species-other passing into loved subject . . . a relationship with the other woman—who is precisely not a child of my body. . . . [but] rigorously distinguished from being motherly or maternal, matronizing, et cetera. Th[is] other woman's age is not specified, only that she is other" (67–68). Accordingly, Cixous is able to turn her philosophy into something "doable" (66), an ethics that makes feminism concrete, locating the site of political action *between* women who are able to recuperate for one another their appropriated selves and bodies through the metaphorical act of support and love from another woman.

It is precisely this complex of "giving the mother" to the other woman that is being staged in Marsha Norman's *Third and Oak:*

The Laundromat, despite the fact that neither woman is actually a mother to the other nor to *any* other. In this brief one-act play, Norman finesses a situation in which two socially inscribed women meet in a corner laundromat to do their husbands' laundry while each hears the other's story and, in so doing, sets in motion the conditions for a recovery of self by the other woman. In the midst of their own unmediated losses, each woman mothers the other across the chasm of economic, social, and perhaps even spiritual disparities.

Recently the women's movement has become painfully aware of its current white middle-class bias and the lack of serious impact upon the world's gender politics outside of that white middle-class arena. To many feminists, it is a time for reassessment. Nancy Fraser and Linda J. Nicholson suggest that past feminist practice relied too heavily upon the academic influences of male professors, which tended to universalize conditions as well as solutions; in addition, today, a feminist praxis must recognize that "commonalities are by no means universal; rather they are interlaced with differences, even with conflicts. This, then, is a practice made up of a patchwork of overlapping alliances, not one circumscribable by an essential definition" (35).

White feminists must continue to be, of necessity, brought to account for extrapolations that generalize class and racial struggle under white middle-class gender experience, only to further marginalize already excluded groups of working-class white women and women of color or ethnic diversity. Like the civil rights movement, the feminist movement has had to acknowledge its own preconceptions and the density of the oppression of women that is still only barely articulated after two decades of energetic investigation.

On the other hand, Susan Bordo cautions that "the dynamics of inclusion and exclusion (as history had just taught us) are played out on multiple and shifting fronts, and all ideas (no matter how 'liberatory' in some contexts or for some purposes) are condemned to be haunted by a voice from the margins already speaking (or perhaps presently muted but awaiting the conditions for speech), awakening us to what has been excluded, effaced, damaged" (138). Nevertheless, the reluctance to theorize gender and political commonalities among the varied groups of women may serve to immobilize feminist practice entirely by reproducing the same "white male knowledge/power" base that feminism has sought to mediate in the past (151). Bordo instructs that the most productive strategies of demystifying "the 'human' [and perhaps, humanist] (and its claim to 'neutral' perspective) through general categories of social identity, which give content and force to notions of social interest, historical location and cultural perspective" are being abandoned to a chronic gender skepticism and feminist fragmentation that short-circuited feminist activity in the earlier part of the twentieth century (153). As the movement teeters on the verge of relinquishing the very methods that have brought about the semblance of success, the dilemma of merging liberation theory with hard-core economic and social differences appears increasingly elusive.

However, one of the most fruitful avenues in which the movement has assessed ideas and promoted the dissemination of information about women's oppression has been through consciousness-raising, supported largely through producing the conditions under which women of various backgrounds could "story" their experiences as women along with those whose experiences and narratives might be terribly different from their own. In discussing the nature of narrative knowledge, Jean-François Lyotard asserts that

narratives allow the society in which they are told, on the one hand, to define its criteria of competence and, on the other, to evaluate according to those criteria what is performed or can be performed within it. . . . [for] a collectivity that takes narrative as its key form of competence has no need to remember its past. It finds the raw material for its social bond not only in the meaning of the narratives it recounts, but also in the act of reciting them. The narratives' reference may seem to belong to the past, but in reality it is always contemporaneous with the act of recitation. (19–22)

In other words, narrative activity serves the collectivity in two important ways. First, in telling stories, members are empowered by a speech act that permits them to organize their experience in a socially recognizable form and to receive acknowledgement for doing so. In listening to stories, members gain insights about the larger aspects of their condition—similarities and differences. In this way too, the act of recitation itself actually allows the narrative to transcend the context out of which it arose to enfold the context of the telling. According to Peter Brooks, "the performance of the narrative act is in itself transformatory, predicating the material of the life story in a changed context," and narratives of the confessional sort— "subordinating all its verbs to the verb 'I tell'" (60)—often serve to solicit conversation from the otherwise silent realms of social affiliation by conveying experience in a way that reveals, exposes, and lays claim to a specific structure of knowing.

Further, because the collectivity of lower-class and disenfranchised minority women are often deprived of successful access to formal education, they often coalesce around the articulation of stories that provide them with their only access to meaningful personal power. As Lyotard suggests, the exchange of stories in the absence of history—for women, class, and race—continues to be a productive means by which to formulate what is and can be done within the collectivity. In this way, minority groups formulate an understanding of their lives as minorities and the lives of those they love or serve, even when they are denied a voice and status in the larger social structure. Indeed, narratives from one woman to another have provided not simply a selected means for understanding women's roles and limitations in culture, but, in fact, the *only* means of discovery available, and probably the only opportunity for exchange between women of differing circumstances.

Nevertheless, the experience they chronicle is not without social prescription. As Joan W. Scott's critique of historical narrativity establishes, "Experience is already an interpretation *and* is in need of interpretation. What counts as experience is neither self-evident nor straightforward; it is always contested, always therefore political" (37). For the truth about social groups is that they organize and understand their experience along already established narrative lines that they, as a group, construct as meaningful. These lines, however, are formalized over time and their repetition as recognizable performance paths imparts an important sense of satisfaction to listeners as well as tellers. In accordance with this process of narrating and listening to stories. then, the collectivity comes to privilege some narrative paradigms over others, and the privileged forms produce a force field that can attract and envelop less privileged patterns, so that the least familiar stories are frequently lost in the force field of those more familiar products.

This operation of assigning privilege to some formats over others is no doubt partly responsible for the silencing of groups of women who have been speaking all along or trying to, but whose voices failed to be heard because the structure of their stories, like the condition of their lives, was different, unfamiliar, and thus, poorly integrated into the larger polemics of feminist thought. Certainly, the narratives selected for privilege in feminism are also due for review. For, when their stories don't suit the social forms already established, members feel stifled, anxious, and even outraged until they too are given their say, enabling them to reinscribe themselves into a more compatible form and content or to alter the current forms in which they may cast their experience. Any serious listening and telling that goes on among women, among feminists in particular, says Scott, must be the sort that "interrogates the process of their creation," not simply of the story but its method of construction (37).

Norman's play, *Third and Oak: The Laundromat* demonstrates both the means and the limits of the conversion of experience into narrative that constitutes the access to difference. By listening and telling stories, Alberta and Deedee, who come from immeasurably antithetical perspectives, are able to make contact and to go their separate ways without judgment, but with a sense of support from the one who is different, who is literally Other. For both women, the listening and telling is difficult because they speak across great divisions. The vast wasteland of social class and generation that separates them from the very instant their paths intersect in the play is not overcome, but investigated by the tenacity of the lower-class woman and the educated experience of the middle-class woman, producing a catharsis for both in the period of the hour in which they meet and exchange stories of their lives.

In her acclaimed novel *Beloved,* Toni Morrison identifies "a woman who is a friend to your mind" as one who gathers "the pieces that I am, . . . giv[ing] them back to me in all the right order" (272–73). This woman-friendship requires listening, hearing anew what is being said, similar to the sensitive activity Cixous calls for of giving back the mother to the other woman. In Norman's early play, the two women, caught in the initial wave of consciousness-raising,

model a kind of listening that allows for the other woman to redis-
tribute her life experience in another order, one that more clearly
returns her "self" to her.

Spivak notes that Cixous, like many French intellectuals, recognizes the Marxist narrative of class struggle as a particularly viable
narrative from which to extrapolate a liberation ethics, and indeed,
Norman has also invoked the touchstone of class struggle in other
plays, which, like *Getting Out*, starkly draw attention to the trap
constituted by poverty and abuse for lower-class women, where "factors that mitigate against Arlene taking charge of her life must be
seen as flaws in the social system . . . [and] a sexually discriminating
legal system" (Scharine 191).

Making the laundromat the locale for the play's development
provides a particularly rich site upon which to foreground the confrontation of the two "socially other" women, as the privatized activity of doing laundry is presented, contrastingly, in a publicly accessible space. In this way, the laundromat not only represents an
intersection for differing social groups of women, but also, of fe-
male-associated activity with male-identified public space. Each
woman's claim to the public space is neutralized in respect to the
other because entry into this sphere is equally accessible, and equally
impeded by their status as women. Further, the initial exposition of
the play makes clear that neither woman is a regular user of the
public facilities, even though Alberta, the middle-class woman, appears far more comfortable there than Deedee. When Alberta enters, she finds the attendant asleep "off-stage" in his office and remarks, "What they pay you to do, sleep? Listen, it's fine with me.
Better, in fact. I'm glad, actually" (5), signaling that the male presence would somehow interfere with the process of getting the job
done. Later, Alberta indicates that being watched by her husband as
she prepared the Thanksgiving turkey was inhibiting because it "made
me nervous" (13). Initially then, Alberta stakes out the jurisdiction
of household activity as distinctly female and separated from public
view, even though the laundromat's peculiar split disposition as public
space, traditionally associated with masculinity and designated by
the male attendant, can only be temporarily recuperated here in the
earliest hours of the morning by the women because the attendant is
asleep.

When Alberta continues that she has never understood why men like to have women watch them work, she again implies the traditionally public nature of male occupations. It is only men's occasional relations with women that are considered off-limits within the public realm. Of course in the usual distribution of power dynamics, a woman's watching of a man will not diminish the man as his watching of her diminishes her. That problematic may also be implicated in Alberta's comment, as well as informing her desire not to be watched by men and not to wake the attendant.

It is significant, too, that Alberta and Deedee abandon their private household space in a time of deep emotion to "go public," so to speak, as though leaving the home provides an arbitration of their conflicting personal feelings. While Alberta selects the laundromat for the anonymity she imagines it will concede to her, she discovers that along with the anonymity comes required social engagement with others inhabiting the public space with her. However, Deedee enters the public space for precisely the opposite reason, to find company, to find another individual to while away the time she spends waiting for Joe to return. As Patricia Williams suggests in *The Alchemy of Race and Rights,* social change demands "the acknowledgement that our experiences of the same circumstances may be very different; the same symbol may mean different things to each of us" (149). Ironically, the larger contradiction here is that both women reveal themselves in the public sphere, but remain anonymous—even somewhat emblematic—to one another despite each being deeply rooted in the specificity of her unique circumstances.

The contradiction of this dynamic of social intercourse among women pervades the play's composition. As a specific woman, each assembles her personal items to be laundered on a particular morning in a certain laundromat located on Third and Oak in order to escape a distinctive personal loss, but like the women before and after her, she is Everywoman doing her husband's laundry, suffering loss alone or in silence, and finding the circumstances of her life unimportant or incomprehensible to the flurry of other lives around her. Norman's choice of location is not simply the early feminist acknowledgement that the personal is political, but an insistence that any airing of female laundry must be given a public forum, even if that forum is only obtained in the momentary absence of male attendants.

While Alberta seems in complete control as the play begins, sorting her laundry and having enough change for the washing and detergent machines, Deedee is immediately dislocated as she enters, stumbling into the room and throwing her armload of shirts across the stage. Indeed, her opening chatter, given the circumstances and the hour, signals her alienation from the activity and the environment. She mistakenly throws a green shirt in with the white ones until Alberta alerts her to the potentially damaging effects. Deedee's discomfort and disorientation, however, catalyzes the discussion between the women and makes for the dramatic movement of the scene in which Deedee's incompetence at laundering is overshadowed by her willingness to expose both her feelings and her life to Alberta.

Fortified in a number of narrative shifts are the differences that constitute the women's circumstances before the other. It is not only Deedee's lack of confidence and skill in the laundromat that are posed in contrast to Alberta's self-assurance there. Alberta is also obviously well-educated, while Deedee is not; Alberta's comment that a former student thought Herbert Hoover invented the vacuum cleaner embarrasses Deedee who, no doubt, thinks the same thing. Alberta has the means available for living in a house with a garden, while Deedee lives in an apartment over a bar. Finally, Alberta appears well-traveled, and her age is closer to Deedee's mother's than to Deedee's. No doubt, Alberta's confidence is a result of her greater experience and education. However, she is not without her own insecurities, which she reluctantly begins to disclose to Deedee over the course of the time they share in the laundromat.

Patricia Williams further maintains that "it really is possible to see things—even the most concrete things—simultaneously yet differently; and that seeing simultaneously yet differently is more easily done by two people than one, but that one person can get the hang of it with time and effort" (150). Williams accomplishes this simultaneous but different "seeing" in her book by listening effortfully to her sister's ideas and by paying close attention to a variety of disenfranchised voices from the homeless, from children, and finally from women of different ethnic or racial backgrounds. Because Williams models the activity throughout her book, she demonstrates that the effort is infinitely rewarding and renewing. Norman's dramatic action of *Third and Oak* reflects an effortful perceptivity engaged by an attentiveness to the unfamiliar, to narrative styles that reveal persistent, even schizophrenic, effects of being a cultural Other. Yet the complex of seeing simultaneously but differently is realized at the end of the play by both women as fruitful and rewarding.

Thus, from within difference, women may understand simultaneously but differently through an effort of listening and accepting the storied experience of the other. This effort is required of Alberta and Deedee and the viewers of the play as they assemble and reassemble the play's larger problematic of difference and sameness. For just as the play has signaled the series of differences between the two women in the beginning, the middle begins to flesh out some of their similarities. With those similarities, however, comes a tempting capitulation to misread, or to ignore what is being said. For instance, when they discover they have the same name—Johnson—Deedee advances, "Hey! We might be related," to which Alberta feels and, more importantly, responds with "I don't think so" (9). In actual fact, the women have very little basis for extrapolating a connection. Their lives do not intersect at all, except in this temporary time and space. At the moment, Deedee's rush to propose a tie between them is, for both women, a reduction of the distinctly different reasons that have positioned them there in the first place. A blindness to difference at this point would make them essentially invisible to one another. Deedee's subsequent observation more aptly acknowledges that a lot of unrelated people probably have the same name.

This is no doubt true for those who bear the name of Woman as well. Indeed, an initial impulse to conflate circumstances subordinates differences by which we identify and locate ourselves in society and time. According to Spivak, a requirement of "decolonized feminism" is the conception of agency as "pluralization, alteration . . . . to split, open, and fill all generalized, unified struggles with plurality" (70). While Alberta and Deedee are, perhaps, in a greater sense part of the same "family," though that family is more global than local, important factors distinguish their relations with the world. Disregard for those differences can seriously thwart one or both of them here.

In a similar vein, both women appear to be in the throes of a loss that goes to the core of their already constructed personal identities: for Alberta the ending of her husband's life, and for Deedee, the exposure of her husband's infidelity. Even here, conditions mitigate similar circumstances. Deedee's attempt to elicit a confession from Alberta that Herb may have been capable of the same offense is cut off, first, by Alberta's confident, "No," and then later, by the acknowledgement that Herb has died, making his possible infidelity a moot point. Here, the two conditions of loss are pervaded with difference. Alberta's is solid and definitive. Apart from the few clothes she is laundering and the collections of household memories she daily confronts, her loss is total and complete. It is, as far as her own actions are concerned, irrevocable, while Deedee's loss is shot through with ambiguity. There is nothing definitive about Deedee's situation which may continue indefinitely, and which she may address in any number of ways, from continued pretense to outright divorce.

Their economic positions, in particular, vis-a-vis the losses are distinct as well. Alberta is a former schoolteacher, probably with retirement savings of her own and a pension, no doubt, commensurate with her husband's successful economic status. Deedee, though young and energetic, has no trade or ostensible skills. If she leaves Joe at this point, she will be forced to return to her mother's home for lack of real income.

Both women depict their mothers as similarly inaccessible, but again, the reasons for the inaccessibility play themselves out differently. Alberta's mother, who is also deceased, Alberta confides, solicited the reading of *Wuthering Heights* five times the year she died. Alberta's mother's comment, "All they had to do was find Heathcliff someplace to go every day. The man just needed a job," belies her inability to imagine or acknowledge the manifestation of deep emotional or psychic loss that the novel renders, as well as her distinctly middle-class belief that work is the solution to any or all personal problems. Following Deedee's inquiry, "What about you?" Alberta too, in saying, "It was a blessing, really" that her mother died, sounds as lacking in compassion as her mother did about Heathcliff.

Deedee's relationship with her mother is characterized with "she don't ever say how she likes seeing me, but she holds back, you know. I mean, there's stuff you don't have to say when it's family" (7). Although Alberta's *Wuthering Heights* story appears to be lost on Deedee, the younger woman actually understands better than it first appears.

Her follow-up comment that "My mom thinks Joe's a bum" (12) connects Alberta's rendering of her mother's inability to "get" the story of *Wuthering Heights* to Deedee's mom's inability to recognize any value in Joe.

In a more fundamental way, Deedee's honesty jars Alberta, who is accustomed to covering up or disregarding her feelings, not because Deedee fails to make sense, but because she actually makes the connections Alberta prefers to avoid. Deedee, in fact, understands her own motivations quite well. While she may be frightened of being alone, Deedee owns very little but her feelings. Given her social and economic position, she hasn't much to lose besides Joe. This is not the case for Alberta, however, who comes to her situation at the end of what was no doubt a comfortable, if not happy, existence. Rather, Alberta prefers keeping the boundaries neat and tidy, sorted, like the laundry, to prevent any bleeding of colors. Even if the distinctions don't work for Alberta, they have become comfortable.

Richard G. Scharine defines a "political" play as one that "shows public policy, laws, unquestioned social codes impinging unfairly and destructively upon private lives. Individual though the protagonist may be, what happens to this character is not an example of isolated fate but rather is the result of historically alterable conditions which are inherently unfair to a segment of society" (186). Certainly the critique of society surrounds the women within the confines of the laundromat. As characters essentially defined by their culture as well as in relation to the men in their lives, they are devalued by the loss of those men. Also, neither woman seems particularly aware of her position in the culture, so immersed is she in the roles that have been assigned her. Neither woman is initially capable of recognizing herself as dispossessed because of her loss of a husband, since up until the moment she enters the laundromat, she has followed the only path she found available to her.

Though Alberta has had a profession, it has been the female-designated one of schoolteaching. When Deedee asks her why she retired from teaching, Alberta replies that the reason was age, "Not my age. Theirs," but when pressed further, she reveals, "Mother was very sick then" (11). Thus, even her retirement was a response to the needs of another, not her own. Deedee's life, too, revolves around the desires of her husband for an apartment over a bar, for a souped-up car, for his late-night bowling soirees with another woman. Because of Joe's need to be the sole provider, Deedee keeps her small source of income a secret, not for the money she receives, since she is unable to spend any of it without Joe learning about the job, but to keep busy, to sustain her in her continual waiting for Joe to get home from work. Clearly, the conditions under which both women live, while different, are brought about by the cultural imperative imposed upon women to serve others. Their own productive emotional or economic fulfillment is absent from either's conception of reality.

Deedee's mother's advice that Joe and Deedee are in the "itch" year of their marriage, the year when his interests are likely to stray for a time, is not only unreliable since the audience and Alberta know that the "itch" is routinely identified with the seventh year of marriage, not the second, but it is also a convenient, if not characteristic, excuse for the patriarchal privilege that underwrites and supports female dependency and male betrayal. Thus, even the maternal advice that Deedee is likely to find consoling is essentially deceptive, a kind of gloss of the actual circumstances of her deteriorating marital union. Deedee's revelation deconstructs the conspiracy women (and especially mothers)[1] create in fostering one another's oppression.

In a close examination of the women's responses to one another, however, it is possible to see what each is avoiding, and what each, in various indirect ways, is able to "give" to the other. This interaction is the play's most crystallizing cultural critique, informing and decolonizing feminist ethical action. Even though both women project denial as they discuss their lives, Deedee's tenacity works to loosen Alberta's grasp on that denial. Though Deedee continues to talk, it is evident that Alberta could probably curtail the younger woman's effusiveness if she were to ignore both Deedee's questions and comments. Instead, Alberta's habitual responsiveness signals her own ambivalence about talking, and stimulates the line of personal inquiry Deedee follows. Eventually, Alberta's awareness of her own situation is revealed to her as she talks to Deedee.

Her own frantic behavior over Herb's cabbage soup-drenched shirt, coupled with the unexpected desire to perpetuate a lie about Herb's current whereabouts, surprises Alberta. It is actually Deedee who precipitates the final catharsis for Alberta, when she misconstrues Alberta's hysteria over the shirt. Her pride wounded, Deedee accuses Alberta with, "You didn't even want me to touch that shirt. Herb's shirt is too nice for me to even touch. Well, I may be a slob, but I'm clean" (23). Indeed, Alberta's constrained and passive existence is truly foreign to Deedee, so much so that she mistakes the reverence for the shirt as a personal slight. What Alberta has bought in return for her pleasant and safe surroundings is her own censorship. In trying to understand the behavior, Deedee explodes with

Herb is so wonderful. You love him so much. You wash his clothes just the right way. I could never drop his shirt in the washer the way you do it. The stain might not come out and he might say what did you do to my shirt and you might fight and that would mess up your little dream world where everything is always sweet and nobody ever gets mad and you just go around gardening and giving each other little pecky kisses all the time. (23)

Indeed, the problem of difference is eloquently represented here in Deedee's misjudgment of Alberta's motivation. Just as Williams' observation earlier suggests, what is symbolic of one thing to one group may have quite different significance to another. When Deedee too easily assumes that Alberta's circumstances are like her own, she misreads the other woman. Because Alberta's life with Herb is incomprehensible to Deedee, the terms under which the older woman remains with Herb appear too great. Yet Alberta's long life with Herb informs her behavior. According to Leslie Kane, Norman's plays often explore the "world of isolation and enforced good cheer" that Norman's own strict fundamentalist upbringing imposed upon her. This appears to be the world that women in her plays inhabit to a greater or lesser degree. For this reason, Deedee's abrasiveness is threatening for Alberta, and the coarse words represent a crude life from which Alberta believes any sensible person would want to flee. Typically, she disdains the lower-class woman's reluctance to remedy the situation by leaving her husband.

Certainly, such interactions between lower- and upper-class women typify their disparate relations with the world. While Deedee's mother's scenario suggests that men are all unfaithful at sometime in their marriages, Alberta's long-term marriage convinces her otherwise. Nevertheless, Deedee's refusal to reject Joe is informed by her poverty, her lack of economic options. Oddly, a return to the mother's home, which is similarly faulty, will become the impetus for action. The compensation for the vigilance and tactfulness Alberta has engaged in through the years, has, up to this point, been acceptable. If Herb had been unfaithful, he had no doubt been discreet about it, and that would have mitigated pain and humiliation. For Alberta, propitious behavior is a requirement for life, and possibly the only excuse for conflict or disapproval. Only when Deedee has gone over the line and cunningly cut to the chase of Alberta's situation is Alberta able to respond with, "What do I have to do to get you to leave me alone?" (23).

Alberta's discomfort with conflict causes her to avoid Deedee's observation that she is the same age as the students Alberta dislikes. Alberta's inability to field confrontative issues in her own life goes to the heart of the atmosphere of delicate decorum in which she has been enclosed. What makes Deedee so explosive is her refusal to let things lie, to wait for things to reveal themselves. Instead, she is constantly interrogating; first Alberta, and then, herself. Finally, she makes a startling reading of all of Alberta's vagueness and alarm in "You act like he's a saint. Like he's dead and now you worship the shirts he wore. . . He is dead, isn't he?" (23).

In just this way, Alberta's conflicting emotions are brought to the surface by Deedee's stunning cross-examination. Evasive answers about Herb's gardening, ("I bought Herb some new tools for his birthday and then he . . . gave it up . . . gardening") are met with Deedee's "Before his birthday? . . . Did you have time to buy him another present?" (14). Later, as the two women exchange barbs, Deedee pursues further with, "You don't even live in this neighborhood, do you? . . . There ain't a garden for miles around here" (18). She refuses to allow Alberta to slip nicely into the fantasy she has constructed for herself and, in so doing, produces the conditions under which Alberta finally acknowledges her loss of Herb. This interrogation of the middle-class woman by the lower class woman represents Deedee's gift to Alberta. Through the insistent examination of her isolation and illusion, Deedee releases Alberta to her grief and fear and from the confinement of her position as the desexualized female icon.

Alberta, too, is an excellent nemesis for Deedee, though her style is not interrogation but reinforcement. In Alberta, Deedee

finds a more competent advisor than her mother. To Joe's excuse
that he has to work lots of overtime due to the demand for trucks
caused by the population explosion, Alberta responds that the excuse is not "true" (7). To Deedee's comment that she could name
the seven dwarfs, but not seven presidents, Alberta encourages,
"you could name seven presidents . . . . try it" (10). Finally, after
Deedee has made the connection that Herb is dead, Alberta responds with "You're not dumb, child. And don't let anybody tell
you are, O.K.?" (23). Despite her obligatory politeness, Alberta
does respond to Deedee's discussion. She is obviously befuddled
by the peculiarity of Deedee's speech and personal denigration,
but Alberta does not withdraw as the audience might expect her to
do. As an older woman, somewhat versed in the language and interests of young adults, Alberta composedly projects enough concern for the other woman to offer intelligible perceptions without
much ego investment of her own.

For instance, when Deedee begins to reveal the truth about her
appearance in the laundromat to avoid having Joe find her at home
crying, Alberta responds, "I haven't cried in forty years," revealing
that, like Deedee, she too has busied herself with household chores
in order to suppress her most delicate feelings. However, in a genuine effort to console Deedee, she recalls the episode forty years earlier when she did cry at the loss of her aunt's rabbit. Explaining the
scene following the animal's death, she reveals, "I helped her bury
him. Tears were streaming down my face. 'Bertie,' she said, 'stop
crying. He didn't mean to go and leave us all alone and he'd feel bad
if he knew he made us so miserable.' But in the next few weeks,
Aunt Dora got quieter and quieter till finally she wasn't talking at
all and Mother put her in a nursing home" (19). Alberta actually
posits a story that parallels her own recent loss, even though neither
Deedee nor the play's audience is aware of the actual dimensions of
that loss yet.

Therefore, when Alberta does finally disclose Herb's death and
her own reasons for coming to the laundromat, this earlier scene
reverberates with profound psychic significance, foregrounding
Alberta's own pain and her fear that, like Aunt Dora, she will end up
disconsolate and catatonic as the result of losing her own beloved.
Alberta's gesture to Deedee, in light of this later revelation, repre-

sents a poignant and relatively unselfish attempt to comfort Deedee, as it vividly calls up Alberta's own buried pain and impending fears. Yet the recollection also provides an articulation of Alberta's need, so that her gift circles back to her as well. Another dimension of Cixous problematic affirms that "the more you have, the more you give, the more you are, the more you give, the more you have" (1986 124). Also, according to Brooks, the narrative act provides a transformation of experience itself, which Alberta is able to make by recognizing the connection between Aunt Dora and herself through engagement with Deedee's confession. Thus, the circulation of give and take, though unexpected for Alberta here, provides comfort to Deedee, the recuperation of Alberta's own past, and the greater apprehension of Alberta's present.

Two of the most telling moments of the play are Deedee's story about Shooter Stevens and Alberta's exit. Here, the engagement of the two women with each other runs squarely in opposite directions. The first threatens the slight connection they have made with each other, while the last implies that the trajectory of their narratives, though running counter to each other, may actually intersect somewhere in space.

The story about Shooter Stevens, the late night disk jockey whose program sign-off launches the play, is told by Deedee following a short diatribe against Joe and Herb: "cause if they were both home where they should be, we wouldn't have to be here in this crappy laundromat washin' fuckin' shirts in the middle of the night!" Here, Norman's notes convey that "Alberta is alarmed and disturbed at the use of the word fuckin'" (16) because Alberta's desire for conciliating behavior is threatened by the word both as language and as the action it represents. The story of Shooter signifies a number of moral and emotional differences between the women. Shooter's sign-off at the opening of the play—"the rest of you night owls gonna have to make it through the rest of this night by *yourself,* or with the help of *your friends*" (5)—and Deedee's story about meeting him trigger the play's final catharsis as well as the many political realities figuring into the intersection of the two cultures of the women. Race, while not at the center of the play, reverberates from the wings as a profound presence, particularly for Deedee and, to a lesser degree, for Alberta.

As a disk jockey, Shooter symbolizes economic and social success to Deedee, while the more sophisticated Alberta would hardly be impressed by either his fiscal or his social stock. As a man who finds her attractive or even interesting to spend time with, Shooter represents the desirability Deedee feels she has lost as the result of Joe's infidelity. Her need for physical intimacy, while not necessarily greater in a younger woman than an older woman, is nevertheless underscored by the circumstances of Joe's rejection of her. Alberta's loss has little to do a loss of affection from her husband. Finally though, as a black man, Shooter signals an immeasurable store of cultural dynamite enclosed by race and caste. Not only is the jealousy game her way of showing Joe her desirability to another man, but, informed by the tremendous anxiety white men show to the legendary standing of black male virility, Deedee levels her revenge upon Joe by choosing or being chosen by a black man (for "Joe hates black people"). In fact, Deedee appears to be aware of the racist dimension of her fantasy, at least at some level, because to Alberta's question, "Is Shooter married too?", Deedee volunteers, "It makes you sick, doesn't it? . . . Me and a black man" (17). However, Alberta, who up to that point has never met Shooter or listened to his broadcasts, could not know that Shooter is black. No doubt Deedee recognizes the "use" she is making of Shooter with her revenge fantasy even though Alberta is responding to the issue of marital propriety, not race.[2]

When the confrontation with Deedee gets heated, Alberta retreats into propriety again to diffuse the conflict. In apologizing, she disconnects Deedee's anger and defensiveness and precipitates Deedee's revelation of her revenge fantasy with, "Might just serve [Joe] right, though. Come in and see me drinkin' beer and playin' pool with Willie and Shooter . . . would teach him to run out on me. A little dose of his own medicine" (18). In this way, Deedee articulates the truth about her relationship with Joe, and she begins to voice her anger and faltering sense of self. Alberta offers Deedee the gift of hearing, of listening to her voiced anger toward Joe, but also toward the circumstances that shape her life differently than Alberta's.

The final exchange engaging the women follows Alberta's confession. Apologies reverse and Deedee responds to the story about Alberta's discovery of her husband's dead body:

D: I'm so sorry.

A: I don't want you to be alone, that's not what I meant before.

D: Looks like I'm alone anyway.

A: That's what I meant.

D: Sometimes I bring in a little stand-up mirror to the coffee table while I'm watchin' TV. It's my face over there when I look, but it's a face just the same.

A: Being alone isn't so awful. I mean, it's awful, but it's not that awful. There are hard things. (79)

The exchange, rather than further configuring their differences, finally allows for a place to confer similarity in their mutual distress. Both recognize their positions as lonely, and they each have something to say about loneliness, about what the possibilities for living with those hard feelings are. Deedee sets up the mirror, and Alberta encourages her with, "Your face in the mirror is better company than a man who would eat a whole fried egg in one bite." Deedee encourages Alberta with, "You better hang on to his hoes. It's getting about time to turn over the soil, isn't it?" (25–26). The final gifts between the two women constitute Deedee's willingness to allow Alberta to leave without giving her telephone number, which has been offered only out of politeness, thereby releasing Alberta from her burdening caretaker role. In response, Alberta makes a gift of the change she gave Deedee earlier, with "Everyone deserves a free load now and then" (26), for the sense of deservedness is very important to Deedee because it releases her from her chronic sense of worthlessness. As the two women part, both take something with them. Alberta acknowledges Deedee's gift by affirming, "I really wanted to be alone tonight. . . . I'm glad you talked me out of it," while Deedee, with a renewed sense of her own competence, retains the laundromat space for herself by refusing to wake the attendant, uncharacteristically preferring her own company. She humorously embraces the possibilities that this new sense of aloneness confers, with "Yeah, peace and quiet. [Pops the top on the Dr. Pepper.] Too bad it don't come in cans" (26), as the stage lights go down.

In a 1986 interview, Toni Morrison stated that her appreciation of the Soviet people had been derived not from the prodigiously propagated government materials of the Soviet Union or the United States, but from the great novels of Dostoyevsky, Tolstoy, Chekhov, and the literary heritage of the Russian people (Epstein 6). Indeed, Morrison implies that attention to a people's storytelling can reveal passions and interests that may be different from our own, and may also be clouded by other political and discursive realities; nonetheless, that people's struggles become apprehensible with the act of effortful reading and listening.

This engagement of woman with another woman is an action enormously important for all who attempt to look out of one context with understanding and acceptance to another, an action that feminists have known and found productive since the very embryonic phases of feminism. Much can be learned about the other woman if her voice can be spoken across the chasms of difference that sometimes separate her from other women. Marsha Norman's one-act dramatizes the intersection of class and age, in a temporarily appropriated public space where two woman tend to their private hopes, fears, and disappointments. Across their differences, they speak and listen to one another to acknowledge and affirm their differences, to make a gift of their differing abilities in their varying needs, to help the other woman regain her body and self from the cultures that have silenced or disregarded her. Theirs is the art of hearing simultaneously but differently. Recognizing the political aspects of their meeting, Norman foregrounds the seriousness inherent in this listening and telling. Deedee and Alberta pose one model from which feminists configure feminist ethical action. Indeed, "what an amazing formulation of responsibility this is, especially since the dimension is inaccessible and therefore the responsibility is effortful" (Spivak 67–68), for, despite this play's enclosure in the context of 1970s feminism, it speaks anew to a decolonizing phase of feminism, a field that is by necessity always at an intersection of differences.

Notes

1.   Kane draws upon Elizabeth Stone's article, "Playwright Marsha Norman: An Optimist Writes about Suicide, Confinement and Despair," *Ms* (July 12, 1983), 59, in saying that "Norman believes that daughters have been betrayed by moth-

ers with the false promise that they will find 'a nice man' and that their lives will
be 'wonderful'" (262). Indeed, mothers in Norman's plays are culpable in sharing
responsibilities over their daughters' failures and unhappiness. While Alberta is
an older woman who might likely be a maternal figure in this play, she is different from Deedee's own mother. Ultimately, I find her responsiveness ends up
being more *responsible* and more like the one Cixous characterizes as woman's
relationship to the Other woman.

2.   Of course, once Alberta does know that Shooter is black she responds typically
with "You were lucky you didn't get raped!" (18), conveying the racist projection
of many white men and women that many black men are rapists and obsessed
with white women.

Works Cited

Bordo, Susan. "Feminism, Postmodernism, and Gender-Scepticism." in *Feminism/
Postmodernism*. Edited by Linda J. Nicholson. New York: Routledge, 1990.
133–156.

Brooks, Peter. *Reading for the Plot: Design and Intention in Narrative*. New York:
Vintage Books, 1984.

Cixous, Helene. "The Laugh of the Medusa." Translated by Keith and Paula Cohen.
Signs: Journal of Women in Culture and Society (Summer 1976): 875–893.

Cixous, Helene, and Catherine Clement. *The Newly Born Woman*. Translated by Betsy
Wing. Minneapolis: U of Minnesota, 1986.

Epstein, Grace A. "An Interview with Toni Morrison." *Ohio Journal* (Spring 1986): 5–9.

Fraser, Nancy and Linda J. Nicholson. "Social Criticism without Philosophy: An Encounter between Feminism and Postmodernism." in *Feminism/Postmodernism*.
Edited by Linda J. Nicholson. New York: Routledge, 1990. 19–38.

Kane, Leslie. "The Way out, the Way in: Paths to Self in the Plays of Marsha Norman."
In *Feminine Focus: The New Women Playwrights*. Edited by Enoch Brater. Oxford: Oxford UP, 1989. 255–274.

Lyotard, Jean-François. *The Postmodern Condition: A Report on Knowledge*. Translated
by Geoff Bennington and Brian Massumi. Minneapolis: U of Minnesota P, 1985.

Morrison, Toni. *Beloved*. New York: Alfred A. Knopf, 1987.

Norman, Marsha. *Third and Oak: The Laundromat*. New York: Dramatists Play Service, 1980.

Scharine, Richard G. "Cast Iron Bars: Marsha Norman's *Getting Out* as Political Theatre." In *Women in Theatre*. Edited by James Redmond. New York: Cambridge
UP, 1989.

Scott, Joan W. "Experience." In *FeministsTheorize the Political*. Edited by Judith Butler and Joan W. Scott. New York: Routledge, 1992. 22–40.

Spivak, Gayatri Chakravorty. "French Feminism Revisited: Ethics and Politics." In
Feminists Theorize the Political. Edited by Judith Butler and Joan W. Scott. New
York: Routledge, 1992. 54–85.

Williams, Patricia J. *The Alchemy of Race and Rights: Diary of a Law Professor*. Cambridge: Harvard UP, 1991.

Revolving It All
Mother-Daughter Pairs in Marsha Norman's
'night, Mother and Samuel Beckett's *Footfalls*

John Kundert-Gibbs

Although the image of a mother with her daughter has historically evoked a sense of domestic peace, the last few decades have seen a revision of this relationship as a more complex, "human" bond that is as fraught with difficulties and potential as its extensively studied and discussed counterpart—the relationship between father and son. This revitalizing humanization of the mother-daughter relationship has certainly found its way into the literature of our day (a popular example is Toni Morrison's *Beloved*), and, more significantly, it has emerged from the privacy and secrecy of the home to become an important part of a most public forum: drama performed on stage. In examining the extent and importance of this new dramatic relationship, it is instrumental to study two seemingly different plays by two very different playwrights (of differing gender)—*'night, Mother*, by Marsha Norman, and *Footfalls*, by Samuel Beckett—in order to see the intimate ways in which the plays are connected by their central mother-daughter relationship.

While Norman's *'night, Mother* is a full-length, contiguous, highly structured narrative[1] centered on a fairly standard (almost clichéd) dramatic action—Jessie's suicide—it is very interesting to note that critics of the play have leveled at it many of the same charges critics of Beckett's work have applied to his plays. Often through quotation of others, critics provide an insight into the problematic reception of Norman's work: "nothing happens" in the play (Spencer, "Norman's *She-tragedies*" 148), it is circular, the characters are flat and uninteresting (Kintz 197), the play is "utterly boring" (Spencer, "Norman's *'night, Mother*" 364), and even that *'night, Mother* should not be "called a drama" at all (Kintz 197).

Are these comments merely a patriarchal backlash at Norman's insistence on studying a female-female relationship (as most detractors of her work—according to Spencer—happen to be male), or are these comments also an indication of something lurking beneath the surface of Norman's "realistic" play that propels it toward a Beckettian universe? To the latter, I say yes.

The staging of the play, of obvious significance to Norman, must be realistic to the point of naturalism in the foreground—this is a "country house" full of real people's clutter and comforts, a house where these two specific characters live—while in the back, near the center of the set, stands a door onto "absolute nothingness" (Norman 4). In a performance, this door acts as a magnetic force, growing in intensity as the evening wears on and pulling Jessie and Mama (and us) out of the naturalistic, "next-door" world we can see into the black unknown world of "threat and promise" (Norman 4) lying only a step beyond. In an interview with Savran, Norman raises the status of this door to the level of another character: "you have Mama and Jessie and the door behind them" forming an equal triangle (Savran 185). As a central dramatic image, the door embodies all the complexities of the women's relationship, as well as death, rebirth, nonbeing, silence, peace, heaven, hell, and much more; it is what makes "this last part so good, Mama" (Norman 75). This pivotal door represents the intimate interdependence between mother and daughter, and the profound differences between the two. The funneling hallway is the center around which mother and daughter revolve and recombine; the door itself is the infinitesimal, infinite chasm which forever separates the two women.

In *Footfalls*, what at first appears to be a very different world is perhaps merely the other side of Norman's bedroom door: mother/ V speaks from a dark distance, awakened from her "sleep" by her daughter May (or M), who paces a slim, shrinking strip of grey light, tracing out a pattern demarking the "sideways eight" of infinity.[2] Here, also, we participate in an intimate, complex portrayal of a mother-daughter relationship (though obviously this time in less conventional surroundings). And once again, a central, dynamic image—of May "revolving" on this strip of light—embodies the paradoxes and complexities of the play in general and the women's relationship specifically. In fact, Beckett has been quoted by several critics as having claimed the "picture" of May pacing the strip is the center around which he constructed the play (see, for example, Knowlson and Pilling 220, and Gontarski 164). Thus we have two very important stage images—the door and the strip of light—that provide a concretization of the complexities of the two relationships between these mother and daughter pairs.

How can we further examine the import of these parallel images on the characters and on the plays themselves? Let us step back for a moment and consider the historically "undramatic" nature of the mother-daughter relationship. From Penelope on, the wife and mother in European literature has been associated with stillness and home, a counterpart to her husband who travels and interacts with the outside world in various ways. The "good" daughter will, of course, follow her mother and perpetuate this counterpoint with her future husband. Thus, in most Western literature, the "normal" female character is relating either with her husband, or with suitors who hope to be her future husband, and she does this either in or near her home—or, as Christendom spreads its influence, in her one other appropriate setting: the church. The proper woman, therefore, relates only with men and does so only at home or in its appropriate extension, the church. Thus, as Spencer puts it, "a woman's scope of action was sorely circumscribed" (Spencer, "Norman's *She-tragedies*" 147). In *Footfalls* and *'night, Mother*, however, this propriety is thrown into question.

In *'night, Mother*, Jessie and Thelma are indeed in the "appropriate" setting—a naturalistic house—yet on this particular night, what takes place around the central and pivotal bedroom door, whose meaning and importance therefore evolves during the evening, forces the audience to reevaluate the apparent humdrum comfort of this home. The comfortable peace the homey setting instills is, in fact, shattered less than ten minutes into the play when Jessie announces her intent to "go into the bedroom and lock the door" and kill herself (Norman 19). From this point on, the household setting becomes much more complex, its everyday ordinary look resonating Jessie's attempts to stay rational and in control on her "big night." Indeed, the house and its necessary routines even set the agenda for the evening: Jessie's need to help her mother order food, setting out candy in jars, cooking and cleaning." [T]he action [of the play] is marked by the rhythm and tempo of domestic work. Thus conversations are motivated, maintained and framed by repetitive, unrewarding, interminable routines that . . . constitute the sphere of female activity" (Spencer, "Norman's *She-tragedies*" 151). Yet at the same time, the house's ordinary look and its repetitive routines act as a referent to the unusual nature of this evening: Everything is just the same, yet everything is fundamentally different because of what will shortly happen. Jessie's suicide will, in fact, rupture the anesthetizing cocoon of isolated routine to which the two have grown accustomed, a daily ritual that protects the women, yet at the same time cuts them off from the outside world—so much so, in fact, that by the end of the play, there almost seems to be no outside world for Thelma to contact.

Perhaps as an outgrowth of the house's isolating qualities, Thelma and Jessie are thrust beyond the world of men as well. Although there is a lot of talk about husbands, brothers, and sons, this evening (and seemingly the house itself) "is private," as Jessie puts it. To a large extent, this separation is the result of both women's failures in their relationships with men: Jessie is divorced with a delinquent son, and Thelma admits she never loved her husband. Yet at the same time, the men referred to in the play would not or could not understand what happens this evening: It is a necessarily segregated time in which mother and daughter can wrestle with their identities *as* and with women, independent of the confusing gaze of men. Mama's confession at the end of the play, "Forgive me. I thought you were mine" (Norman 89), indicates the essential problem the two face: Neither mother nor daughter can (at least until this point) separate her sense of identity from that of the other. This concept is certainly not new:

Nancy Chodorow, a leading spokesperson for early socialization experience of females, proposes that the mother-daughter relationship is characterized by an essential continuity not present in mother-son relationships. While mothers treat sons as separate beings, encouraging their autonomy, mothers identify with their daughters, treating them as extensions of themselves. (Browder 111)

Thelma and Jessie are locked in a struggle that precludes and excludes men, necessitating their isolation on this most important evening. Furthermore, men like Jessie's brother, Dawson, are seen either as external threat or support, but are not absorbed into the household that the two women share (even Thelma's husband almost ceased to exist in the house: He was merely the "faded blue man in the chair" (Norman 47). Thus, the house becomes both a sanctuary from the pressures of the external (male) world and a private, closed arena in which mother and daughter are permanent combatants. Drawn and/or forced back to this house and to each other, neither woman is able to succeed according to the rules set up by the male world outside. Mother and daughter must iron out their samenesses before either can move out of this apparently peaceful, but deadly, routine of female home life.[3]

Though, as noted, it is apparently very different from 'night, Mother, Footfalls produces almost the same sensations of isolation, routine, and conflict that we have just discussed. Through the slow, yet implacable movement of May and the repetitive accumulation of information that becomes the sad story of a daughter who "was never there" (Beckett 243), we again find ourselves in a world where mother and daughter compete for identity and control through each other. As in 'night, Mother, we are at first presented with a daughter who is essentially mother to her mother. Like Jessie filling candy jars and taking care of shopping for her mother, May has to take care of her presumably bedridden mother: "Would you like me to change your position again? . . . Straighten your pillows? [Pause.] Change your drawsheet? [Pause.] Pass you the bedpan? . . . " (Beckett 240). In both cases, the mother is unable to take care of herself, relying on her daughter as a child would on her mother. Yet again, as in 'night, Mother this daughter-mother inversion seems to appeal to the daughter as well, as it covers over May's and Jessie's failures in becoming fully independent and alive.

Beckett's critics, for whom biography is of great significance, have learned (from conversations with the playwright) that the impetus for May's character was a young woman about whom he heard Carl Jung lecture in the 1930s, a woman for whom Jung said he could find no cure because she had "never really been born" (Knowlson and Pilling 222; quotation is from All That Fall). This makes explicit what is certainly at the heart of the play and leads to its final tableau: May is not really "there," or alive, having never been born. In fact, both mother and daughter eschew referring to May's beginning as a 'birth,' alluding to the event instead with lines like "Where it began" (Beckett 241). May's confined pacing on a surreal strip of grey light is, indeed, akin to a Dantean purgatory for the unbaptized children of the world—those who were never properly born. And this religious undertone is made more explicit in May's third-person narrative in which she claims the site of her pacing is on "his [Christ's] poor arm" in "a little church" (Beckett 242), a reference which places this scene in one of the two appropriate venues for a female in a male-dominated world. Her mother's narrative, however, places May's restless pacing in the other proper female place: inside her house, where there was once "a deep pile" carpeting. Although we will never be sure which is May's true location, we are again locked into a world in which these women (can) only appear in the church or the home. And once again, the intimacy of the place (wherever it is) seems both to protect their privacy and to force them to confront one another in a constant telling and retelling of what has and is happening.

While May is imprisoned within a grey strip of light, it seems her mother gets the worst of it, as she is reduced to a voice from the darkness, her very existence questionable (some critics indicate that she is only a ghostly memory within May's mind). Is it possible for the mother in *Footfalls* to compete with her daughter for identity in a fashion paralleling Thelma and Jessie's conflict? It appears from the evidence that she can. Whether or not she truly exists anymore,[4] mother is definitely competing (at least in May's mind) for control of their identities. However, in apparent opposition to Thelma, who seems to try to keep Jessie "hers" through more naturalistic means involving guilt and threats, mother/V works to control the narrative of her daughter's story. By producing the "facts" of her daughter's story, mother can control how May's history, and therefore May herself, evolves. By observing May's alternate periods of pacing and stillness and retelling an apparently objective third-person narrative (she refers to herself as "the mother"), mother/V can construct a "factual" frame of reference from which to observe May, one that she (mother) controls.

Interestingly, although it is not as obvious in *'night, Mother*, Thelma attempts the same control of narrative that mother/V does in *Footfalls*. By telling the story of her friend Agnes' pyromania (which she later admits is a falsification), informing Jessie of her long-term, inherited, epilepsy, and even in producing the story of how she walked in on Jessie's husband, Cecil, and "Agnes' girl" having an affair, Thelma tries to control the flow of information and therefore the "truth value" of the world in much the same fashion as does the ghostly mother in *Footfalls* (even the stage directions point out that Thelma "believes that things *are* what she says they are" [Norman 2]). The result of this is that in both plays we are at first led to believe the mother's vantage point as the true and rational one. However, as their respective daughters question (either through direct questioning or by retelling the story) the validity of their mothers' statements, we find that the mothers may not be as trustworthy as we at first thought. In the case of *'night, Mother,* Thelma's later admission that she was grossly exaggerating her story of Agnes' madnesses throws the validity of her later stories into question. Although there is a great deal more reason to believe Thelma's later statements concerning Jessie's epilepsy and her husband's affair, we now know that she will bend the truth to suit her immediate needs and thus we can never again be quite certain she is being reliable. In *Footfalls*, May's recasting of the story of her pacing in a much more religious light (both in location and in the added conversation between "Amy" and "Mrs. Winter") leads us here as well to question whether or not mother is telling the whole, objective truth.

When, near the end of the plays, each daughter is allowed to tell her own story, both are caught up in the idea of nonpresence, an idea which is linked by them to their mothers. Jessie, just before the final "push" toward the bedroom where she will kill herself, tells her mother,

I am what became of your child. . . . I found an old baby picture of me. And it was somebody else, not me . . . that's who I started out and this is who is left . . . I'm what was worth waiting for and I didn't make it. Me . . . who might have made a difference to me. . . . I'm not going to show up, so there's no reason to stay, except to keep you company, and that's . . . not reason enough because I'm not . . . very good company. (Norman 76)

Surely Jessie here expresses for the first and last time her inability to separate from her mother's image of herself (the picture), and her consequent feeling of nonidentity. She is not going to "show up" because she never really had a chance to exist as a fully individuated person.

In *Footfalls*, May makes essentially the same confession, though in more couched terms. Describing herself (interestingly, her outward appearance—as she seems unwilling or unable to come to terms with any inner description of herself) for us, May says,

The semblance. . . . Grey rather than white, a pale shade of grey. [Pause.] *Tattered.* [Pause.] *A tangle of tatters.* [Pause.] *Watch it pass*—[Pause.]— *watch her pass before the candelabrum, how its flames, their light . . . like moon through passing rack. (Beckett 242)*

Describing herself in terms reminiscent of *The Tempest's* "insubstantial" pageant of spirits (with the obvious connection to life itself), May calls herself a mere "semblance"—the imperfect image of the only other character in the play: her mother. And, in the only emotional "crack" in the play, May describes her anagrammatic self, Amy, as "[*Brokenly*.] . . . dreadfully un—. . ." (Beckett 242), leaving, in this dangling negative, potential for words such as unloved, unfulfilled, even unformed. Perhaps, though, it is just the negating prefix that is necessary: May feels herself to be a negation, a "ghost" before her mother.

The daughters, then, compete for storytelling space within their isolated, two-character worlds, but they only succeed in these moments in reinforcing their inadequacies—Jessie through her shame and desperation at no longer being her mother's "pink and fat" baby, and May through her absorption of her mother's speech patterns and rhythm[5] and her inability to talk of and even directly about herself.

In both plays, then, we have a competition for identity through daughter-mother inversion (the daughter caring for the mother) and through control of the memories of their shared past, all in the repetitive, private, seemingly inescapable arena of home. And what grows out of this desperately repetitive competition is a sense that "it" must end. In *'night, Mother*, Jessie tells her mother "I'm tired." To her mother's question, "Tired of what?", Jessie responds, "It all. . . . I can't say it any better" (Norman 28). As the play progresses, we find that her exhaustion with "it all" is essentially at the heart of Jessie's intention to kill herself. In *Footfalls*, this "it all" becomes a litany repeated as the final words of each section. For example, in section three, May, subsuming her mother's role with her own, repeats exactly the dialogue that ended section one (with the exception of the permutation of her name into Amy):

Amy. [Pause. No louder.] *Amy*. [Pause.] *Yes, Mother*. [Pause.] *Will you never have done?* [Pause.] *Will you never have done . . . revolving it all?* [Pause.] *It?* [Pause.] *It all*. [Pause.] *In your poor mind*. [Pause.] *It all*. [Pause.] *It all*. (*Beckett 243*)

Interestingly, at the end of the mother's monologue in section two, mother/V claims that May sometimes "tries to *tell* how it was" (Beckett 241; my emphasis), which seems to introduce May's long, somewhat abortive "sequel" immediately following. Regardless of how exactly it is expressed, however, this cogitating on "it all" is obviously central to *Footfalls* as well, so "it all" is at the heart of both plays. As one of the most ambiguous words in the English language, though, "it" really opens room for more questions rather than providing answers to what drives each play. We might ask why these two playwrights could not come up with more specific reasons for their two daughter characters to worry, yet, as Jessie states and Beckett has often quipped about his writing, "I can't say it any better" (Norman 28).

If this indefinite pronoun is the best either character can do to voice her opinion of her universe, we will not be able to pin down exactly what is at the heart of their troubles, yet a word like "it," in context and followed by the all-encompassing word "all," can provide a vivid insight into the emotional turmoil each daughter is experiencing. Furthermore, the vague reference to whatever constitutes the hell of their existence is truly more appropriate and universal than any specific problem they could vocalize. It would belittle their troubles if either May or Jessie could explain exactly what was bothering her—indeed, the plays would become rather melodramatic if either succeeded. It is their universe, their entire being (or lack thereof) which is "Not enough" (Beckett 241). And by the time we see them, neither Jessie nor May can find subsistence to continue their struggle for selfhood. Jessie says that ". . . maybe if there was something I really liked, like maybe if I really liked rice pudding or cornflakes for breakfast or something, that might be enough" to continue (Norman 77).[6] And May finds her pacing is "not enough" to get her through her life. She tries removing the "deep pile" carpeting (at least in her mother's version of the story), but even hearing her feet, "however faint they fall" (Beckett 241), seems not, in the end, to be enough: When Mrs. Winter asks Amy if she saw "anything . . . strange at Evensong" (Beckett 243), apparently referring to May's ghostlike pacing (Knowlson and Pilling 226), Amy responds that she didn't because she was "not there." Thus, the two daughters seem unable to grasp enough to "like" out of existence to forge ahead and to grow.

In the end, Jessie and May also follow similar paths toward nonexistence. Jessie pulls her "disappearing act" through the more naturalistic, psychologically motivated action of locking herself within the "absolute nothingness" of her bedroom and killing herself. May, while not specifically motivating her disappearance, seems to follow in the "footsteps" of her story, gradually fading out as lighting on her is reduced, until at last she is not there at all in the fourth section of the play; all that is left is the dimly lit strip to echo her insubstantial revolutions.

The latter stages of these two plays are, however, very differently charged emotionally. Jessie fights her mother, finally forcing her back into the hallway as she shuts the door to her bedroom and shoots herself, while May finishes her story in lines that fade into silence; she then simply disappears. Thus, *'night, Mother* winds itself tighter emotionally as the end draws near and we and Thelma realize in shocked silence that "the moment" is now, but *Footfalls* seems to wind down into stillness and silence, with May pacing less and less and her monologue finally filled with as much silence as speech. However, while *'night, Mother* employs a traditionally emotional climax and *Footfalls* something more akin to a disintegration of structure and movement, both rely on revolution—a revolving motion (and, more subtly, its other meaning)—to achieve their ends. In *Footfalls*, the obvious revolution is May's continuous pacing of the grey strip of light, slowing and finally stopping as the third section comes to an end.[7] In *'night, Mother,* Jessie and Thelma parallel this physical revolution in their motions about the living room, which eventually contract into a spiral around the door to Jessie's bedroom as the evening approaches its inevitable conclusion. Thus, although at very different pace, each play relies on a revolution about the most significant set element on stage (door and strip of light).

This circular motion is not limited to the blocking of the characters on stage; it acts as a key to the emotional, factual, and even symbolic levels of the plays as well. First of all, there is the process of mental revolution in each daughter. Once again, this is more explicit in *Footfalls*, where sections one and three end with the question, "Will you never have done . . . revolving it all? . . . In your poor mind" (Beckett 241). Obviously, for May the pacing motion and her constant mental turmoil are linked in deep ways, as she is driven to do both by the same underlying fear of nonexistence. For Jessie as well, thought keeps pace with her "circular" motion of filling candy jars: From Christmas onward (apparently several months at least), she has worked over and over her plans for suicide, and questioned whether anything could revive her exhaustion with "it all." In a constant round that keeps pace with their movements, then, the two daughters turn their thoughts inward, working over the same fears and hopes again and again.

The daughters are not, however, alone in this revolving motion. As we have examined before, both sets of mothers and daughters tell stories, and they do so in a round. Essentially, each woman wants control over the script that is her daughter's life. In *Footfalls*, this script is the mostly historical tale of "what happened" to May (and, to some extent, why), a story that through its odd presentation and archaic language seems very distant from the characters, yet what we see on stage and May's emotional cracking show how near this story is to their hearts. In *'night, Mother*, there are many more stories, yet they tend to focus on Jessie's epilepsy and who (mother or father) is to blame for it (even the story about Agnes turns out to be an evasion on Thelma's part of the real reason Agnes will not visit when Jessie is around). So both Jessie and Thelma, and May and mother/V, take turns casting and recasting the daughter's story (perhaps each of their stories is a perversion of a "coming of age" story), the mothers hoping to maintain the status quo, the daughters trying to move beyond their mothers' views of them.

In light of the daughters' attempts to alter the status quo, it is interesting to note that both Jessie and May tell a story of future events as well as retelling those of the past. Jessie, by mapping out her mother's actions for the moments to years after her suicide, changes the balance of control over "their" story.[8] And in the final seconds, we see Thelma begin following the "script'" that Jessie has set out for her, washing the hot chocolate pan and calling her son. Though it took her death to do it, it is now Jessie who controls the future (and therefore the past) of the two of them. May, as well, talks of the future—in her case, she predicts her imminent disappearance in her story of Amy and Mrs. Winter. The crux of this story is the daughter's claim that she could not have seen anything at Evensong because she was "not there" at all, having disappeared from her mother's side. Mrs. Winter's only response is that Amy must have been with her because she heard her daughter say "Amen" to the prayer being said.[9] In this story, we "see" Amy's disappearance in defiance of what her mother claims, an act that we see repeated in May's disappearance moments later. Thus, in each case, the daughter has shaken herself loose from her mother's control by "revolving" their plot forward—taking authority over the future "script" of the pair.

In working on the revolving physical and mental actions and storytelling, we have verged on another, very important instance of circular movement: that of the daily (or nightly) routine of events in these women's lives. As we have discussed above, these mothers and daughters live a life of private repetition, going through the same motions day after day in a cycle of habit that crushes the women, yet is sought after for its familiar safeness. When Jessie tells Thelma that Dawson cannot come over because, among other things, it is Saturday night, Thelma knows exactly what Jessie means, as all of their Saturdays are the same. When mother/V describes May's nocturnal pacing, it is clear that what we see May doing has been going on for a long time (somewhere over thirty-five years, to be more precise). Just as much as the places in which they live, this repetition traps these women in a cocoon beyond which they seem unable to stray.

Moreover, it is not simply the characters' lives that revolve constantly: each playwright seems to understand the need to reinforce this sense of

circular repetition through stage effects. In 'night, Mother, Norman specifies that the bedroom door should, through lighting effects, alternately
disappear and become the focus of attention. In Footfalls, Beckett repeats the same sound and light sequence at the beginning of each section, the chime and fade-up altered only in their gradual lessening. Thus,
each play cyclically alternates light and shadow (and sound and silence)
to solidify and concentrate the sense of repetitious revolution that is at
the center of each mother-daughter pair's struggle.

Even mother and daughter are, in fact, in revolution: as we have
discussed, there is an inversion in both plays wherein the daughter
plays mother to her mother. This inversion in itself is, however, a
cyclical one. Whereas May states her willingness to care for her mother
in section one, thereby acting as mother, in section two, mother/V
recovers her motherhood: In telling the story of her daughter's development, and in her pride in observing May's pacing ("how feat
she wheels" (Beckett 241)), mother/V shows herself to be the proper
mother to May. Section three tightens this revolving inversion, as,
through May's voice, mother and daughter vie for motherhood. With
Jessie and Thelma, we quickly become aware of how much Thelma
is like a child with her daughter—Thelma needs Jessie to supply her
with "treats" (Norman 5)—and, as the play progresses, we see that
Thelma feels herself unable to function without Jessie to organize
things and tell her what to do; she even pouts like a child when
Jessie starts cleaning out the pots and pans in the kitchen. Yet at
times, Thelma more or less successfully takes on the role of mother.
In one abortive instance, she claims that she can "fill pill bottles . . .
and change the shelf paper and wash the floor" (Norman 32)—that
she will, in essence, be mother—if Jessie will choose to remain alive.
Thus in both plays there is a circularity to the characters' role playing, as each perhaps tries to find something that is missing from her
life in her societally assigned role.

There is even, on a more symbolic level, a revolution of life and
death in each of the plays. In biological and societal terms, the mother
is to pass her life on to her daughter, dying, if necessary, in the process. In neither play, however, is this transfer completely successful:
Neither daughter has had a "proper" life and both May and Jessie
seek death (in May's case, we can see this from her despair at only
being middle-aged). Instead, it is the mother who clings to life.

Thelma tells Jessie that "I will stay here until they make me go, until they drag me screaming and I mean screeching into my grave" (Norman 78), while mother/V calls from the darkness, taking life either through May's mind (Gontarski 167) or clinging to her nebulous existence as best she can. Beyond this, Jessie's death is an actual rebirth for Thelma:

Mama's slow acceptance of Jessie's decision to die is a movement toward acceptance of her own mortality. That this is a life-giving experience becomes clear as Thelma begins to accept the impending separation and hence the death of her dependency. . . . Mother and daughter merge as they separate, the death of one giving life to the other. (Burkman 260)

And, although the ending of *Footfalls* is much less conclusive than that of *'night, Mother*, there is nevertheless the potential for mother/V's rebirth in the transposition of the two in the story May tells in her monologue: If Mrs. Winter is the one present at Evensong while her daughter subsides into a mere sound, the mother has perhaps gained substance at the cost of her daughter. In both cases, the "suicide" of the daughter takes on the religious/ritual significance of a sacrifice for her mother (cf. Jessie's exclamation, "Jesus was a suicide, if you ask me" [Norman 18]), a voluntary death infusing within the dead (or nearly dead) a new life.

This last revolution—of life and death—brings up a final, very significant point: the painful, monotonous cycle of habit, movement, light, roles, and even existence is coming to an end "this evening." In each play there is ample evidence of finality, as if this is the end of a very long routine. When Jessie says, 'night, Mother," she has entered the "still point" of "nothingness" within the bedroom at the center of the set, a place where the revolving wheel stops spinning and her "poor mind" (Beckett 243) will be at rest. Likewise, in *Footfalls*, May has escaped through the point at the center of the infinity that she traces out into the darkness (where she will either join her mother or simply fade away), a still emptiness in which May need no longer pace back and forth. In the fourth section, her cocoon, the grey strip of light, is quiet, her footfalls now an echo in our minds.

Mother *and* daughter are able to escape the life-in-death revolution of habit through the daughter's actions: May and Jessie cast off their corporeal existences while Thelma and mother/V receive a more meaningful and "true" existence. If, then, the murky and revolving world in which these women are trapped is essentially the female corner of a male universe, the ending of both plays is a positive step toward liberation from the limitations placed on the mother-daughter pair in society. The separation of daughter from mother is achieved through a merging of the two in a unique, final moment that is not "proper" to a woman's prescribed existence of monotonous, repetitious duty. These characters achieve a deeper humanity (a humanity without the common dichotomous pigeonholing of women) in a moment of self-sacrifice and selfishness; a moment both positive and negative (and therefore of positive value both for them and for us); a moment that is, in effect, the painful, hopeful, essentially female act of motherhood—birth. If the end of *Footfalls* and *'night, Mother* point to a way to cease "revolving it all," then these plays are truly a revolution in drama.

Notes

1. See Savran 182–183, for Norman's discussion of the underlying structure.
2. See Brater, 60ff. for a more complete discussion of this image.
3. Interestingly enough, even the all-important issue of food in the play clues us into the "unnatural" and "inappropriate" nature of Thelma and Jessie's home life. While preparation of wholesome food is the hallmark of the proper wife in the home, Jessie has no appetite for food at all, while Thelma wants only prepackaged sweets to eat. As Katherine Burkman points out, this links the two in a death-in-life existence in which "all nourishing foods" are rejected (258), leaving them "useless women."
4. It would make for an interesting interpretation if neither mother nor daughter really existed.
5. See Gontarski 168, and Brater 68, for example, for thoughts on the importance of the relationship between mother's and daughter's speech patterns to this play.
6. Once again, it is an appetite for food (or in this case a lack thereof) that resonates this mother-daughter pair's relationship with life.
7. In section one, the shortest of the play in terms of time, May performs three (plus) "walking units"—pacing four lengths from right to left, left to right, right to left, and left to right (I choose this particular grouping of four lengths as a unit because it is performed as a whole before either character begins to speak). In section two, she walks only two units. In section three, the longest section, only one and a half; and in section four (fade up on blank stage), none. Thus, the motion of the play, as well as the lighting, tends towards (and achieves, in this case) zero.
8. This idea was suggested to me by Susan Chast, a professor in the theater department at the College of William and Mary, in a discussion in July 1993.
9. This reversal of who is seen and heard in May's tale is very thought-provoking, as mother and daughter have traded places from what we see on stage (the mother present in the light, the daughter in the darkness only heard as a voice).

METHODIST COLLEGE LIBRARY
Fayetteville, N.C.

As a result of this, should we conclude that May has traded places with her mother when we find her absent in section four of the play?

Works Cited

Beckett, Samuel. *Footfalls*. In *The Collected Shorter Plays of Samuel Beckett*. New York: Grove Press, 1984. 236–243.

Brater, Enoch. *Beyond Minimalism: Beckett's Late Style in the Theater*. Oxford: Oxford UP, 1987.

Browder, Sally. "'I Thought You Were Mine': Marsha Norman's *'night, Mother*." In *Mother Puzzles: Daughters and Mothers in Contemporary American Literature*, edited by Mickey Pearlman. New York: Greenwood Press, 1989.

Burkman, Katherine H. "The Demeter Myth and Doubling in Marsha Norman's *'night, Mother*." In *Modern American Drama: The Female Canon*, edited by June Schlueter. London: Associated UP, 1990. 254–263.

Gontarski, S.E. *The Intent of Undoing in Samuel Beckett's Dramatic Texts*. Bloomington: Indiana UP, 1985.

Kintz, Linda. *The Subject's Tragedy: Political Poetics, Feminist Theory, and Drama*. Ann Arbor: The U of Michigan P, 1992.

Knowlson, James, and John Pilling. *Frescoes of the Skull: The Later Prose and Drama of Samuel Beckett*. New York: Grove Press, 1979.

Norman, Marsha. *'night, Mother*. New York: Hill and Wang, 1983.

Savran, David. *In Their Own Words: Contemporary American Playwrights*. New York: Theatre Communications Group, 1988.

Spencer, Jenny S. "Marsha Norman's *She-tragedies*." In *Making a Spectacle: Feminist Essays on Contemporary Women's Theatre*, edited by Lynda Hart. Ann Arbor: The U of Michigan P, 1989. 147–168.

———. "Norman's *'night, Mother*: Psycho-drama of Female Identity." *Modern Drama*, 30,no.3: 364–375.

A Place at the Table

Hunger as Metaphor in Lillian Hellman's *Days to Come* and Marsha Norman's *'night, Mother*

Linda Ginter Brown

> *Food is my drug of choice.*
>
> —*Oprah Winfrey*

One does not have to search far to find examples showcasing contemporary society's love affair with food. Store shelves contain abundant supplies for those with the wherewithal to purchase. Restaurants cater to clientele all along the economic spectrum. Bookstores report continually increasing cookbook sales even in shaky financial times. Television shows featuring cooking segments garner large audiences.

At the same time, more than ever before, health problems related to diet demand attention. Rising numbers of anorexics, bulimics, and compulsive overeaters struggle to survive their twisted relationship with the food necessary to sustain their existence. Women comprise the majority of this struggling population. These battles belie the real issue—the need to find a true self in the midst of a false society. The hunger that haunts these women is not of physiological origin. It does not connote any quest to appease what Maslow calls the most basic human need[1], but rather a psychic one. Perched on the edge of the twenty-first century, women hunger to heal that "hole in the soul." They fight not to fix their Oedipal crisis, as Freud posited, but rather to find their true selves. Fragmented and confused, they search for the missing piece. Like Humpty Dumpty, they have fallen from the wall and cannot put themselves together. Psychically, they long for a cohesive self.

Food metaphors depicted in women's writing reflect that psychic search. Both Lillian Hellman and Marsha Norman use this "culinary approach" to foreground a number of their female characters' struggles with psychic issues. By examining their works, one can see how certain female characters use their relationships to food to symbolize the gnawing psychic hunger each experiences.

Reading Hellman's memoirs is tantamount to sitting at a banquet of culinary metaphors. Hellman's passion for food permeates many pages, starting with her childhood memories in New Orleans and ending with her last publication, *Eating Together: Recollections and Recipes*, a cookbook coauthored with Peter Feibleman and published after her death. In *Unfinished Woman*, she relates how she cleaned the crayfish for the delicious bisques her aunts would make and how she learned to kill a chicken without "any ladylike complaints" (13). Her reputation for hospitality is well known, along with marvelous parties at her home on Martha's Vineyard. Robert Brustein attributes her preoccupation with nourishment as "perhaps reflecting her blocked maternal instinct."[2] Even Marsha Norman, who interviewed Hellman shortly before she died, was invited to bring her husband and come back for dinner when Hellman was better able to cook. Her penchant for parties is well documented, for, unnurtured herself, Hellman sought to appease others' hunger. Her writings attest to that commitment.

Ironically, one of Hellman's weakest plays contains an abundance of food images. *Days to Come*, Hellman's second play, opened in December 1936 to generally negative reviews. Hellman's uneasy fears about the play turned to horror on opening night. Her inability to "stomach" the production manifested itself as she vomited in a side aisle near the back of the darkened theater. Audience response ranged from lackluster to outright disgust, with William Randolph Hearst leaving, with six friends, during the middle of the second act. *New York Times* critic Brooks Atkinson condemned the play[3], charging Hellman with laborious writing and confusing plots and counterplots. Robert Coleman, *New York Daily Mirror* critic,[4] contended that Hellman used "staccato and stuffy dialogue." Charles Dexter, writing in the *Daily Worker*,[5] noted that Hellman sympathized with the worker's plight, but was unable "to get under the skin of her characters."

This unsuccessful effort centers around the Rodman family, owners of a brush manufacturing company in Galion, Ohio, and foregrounds the inherent conflict between management and labor.

Although company CEO Andrew Rodman abhors the thought, a team has been brought into break up a strike. Because Rodman has known the townspeople all his life, he believes reason will prevail. A weak and ineffectual man, he fails to see that his wife, Julie, is having an affair with family friend and lawyer Henry Ellicott. However, Ellicott "owns" more than just Rodman's wife. He has manipulated Rodman into borrowing funds to keep the company afloat, taking company shares as collateral.

Whalen, a union organizer, counsels company workers to refrain from fighting with Wilkie, the strike buster who arrives in town with two thugs, Mossie and Easter. Mossie kills Easter during a card game and plants the body at union headquarters to implicate Whalen. Julie, who hopes to initiate a "friendship" with Whalen, witnesses the plant, as she is at his office when it occurs. Whalen is jailed, and in the ensuing ruckus, a company worker's child is killed. Firth, the child's father, confronts Rodman at the family home. Wilkie is ordered to leave town.

During the entire episode, Cora Rodman, Andrew's maiden sister, worries about losing the company and how the strike will affect their family. Intensely jealous of Julie, she finally tells Andrew about his wife's lengthy affair with Henry Ellicott. After Ellicott leaves, Julie offers to leave or give Andrew a divorce, but he declines. As the curtain descends, he rather pitifully attests that they will live, "just as 'half-people' the rest of their lives—for days to come" (133).

While the political machinations of both management and labor obstensibly constitute the play's central action, the most interesting struggle, from a critical standpoint, focuses upon Cora Rodman, Andrew's spinster sister. While lamenting Hellman's ill-fated choice to include so many issues in one play, critics seldom mention Cora, whom Grenville Vernon called an "acidulous old maid."[6] Carl Rollyson, in his lengthy study *Lillian Hellman: Her Legend and Her Legacy*, terms Cora "a puzzle in the play" (95) and suggests that Cora is tormented by the same issues as the other characters—what the strike means and how management and labor can find a way to coexist (95). He rightly observes that "She does not know how to begin to live her own life" and "she exemplifies critic Joseph Wood Krutch's observation that Hellman is a 'specialist in hate and frustration, a student of helpless rage'" (95). However, Cora's torment goes much deeper than the family's trouble with the strikers, and her ceaseless preoccupation with food and its preparation signals the reader that Hellman, once again, is presenting a fragmented self in search of cohesion. Cora's continual focus upon food symbolizes her struggle for personal power, an identity, and the need to fill the "gnawing psychic hunger" she experiences as part of the Rodman family structure. Clearly, getting to eat what she wants when she wants it metaphorically symbolizes filling a psychic void. In her work *The Hungry Self*, Kim Chernin quotes a client who relates, "There is no I . . . There's just an immense hole at the center. An emptiness. A terror. Not all the food in the world could fill it. But, I try" (20). Cora also tries. From act 1, scene 1 where she berates Hannah, the housekeeper, for cutting her piece of cake too small, until the last scene of the last act, where she takes a bite of toast and chides everyone for "getting too excited," it is quite apparent that something is "eating" her.

That "something" is her response to the powerlessness she feels. More than anything, she desires a "place at the table," to be part of some satisfying relationship, to be acknowledged as a person. No one, either in or out of the household, supports her emotionally. Consequently, her manipulative behavior reveals a desperate woman posturing for attention, begging to be heard, but mostly being ignored. Like numerous other female characters of Hellman's, such as Martha in *The Children's Hour*, or Anna and Carrie in *Toys in the Attic*, or Regina in *The Little Foxes*, Cora struggles to find some measure of personal power denied her in the patriarchal culture within which she must exist. Her relationship to food illuminates that struggle.

A thin, nervous woman of forty-two, she has never married but lives with her brother Andrew and his wife, Julie, in the house left by their parents, the founders of the Rodman family business. She snipes. She carps. She criticizes. Her behavior belies an unhappy soul, whether she harangues Hannah, telling her, "You didn't bring me enough butter on my tray this morning and I had a roll left over . . . there always seems to be something wrong with the breakfast tray" (79), or whether she tells Henry Ellicott, the family lawyer, "I shall eat as much as I please. Just as much as I please" (130). Cora fears being shortchanged. Like Beckett's Hamm in *Endgame*, she worries that supplies are running out. She fears that nothing can satisfy, that there will never be enough. Her nervous stomach mirrors her inward turmoil. Outwardly, she attempts to soothe herself with chocolate pepsin drops prescribed by her doctor—even medication meant to calm digestion needs a "sweet" coating. Cora cannot accept life "straight." She must seek solace in food for she cannot face the truth of a meager existence. Even sleep escapes her, for, as she relates, "if a pin drops, it wakes me. I've always been like that" (81).

Interestingly, Cora has never married, nor has she "reproduced" herself through the birth of a child. Like her creator, she seeks nurturance from an Other who is missing from the picture. Although Hellman married Arthur Kober, the marriage was brief, and the child they conceived beforehand was aborted. Yet Hellman never stopped seeking nurturance, psychic food that would enable her to survive. Her relationship with Dashiell Hammett, her "idealized other," assuaged some of that hunger, but as Rollyson rightly suggests, "Always, something was missing for Hellman" (8), and "she was—even later in life—the type of person who liked to dress elegantly for dinner and then complain about the 'rat-fuck' food she was eating" (35).

Perhaps Hellman's attempts to find satisfying food belie a deeper fear—of losing herself *or* reproducing herself. In her ground-breaking book, *Bitter Milk*, Madeline Grumet describes this fear when she describes childbirth as "the wrenching expulsion of the infant" that "physically recapitulates the terrors of coming apart, of losing a part of oneself" (10). Perhaps Cora, as well as her creator, fears reproducing herself. If her search for a "replacement umbilical cord" has thus far been unsuccessful, she risks being unable to nurture any mirror image she may reproduce.

A useful construct to more fully illuminate Cora's struggle for a cohesive self is time—whether past, present, or future. In the past, Cora's family unit was intact. Her biological mother was present, and the interloper, Julie, who marries her weak, ineffectual brother, had not yet intruded. Papa, who "knew how to run the company," was alive and was certainly more effectual than his son, who has endangered the family fortune through his *laissez-faire* attitude. However, Andrew's climactic speeches at the play's end reveal the loathing and contempt he harbors toward Cora, as he tells his sister, "You hate me and I hated you from the day I was old enough to think about you." (132). His uncharacteristic venomous outburst certainly suggests that Cora's childhood was less than ideal.

What Cora needs more than anything is a supportive relationship with a nurturing mother figure. If she can obtain this necessary connection, she stands a chance to become psychically whole. Without it, she risks continued fragmentation. As Chodorow notes, "a girl cannot and does not completely reject her mother in favor of men but continues her relationship of dependence upon and attachment to her" (53).

Hellman is strangely silent concerning the biological mother. No mention of her is made during the entire play, but a surrogate mother is present in the character of Hannah, the housekeeper. Arguably the play's strongest female character, Hannah bows to no one, not even Cora. Perceptive as well as powerful, she usurps pantry supplies to support the striking workers. Unlike Andrew Rodman, the company CEO, Hannah has a much more realistic view of the situation, realizing that a confrontation is coming. She notes, "I haven't lived in this house twenty years for nothing" (78). When Wilkie arrives with his mafioso thugs, she refuses to answer the door. Even Andrew acknowledges her role in the family's structure in the last scene, as he relates, "Hannah shares the secrets of all of us. That's why Cora can't get rid of her, isn't it, Cora?" (132).

Cora and Hannah's relationship centers upon food. In Cora's first speech, she asks Hannah, "Did you make something sweet?" to which Hannah accedes, "Chocolate cake. All over" (79). Characteristic of an adult's desire to reestablish a childhood memory, Cora seeks something sweet, not a vegetable or salad, which might be better for one's arteries, but something like "mama used to make." Her food fixation leads her to inventory the food supply and her discovery that supplies are, indeed, low, sends her to Mossie and Easter for help in catching the responsible criminal. She concedes, "very funny things are happening here. Things are missing from the pantry. Or is that too unimportant work for you? . . . When I looked into the closet I was amazed to find at least eight or ten dollars worth of canned goods" (99).

As a surrogate mother figure, Hannah embodies what Melanie Klein referred to as a "good breast, bad breast" image[7]. Klein, in opposition to her mentor, Freud, focused upon an infant's preoedipal, rather than oedipal, development. Because the infant cannot distinguish between the mother and the breast during the earliest stages of development, the infant is inevitably frustrated and splits this "object" into a "good breast" and a "bad breast" in order to preserve it psychically. Hannah, as "keeper of the food supply," controls Cora's physical nourishment. Moreover, when confronted about the thefts, she shows not one iota of remorse. Instead she insists, "I wish I could have taken more. People need it. Do what you want about it, Mr. Andrew" (100). Cora's concern that there be enough food available does not impress Hannah in the least.

Hannah's position as a surrogate mother figure only enrages Cora. She finds no sustenance in their relationship, nor does she have anyone else who can meet her needs. As Chodorow posits, "women, therefore, need primary relationships to women as well as men" (53). In this motherless world (for Hannah refuses to fulfill her potential as a nurturing mother), Cora is bereft. If the past precluded any basis upon which to build the underpinnings of emotional stability, the present presents little hope either. The sad reality is that Cora is pushed aside. Andrew's tired answer that he will not do anything about the theft further humiliates Cora and serves as a stunning example that Cora deserves no place at the family table. Her opinions and actions are of no consequence. Just as she has no say in corporate decisions affecting family business, she has no say in the day-to-day management of the household budget. This "bread and butter" is off limits. Indeed, Cora has no say in anything that occurs in the Rodman household. Because she feels so powerless, she lashes out at each combatant and then seeks solace in food. As Cherin suggests, an association exists between a woman's eating habits and her struggle for identity (xi); she maintains that a woman must return to her roots to find what keeps her developmentally weak, "the hunger knot in which identity, the mother-separation struggle, love, rage, food, and the female body are all entangled" (xiv). Cora fits Chernin's definition of a woman with an eating disorder, one who is "trying to fill an ill-defined 'gnawing hunger' whose real nature she cannot admit to herself" (24).

Even the murder of Wilkie's thug, Mossie, right in the Rodman home, cannot keep Cora from her appointed snack. In Cora's view, nothing can be done for a dead man, but hunger can be appeased.

Loudly ringing the bell to summon Hannah, she insists, "My milk and fruit aren't upstairs. We can't help it if he got killed. Whatever we do now isn't going to do him any good. . . . You forgot it, didn't you?" (117). Hannah's cryptic reply that, "I didn't think you'd starve. . . . Funny, how you drink it. Just like you need it" (117), reveals not only Hannah's hard-hearted approach, but also Cora's overriding need for nurturance. To borrow a line from Arthur Miller's Linda Loman, "Attention must be paid." In this case, Cora's starving self demands it. While the others gather to discuss the previous night's horrific events, she sends back the improperly made hot chocolate. Her curt reply to Ellicott's query as to whether she must have her breakfast in the library symbolizes her attempt to sustain structure in her power-less life, as she demands, "Mind your own business. I've had it here for thirty years. I shall continue" (130). Family and friends may manipulate her position, but Cora will not cave in so easily. If the hot chocolate will not soothe her psychic aches and pains, she will send it back to the kitchen until Hannah "gets it right." Just like Jessie in Marsha Norman's 'night, Mother, Cora longs for the days when warm cocoa with Mama would take care of life's woes. The fact that those days are a fantasy is beside the point. One can try. One can demand one's place at the table as long as one's strength holds.

Cora's present sense of power is further diminished by her brother's wife, Julie. Before Julie married Andrew, Cora could func-tion as the household's mistress. Her constant criticism of Julie's ability to coordinate household functions reveals her rage at being displaced. She loses no opportunity to illuminate Julie's incompetence, as evi-denced by her remark to the man who comes to plant the trees. Cora notes, "I told him that you always did that. Forgetting about things" (82). She further establishes her fear at relinquishing her perceived place as mistress of the household when she deliberately snubs Julie's hoped-for paramour, Leo Whalen, the union organizer. Julie's immediate caustic attack as she demands, "Don't do that in my house again" (92), only enrages her more. Cora does not accept Julie's place in the Rodman household. She underscores the rage she feels as she shouts, "How dare you talk that way? So now it's your house? My father built it, but it's YOUR house now" (92). As long as Julie remains, Cora's place at the table remains in jeopardy.

Cora holds a losing hand in this game with her sister-in-law unless she plays her high card and reveals Julie's longstanding affair with the family lawyer, Henry Ellicott, as well as other clandestine liasons. However, her decision to reveal Julie's extramarital liaison with Ellicott, causing Julie's fall from grace, backfires. Metaphorically speaking, Cora feels that if she can pull the chair out from under Julie, she can regain a place at the family table. Unfortunately, for her, the plan fails. Whether Andrew knew or did not know of his wife's deception is of no consequence to him now. In view of the fact that he bears responsibility for two murders, he has neither the energy nor the inclination to demand an explanation from Julie, even though Julie insists, "Let her say it. She's wanted to for a long time" (130). Andrew's lackluster reply, coupled with Julie's taunt, causes an emotional explosion that serves as a catalyst to bring the missing ingredient to the table—truth.

When Cora acknowledges that she has known about Julie's extramarital behavior for years, she pinpoints the powerlessness his marriage has supposedly placed upon her. What has eaten away at Cora's insides is that Andrew has, unashamedly, squandered family money (half of which belongs to Cora), upon European trips, fashionable clothes, and a year's study in Paris for his wife. Cora resents that Andrew has had to borrow thousands and thousands of dollars, resulting in deep debt, to make Julie happy.

However, Cora's bare-bones approach to truth elicits no appreciation from Andrew—or anyone else. Her strategy falters, and, as a result, her future as a Rodman family member appears dubious, at best. Each one harbors resentment about her revelation, but Andrew's response epitomizes the seething hostility present, as he insists, "It wasn't your business. It isn't your business now" (131). Instead, he discloses the denial in which each one, as well as Henry, participates, noting "It was all there before. It can be said now" (132).

Sadly, Cora's response to the debilitating diatribes indicates no success on her part at assuaging the ill-defined "gnawing hunger" that eats aways at her psyche. Her last speech, in which she mildly suggests, "Things went entirely too far. It comes from everybody getting too excited. Now you go to sleep and nothing will seem as bad when you wake up. People said a lot of things they didn't mean. A lot of things they didn't mean. I'm sure of that" (133), indicates her inability to accept the truth. Her final gesture, summarily chomping down on a bite of toast, signifies her continuing turn to food. Food denotes sustenance. It comforts. The hot chocolate like Mama used to make or the tea and toast she brought when you were ill conjure up a time—far removed—when needs were met, when hunger was fed. Cora's fixation on food represents an attempt to obtain the nurturing she never experiences in the Rodman family. Tragically, the food can never satisfy. It must be perfectly presented, and it must be in abundance. Supplies can never run out.

However, no abundance can ever appease the appetite within Cora. Hellman's characterization illustrates one way a woman may respond when confronted with the powerlessness of her life. As Chernin notes, these women are "filling the emptiness with food" (25). This preoccupation, for Cora, signifies the fear she feels when confronted with the obstacles before her— obstacles that leave her economically dependent as well as emotionally bereft. Cora wants what most women want—an identity that affords them some measure of power; a place at the table—but, just as other female characters in Hellman's works, she finds her chair missing. Like Lavinia in *Another Part of the Forest,* who escapes her confinement through fantasies that substitute for the reality she finds unbearable, or Regina, in *Little Foxes,* who responds to her powerlessness by, in effect, murder, so Cora escapes through food.

In this motherless world, Cora has no means of escape. She has no idealized other with whom she can bond. She will simply, as millions of her sisters throughout centuries, have to make the best of a brutal situation. In order to do so, she will continue to keep the food pantry, and the hostile Hannah, under surveillance. In this play, which William Wright terms "Hellman's most political play," Cora's character has no power base from which to muster a fight. Instead, she continues to struggle in a hostile and stifling environment. No other choices exist. Like her creator, Cora must remain "an unfinished woman," never finding the truth she needs to satisfy her appetite—the truth she needs to become psychically whole.

Like her literary progenitor, Marsha Norman also foregrounds food in her plays, particularly the two most successful, *Getting Out* and *'night, Mother.* Both female protagonists search for sustenance and nurturance. Arlene, in *Getting Out,* longs to be invited for her mother's Sunday pot roast dinner, and even though her mother ultimately rejects her, Arlene finds a friend, Ruby, an upstairs neighbor, with whom to break bread. Jessie, in *'night, Mother*, is not so fortunate. She can find no food that will satisfy, and even though her mother tries valiantly to stop her, she kills herself in order to gain control over her meager existence.

In this Pulitzer–Prize winning effort, Norman, true to her "calling" as a storyteller determined to give a voice to people not normally heard, presents the painful existence of Jessie Cates, a woman without hope—without a "self" for which she constantly hungers. Critics categorically raved about this ninety minutes of intermissionless, riveting theater. Brendan Gill, writing in the *New Yorker*, termed it "a very good play indeed," and *Louisville Times* critic Dudley Saunders saw its Broadway opening at the Golden Theatre as "refreshingly clean, honest and straightforward." Drama critic for the *New York Times* Mel Gussow, allowed that "the play stands out as one of the season's major dramatic events," and described Norman as a powerful dramatist. Robert Brustein, writing in *Who Needs Theatre*, likened Norman's technique and effect to that of Chekhov and O'Neill, while noting that Norman's scene depicting the attempt to make hot chocolate "the old way" is her version of "J.D. Salinger's consecrated chicken soup" (66, 67).

Mother and daughter, Thelma and Jessie Cates, live isolated existences in a nondescript house on a lonely country road. Jessie, an unhappy overweight woman, about forty, suffers from epilepsy, but the "disease" that drives her to take her own life is far more insidious than this lifelong affliction. Jessie starves for a cohesive self, a sense of personal autonomy, which has thus far escaped her. Because she has no "appetite" for life, she opts for death.

However, although suicide is certainly a factor, this play is *not* about suicide. Indeed, those who see it merely as a "death watch," instituted by a cruel daughter determined to "pay back" her mother for a lifetime of wrongs, err in their judgment. *'night, Mother* is a play about mother and daughter relationships, about psychic hunger, about tragedy, but also about triumph. With the final gunshot, Jessie assumes control over her life, and during the play's action she and Thelma connect in a way they never could before. At the same time, she separates from her mother—a task she has heretofore been unable to accomplish—and Thelma learns to let her daughter go.

Hunger, and the need to appease it, form the play's central metaphor. Both women experience psychic hunger brought about by the helplessness women have historically experienced as part of a patriarchal culture that offers little hope for personal power. However, Marsha Norman's female characters differ from Lillian Hellman's. Unlike Cora Rodman in *Days to Come*, Jessie Cates does not hopelessly vegetate in a powerless position at the play's end. Ultimately, she gets what she wants—death— which releases her from the incredibly boring existence she would have experienced if she had opted to live. And actually, Mama also gets what she wants, too. She finally communicates in a powerful way never before possible. Some mothers live and die without ever communicating with their daughters at such a deep level.

The kitchen becomes a metaphor for the play's action. Traditionally, we tend to view the kitchen as the heart of the house, symbolizing mother, warmth, and nurturance. We break bread, which mother prepares, in the bosom of our family. We experience connection and relationships that sustain our survival in the outside world. The kitchen, usually smaller than the other rooms in the house, functions as a womb—a warm and safe place. Memory conjures up images of mother fixing breakfast for us before we trudge off to school and taking cookies from the oven upon our return.

Norman begins the play's action in the kitchen, where Thelma searches for the sugary snowballs she loves so well. The kitchen serves as a base from which to launch the battle to save the mother/daughter relationship. Here they will attempt to recapture what never existed through the cocoa-making ritual. The living room, as Jenny Spencer points out in *Modern Drama*, "underscores our sense of physical entrapment and psychological impasse in the ensuing action" (365). Their separation and Jessie's eventual stand for autonomy, however, are symbolized by Jessie's departure to the locked bedroom, which Thelma cannot penetrate.

Thelma, too, starves for fulfillment. Norman's first stage directions tell us that "Mama stretches to reach the cupcakes in a cabinet in the kitchen. She can't see them, but she can feel around for them, and she's eager to have one, so she's working pretty hard at it" (5). Finding only a partial package with the coconut fallen off symbolizes Mama's life. Although she has never heard of Betty Friedan's *The Feminine Mystique*, she most assuredly knows something's amiss. The "coconut is always falling off" for Mama, and this confrontation with her only daughter who is determined to kill herself will only confuse Mama more. Thelma loves candy; its sweetness temporarily satisfies, and she must see that the supply continues. The play's first speech solidifies this position, as she tells Jessie while unwrapping a cupcake:

Jessie, it's the last snowball, sugar. Put it on the list, O.K.? And we're out of Hershey bars, and where's that peanut brittle? I think maybe Dawson's been in it again. I ought to put a big mirror on the refrigerator door. That'll keep him out of my treats, won't it? You hear me, honey? (Then more to herself) *I hate it when the coconut falls off. Why does the coconut fall off?* (5)

Isolated upon a country road and burdened with an epileptic daughter who never communicates, Thelma lives a meager existence. Candy, her little "treats," become a crutch to help her survive. As Sally Browder notes in *Mother Puzzles*, Thelma, too, "has had her share of disappointments" (110). Rejected by a "silent" husband who refused to even talk to her upon his deathbed, Thelma endures her pyromaniac, okra-eating friend, Agnes, just to have someone who will talk to her. "Sweets . . . provide Mama with the sensual gratification, and the sense of fullness she failed to obtain from her marriage" (Morrow 24). Once again, Kim Chernin's patient probably focuses upon Thelma's pain best: "There is no I . . . There's just an immense hole at the center. An emptiness. A terror. Not all the food in the world could fill it. But, I try" (20).

Food functions as a complex metaphor here, and Thelma's psychic hunger begs for appeasement. Chernin's assessment crystallizes this "psychic gnawing" for all women, as she relates:

For food, after all, has defined female identity. . . . It has defined more even than the history of mother/daughter relations and that early sorrow and disorder that began, for many of us, at the mother's breast. Dating back to our earliest impressions of life, recorded in the symbolic code of food imagery, the vanquished story of female value and power returns to us again and again in our obsession with food. . . . (197)

Rather than see Thelma as a "dodo" or a "caricature of a self-centered old baby" (Kauffman 48), we need to understand her position in the play as well as Jessie's. Because she views Jessie as an extension of herself, she finds herself upon the horns of a major maternal dilemma. Now that her "extension" has announced plans to blow her brains out with "Daddy's gun," Thelma faces losing a part of her self, her daughter. At the same time, she also risks repudiation of her entire existence as a mother. As Chodorow asserts, a mother, "tends to experience boundary confusion with her daughter, and does not provide experiences of differentiating ego development for her daughter or encourage the breaking of her daughter's dependence" (59). Thelma valiantly tries to forestall the inevitable, to find something that tastes good to Jessie, but Jessie rejects all offers. However, as they attempt to work through the psychological baggage that underlies every mother and daughter relationship, Jessie mounts an all-out effort to connect and make her mother understand this shattering decision. Ninety minutes of anger and accusations finally give way to acceptance and understanding.

Indeed, Jessie hungers for understanding, but more importantly, control. She loves her mother, but, ultimately, she leaves her. Unlike her mother, Jessie cannot subsist on the likes of sugary snowballs, peanut brittle, and Hershey bars. She now knows that this present life will never provide the nurturance she needs to be a truly autonomous self. Her only hope is to separate from her mother and reunite with her father—in death. But before she goes, she "mothers" Mama by preparing her sweet supply. She also lists Christmas presents for Mama to give and explains directions for disposal of her body and funeral etiquette.

While some may think Jessie incredibly selfish for subjecting Thelma to such agonizing torture, the fact is that Jessie cares deeply for Thelma. Her carefully planned evening reflects a desperate attempt to explain why no food, not even rice pudding, can make such an isolated existence bearable, as Jessie suggests, "How would you know if I didn't say it? You want it to be a surprise?" (13). Jessie's refusal to allow Thelma to call Dawson, Jessie's brother, underscores the fact that what occurs, this night, in this house, is for mother and daughter alone. As Jessie notes, "If Dawson comes over, it'll make me feel stupid for not doing it ten years ago. . . . I only told you so I could explain it, so you wouldn't blame yourself, so you wouldn't feel bad. There wasn't anything you could say to change my mind. I didn't want you to save me. I just wanted you to know" (17, 74).

Jessie wants Thelma to know that a place at her mother's table has not satisfied the psychic hunger she endures. No option Thelma offers appeals to Jessie. Supplies have run out. However, as Jessie methodically lines up the bags of sour balls, red hots, and licorice, she makes one last attempt to answer her questions and to recreate a sense of safety that never really existed. As she tells Thelma, "We could go on fussing all night. I mean, I could ask you things I always wanted to know and you could make me some hot chocolate the old way" (36). She adds a caramel apple to her request, and Thelma, who allows that she "makes the best caramel apples in the world" (37), willingly accedes to Jessie's wishes. No request is too difficult for Thelma, who desperately wants Jessie to stay as she asserts, "It's no trouble, what trouble? You put it in the pan, and stir it up. All right. Fine. Caramel apple. Cocoa. O.K. (37). Interestingly, this pan is the one Jessie instructs her to hold when she calls the police to report Jessie's death. Norman's stage directions tell us she grips the pan tightly "like her life depended on it" (89). As Lynda Hart notes, "Jessie's last request from her mother is for food. . . . This last bit of sustenance that mother and daughter share is highly charged with symbolic meaning as the pan Thelma uses to warm the milk becomes the object that will occupy her after Jessie's death" (76). However, Hart pinpoints the problems daughters have in separating from mothers when she suggests that Thelma's insistence that Jessie have three marshmallows in her cocoa reflects Thelma's attempt to retain maternal control over Jessie. As Hart asserts, "Even with the knowledge of her daughter's imminent suicide, Mama cannot acknowledge her daughter as a separate adult. . . . In this most basic of ways, Mama is asserting her power and denying her daughter's initiative" (76).

Mama wants to return to the "old way," in which she retained control over her daughter. Now, the table is turned as Jessie asserts her autonomy through her refusal to eat even though she starves psychically. In this battle over what and how much to eat the two wills clash:

The child's efforts to impose her own will upon the world and to ma-
nipulate her environment are directed towards food very early in the
development of a separate self. What will be eaten and how it will be
prepared are questions that often form the basis of mother and daughter
struggles.(Hart 76)

Unfortunately, however, their attempted ritual to recover their symbiotic relationship ultimately fails, as both mother and daughter realize the cocoa cannot satisfy the deeper longing. Significantly, the milk makes it taste bad. As both mother and daughter concede that it is, indeed, the milk, both women, together, confront their unfulfilled lives. Their mutual dislike of milk is one of the few traits mother and daughter share (Morrow 24).

Mama's avowal that "It's a real waste of chocolate. You don't have to finish it" (45) comprises one of the most important lines in the play. This statement suggests, at least on some level, Jessie's decision to halt her psychic "forage for food"; it also provides a connection to the play's last line, "Forgive me. (*Pause*) I thought you were mine" (89), where Thelma ultimately realizes that she and her daughter are not one, but two separate people.

While her dislike of milk reflects her rejection of the unadulterated and healthful, it also suggests "her dissatisfaction with motherhood which has proven no more rewarding than marriage" (Morrow 26). Now she faces coming to terms with a daughter's decision to reject the woman who bore her even though the men in her life, and not her mother, have abandoned her.

Thelma's rage at the realization that Jessie will never have an appetite for options her mother may offer erupts, as she complains, "I should've known not to make it. I knew you wouldn't like it. You never did like it" (45). Nothing Thelma can do will satisfy Jessie, and knowing that compels her to lash out in a tyrannical rage, threatening never to cook nor drink milk again. Her existence will be bolstered only by candy and tuna, and Jessie's maternal avowal that "You should drink milk" is met with a firm, "Not anymore, I'm not" (54). Moreover, she demands an accounting from the flesh and blood that has turned on her, as she insists, "Nothing I ever did was good enough for you and I want to know why" (55). Characteristically, Thelma assumes, as a mother, it must be her fault if her daughter refuses the food proffered. Thelma cannot accept that Jessie feels that "I cannot do anything either, about my life, to change it, make it better, make me feel better about it" (36).

No one has really taken time to know Jessie on any level except a surface one. All the men in her life, including her beloved father, have fled. Indeed, Jessie's identification with him, the "big, old faded blue man in the chair" (47), is so strong she uses his gun to complete her mission. Jessie could talk to him, even if it was only about why "black socks are warmer than blue socks" (48). Like her father, Jessie is both an epileptic as well as an introvert. Her desire to rejoin him in death is reflected by her wish to "hang a sign around her neck, 'Gone fishin,' like her daddy's" (29). Jessie does not wish to stay around and chat forever. "Unlike Mama, Jessie accepts her father's introversion and complexity because she recognizes the necessary (and desirable) limitation of our ability to communicate with others" (Morrow 29). Jessie wants out, and she wants out tonight.

Although her father leaves her through death, Cecil, Jessie's husband, leaves because, as Jessie tells it, he "made her choose between him and smoking" (56). Interestingly, although Jessie may refuse food, she enjoys smoking—an oral fixation. To Jessie this addictive but non-nourishing habit signifies "the only thing I know that's always just what you think it's going to be. Just like it was the last time, right there when you want it and real quiet" (56). Jessie associates smoking "with power and self-determination . . . smoking offers Jessie a sense of predictability and control—if only negative control—over her destiny" (Morrow 29). Even this failed relationship reflects back upon Thelma because she is the one who engineered it in the first place. Afraid that Jessie would have a hard time "catching" a man, Thelma contracted with Cecil for a porch and ended up with a son-in-law who left her daughter for another woman. Like Cecil, Jessie's juvenile delinquent son Ricky also leaves her.

An incorrigible youngster, he steals, does drugs, and may commit murder in a matter of time. Jessie has given up any hope for Ricky, much as she has for herself. Still, she recognizes his shortcomings are hers too, as she notes, "Ricky is as much like me as it's possible for any human being to be. We even wear the same size pants. These are his, I think" (59). Likewise, she realizes her maternal failure with Ricky, as she tells Thelma, "You know who laid that floor. I did" (60), much as Thelma failed in building a proper foundation for her. Even so, Jessie reaches out to nurture Ricky through her decision to leave him her watch. When Thelma complains that he will just sell it Jessie admits she hopes he gets a good meal, and if he buys dope as Thelma threatens, she hopes "he gets some good dope with it, Mama. . . ." (85).

The other man in her life, her brother Dawson, offers her no familial sense of community. In Jessie's view, Dawson calls her Jess "just like he knows who he's talking to" (23), and he and his wife, Loretta, invade Jessie's privacy by opening the package containing her mail-order bra, the one with the "little rosebuds." The grocery account bears Dawson's name even though Jessie orders the weekly food, and she is tired of dealing with her own brother, who gives her houseshoes every Christmas which never fit.

Aside from family relationships, Jessie has no standing in the community either. Isolated, out in the country, her life consists of day-to-day rituals such as changing shelf paper, washing floors, and coordinating grocery deliveries. She cannot hold a job, not the telephone sales job nor the one at the hospital gift shop where she made the people "real uncomfortable smiling at them the way I did" (35). The one satisfying job she liked, keeping her father's books, ended with his death. Jessie has had no real opportunity to practice socialization skills either, since she has never really been around people except in the hospital after a seizure. People avoid her. Even Thelma's okra-eating friend, Agnes, will not come to visit because she senses "Jessie's shook the hand of death and I can't take the chance it's catching. . . . I'll come up the driveway, but that's as far as I go" (43).

As Jessie sees it, her best bet is to leave this incredibly boring life. She has had enough of being subject to the convenience of other people's schedules and ideas of where her best interests lie. She has had enough of being at the mercy of possible epileptic seizures even though she has not had one in a year. On this particular night, she maintains perfect control. This control is reflected in her statement, "Whenever I feel like it, I can get off. As soon as I've had enough, it's my stop. I've had enough" (33). Her search for a cohesive self has ended in failure, and Jessie knows it. As she explains to Thelma, "That's what this is about. It's somebody I lost, all right, it's my own self. Who I never was. Or who I tried to be and never got there. Somebody I waited for who never came" (76). Jessie is a woman "in whom all desire is spent, not through satiation, but through the clear understanding of the world's false nourishment" (Hart 75). The only reason she remains is to make her mother understand why she had to make this radical decision. At the same time, she wishes to have her mother accept her as an autonomous adult and not the child she once was. "Through both her actions and her words, we sense Jessie's sincere desire to make some connections with her mother as a fully separate human being before she goes" (Spencer 366). Even though Thelma makes one last-ditch effort to assert her maternal power by proclaiming the inescapable eternal mother/daughter connection, as she insists, "Everything you have to do has to do with me, Jessie. You can't do *anything*, wash your face or cut your finger, without doing it to me" (72), Jessie retains the upper hand. In a poignant moment, Jessie reveals the enormity of her newly-found independence by insisting, "Then what if it does! . . . What if you are all I have and you're not enough? . . . What if the only way I can get away from you for good is to kill myself? . . . I can still do it!" (72).

In this gripping speech, Jessie speaks for all daughters everywhere. Her outburst metaphorically reflects the anger we feel toward the woman who can never fulfill our fantasy of the perfect mother. Jessie wants her mother to feed her, but Thelma is unable to provide the necessary nurturance. Her failure incurs Jessie's wrath:

Jessie expresses anger at her mother for not being able to fulfill her insatiable demands (you're not enough), anger at feeling powerless to change her situation any other way. . . anger for not providing her with an adequate sense of self, for controlling her life without giving it meaning. For women in the audience, it is anger that each of us has experienced. (Spencer 368)

Jessie's carefully orchestrated suicide finally separates her from her mother. She will not opt for a life of desperation like Thelma. Unlike her mother, she will not seek succor in sugary sweets, and if she cannot control her life, she will certainly control her death. She has waited until the time was right, for as she sees the situation, "I'm feeling as good as I ever felt in my life" (66). "She is convinced that suicide is the only authentic act available to her" (Keysser 165). With this courageous rebellion, Jessie repudiates the false self assigned to

her by others. She becomes the director in her own life's drama; she
establishes the boundaries between mother and daughter as she responds to Thelma's poignant plea, "You are my child!" with the firm
revelation, "I am what became of your child" (76). The infant self
that drooled on the sheet and felt its mother's hand tucking in the
crib quilt never progressed to any sense of psychic wholeness, never
acquired a true sense of self. In Jessie's view, "I'm not going to show
up, so there's no reason to stay, except to keep you company, and
that's . . . not reason enough . . ." (76). No cupboard held the requi-
site food needed to nourish Jessie's self. Nothing, not even cornflakes
for breakfast, can keep her here.

    As the play's action moves closer and closer to the bedroom
door with each ticking of the clock, Thelma faces the awful moment
of truth. Desperate and scared, she has summoned every conceiv-
able argument to place before Jessie's metaphorical plate, only to
have them pushed aside. She realizes her loss as she tells Jessie, "Who
am I talking to? You're gone already, aren't you? I'm looking right
through you!" (78). This statement by Thelma establishes her realization that Jessie has now smashed the mirror that bonds them together. Thelma, in looking at her daughter, no longer sees her own
reflection. She sees a separate person. In an interesting anecdote,
Madeline Grumet focuses upon this shattering truth in *Bitter Milk,*
wherein she speaks of being surprised after childbirth as she looked
in a mirror and saw her own reflection and not her child's (10). This
cohesion, the "you are mine and I am yours" feeling, is so prevalent
in mother/daughter relationships because of the way mothers view
their daughters as extensions of themselves. The connection is so
powerful that when they look at their daughters, they see themselves. This continuity is not present, as Chodorow attests, in mother/
son relationships. Only by "smashing" that mirror can the daughter
eventually own her reflection. As Sally Browder suggests, "Without
some objective reference, some sense of oneself apart from others,
one is totally at the mercy of others' experiences. One's sense of meaning is defined by others' choices. One's value is determined by how
well one serves or provides for the needs of others" (111). In the
end, Thelma realizes that she cannot possess Jessie, no matter how
much she loves her. The action that began in the kitchen ends with
Thelma screaming and pounding at Jessie's locked bedroom door.

With her anguished confession, "Jessie, Jessie, child. . . . Forgive me. (*Pause*) I thought you were mine" (89), she faces the fact that she finally must relinquish control. Even so, the symbiotic bond remains. The bullet that pierces Jessie's brain symbolically rips through Thelma as well. As critic Leslie Kane points out in *Feminine Focus: The New Women Playwrights*, Thelma's physical reaction to Jessie's shot—her body crumples against the door—confirms Thelma's previous statement about mutually felt pain (267).

Interestingly, in the film version, for which Norman wrote the screenplay, the last crucial line is omitted. According to Stanley Kauffman, through this omission Norman avoids suggesting the dramatic work that it could have been, because:

> *If the play were true—to Norman's characters as she wants us to think of them—it wouldn't exist. Either Jessie would shoot herself before it begins, or as soon as she discloses her plans, Thelma would collapse . . . Thelma's one impeccable line comes right after the shot. Against the locked bedroom door she sobs: "Forgive me. I thought you were mine." The drama that really leads to that line—of a clawing Electra complex, of the mother's mirror-image hatreds, and of pity overarching both—has not yet been written. (26)*

Unfortunately, Kauffman misses the point here. Rather than improve the play, this omission weakens the important truth Thelma realizes while drinking the cocoa at the kitchen table—no mother can own her daughter. Ultimately, she must relinquish control no matter how much it hurts. That poignant realization constitutes the true drama of the play—not a "clawing Electra complex."

Norman, however, offers a more pragmatic reason for the omission. In personal correspondence with me (through her agent, Jack Tantleff), Norman concedes:

> *I chose to omit the last line because that kind of line is only permissable in the theatre, where the line between the real & the imagined, the said & the unsaid is more blurred. The line, as a piece of poetry, does not belong in the realism of the film. . . . It was always my feeling that the line was what Thelma thought or felt at the moment. The only reason we hear it in the theatre, is because we are in the theatre.*

Even so, whether or not Thelma only thinks or feels that she can no longer "own" Jessie, she still confronts that realization.

With the curtain's descent, Thelma grips the cocoa pan tightly as she calls Dawson for help. Jessie's journey, which began in the kitchen and ended in her bedroom, is now complete. Nevertheless, both mother and daughter have connected in a way never before possible. They work through their mutual anger, digging through layers of guilt and remorse in order to salvage nuggets of truth. Each forgives the other. Jessie shows love for her mother by the acts she performs during these last two hours of her life. She prepares Thelma for the inevitable truth—that Jessie must assume autonomy regardless of personal cost. Thelma, through overwhelming grief, finally does let go. Both communicate on a level many mothers and daughters never experience.

Neither is really to blame for the personal realities that bring them to this place on this particular night. Thelma, like many mothers, can only offer what she has. As a participant in a patriarchal culture that places women in this no-win situation, she can hardly do more. Jessie, as a daughter, has to seek her true self—even if that quest ends in death. Both must seek their nurturance in the ways they know best. In this play, where hunger provides the controlling metaphor, Norman provides a tremendous sense of catharsis. However, she provides no answers to the contradictory lives mothers and daughters live as long as women remain the primary caretakers of children. She offers no solutions to unfulfilling lives due to societal constraints. She fails to challenge, as Jenny Spencer notes, "in any fundamental way the prevalent image of women in society—as those who reproduce, consume, and are consumed, who are powerless, inadequate, unworthy, and mutually destructive" (370).

Both Hellman and Norman, through these two plays, create representations of women working to fill that psychic hunger experienced when faced with the limited options for self-determination present in patriarchal society. Hellman's character, Cora Rodman, remains powerless, still striving at the play's end to control her psychic food supply through manipulation of family members. Norman's character, Jessie Cates, assumes control of her life and chooses death rather than face an unfulfilled life like her mother's. Even though Jessie chooses death, she triumphs because she, alone, decides what constitutes her proper nourishment.

Notes

1. I am referring here to Maslow's "Twelve Steps to Self-Actualization," where he gives the basic hierarchy of human needs; hunger is the most basic.
2. See Robert Brustein's "Lillian Hellman: Epilogue to Anger," in *Who Needs Theatre: Dramatic Opinions*, Atlantic Monthly Press, New York, 1987.
3. Brooks Atkinson, "The Play," *New York Times* (December 16, 1936), 35.
4. Robert Coleman, Review of *Days to Come, New York Daily Mirror* (December 16, 1936), 19.
5. Charles Dexter, "Strikes and Strikebreakers Viewed by Lillian Hellman," *Daily Worker* (December 18, 1936), 7.
6. See Grenville Vernon's review, "The Play and Screen: *Days to Come*," in *Commonweal*, 25 (January 1, 1937), 276. Vernon focuses on Hellman's unfortunate attempt to make the play more than just a "melodrama with a purpose."
7. For a cogent discussion of Melanie Klein's work, I suggest the reader consult *Introduction to the Work of Melanie Klein* (New York: Basic Books, 1974) by Hannah Segal. This work is a compilation of several lectures given at the Institute of Psycho-Analysis in London by Segal illustrated by her clinical experiences. In Chapter 3, "The Paranoid-Schizoid Position," Segal more fully explains Klein's view of how the infant splits the mother's breast.

Works Cited

Atkinson, Brooks. "The Play." *New York Times* (December 2, 1934): 10:1.

Brustein, Robert. "Lillian Hellman: Epilogue to Anger." In *Who Needs Theatre*. New York: Atlantic Monthly Press, 1987.

Chernin, Kim. *The Hungry Self: Women, Eating, & Identity*. New York: Harper and Row, 1985.

———. *Reinventing Eve: Modern Woman in Search of Herself*. New York: Harper and Row, 1987.

Chodorow, Nancy. *Feminism and Psychoanalytic Theory*. New Haven, Conn.: Yale UP, 1989.

Coleman, Robert. "Review of *Days to Come*." *New York Daily Mirror*, 4, 1936.

Dexter, Charles. "Strikes and Strikebreakers." *Daily Worker*, 7, 1936.

Grumet, Madeline. *Bitter Milk: Women and Teaching*. Amherst. U of Massachusetts P, 1988.

Hellman, Lillian. *The Collected Plays*. Boston and Toronto: Little, Brown, 1969.

———. *An Unfinished Woman: A Memoir*. Boston and Toronto: Little, Brown, 1969.

Murray, Edward J. *Motivation and Emotion*. Englewood Cliffs, N.J.: Prentice-Hall, 1964.

Norman, Marsha. *'night, Mother*. New York: Hill and Wang, 1983.

Rollyson, Carl. *Lillian Hellman: Her Legend and Her Legacy*. New York: St. Martin's, 1988.

Segal, Hannah. *Introduction to the Work of Melanie Klein*. New York: Basic Books, 1974.

Vernon, Grenville. "The Play and the Screen: *Days to Come*." *Commonweal*, 25 (January 1, 1937): 276.

"And the Time for It Was Gone"

Jessie's Triumph in 'night, Mother

Anne Marie Drew

"But the word was not spoken, and the time for it was gone."
—*Charles Dickens, David Copperfield*

When David Copperfield returns from boarding school to find his beloved mother unexpectedly remarried to the menacing Mr. Murdstone, he feels as if his whole world has been stripped away from him. Desperate for some word of comfort or reassurance, the little boy, with a tear-streaked face, stands in the family parlour. In remembering these forlorn moments, the adult Copperfield says:

God help me, I might have been improved for my whole life, I might have been made another creature perhaps for life by a kind word at that season. A word of encouragement and explanation, of pity for my childish ignorance, of welcome home, of reassurance that it was home. . . but the word was not spoken, and the time for it was gone. (56)

The young David learns to adjust to life without warmth and hope, and although he will eventually face great hardship in his life, time, for him, is ultimately benevolent, offering the success and love and the happiness he longed for as a child.

Jessie in 'night, Mother has no corresponding sense of time as benevolent. It has, as Ulysses suggests in Shakespeare's *Troilus and Cressida*, a wallet at its back, swallowing up every good thing. Jessie cannot look forward with hope. Nothing in her universe makes her believe that time will improve things. Thus, she embraces suicide as her way of triumphing over time. As Sally Browder asserts, "Her suicide arms her with a power, a sense of control over her life" (110). Raynette Halvorsen Smith argues convincingly that, almost against our own will, we find ourselves "rooting" for the suicide as a "bold act of emancipation" (287). Her suicide, I have come to believe, must not be viewed as a negation but rather as a triumph.

It is indeed hard to view suicide as a triumph when most people who commit suicide leave behind them grieving relatives and eternally unanswered questions. No one who has ever read a suicide note forgets the horrifying finality of the message. There is in all of us an instinctive rebellion against self-destruction. For many, suicide is a sin of despair—an acting out of the belief that we are past the saving reaches of God. But God and grieving relatives are not a consideration for Jessie. Her universe, as she sees it, holds no hope for her. We may instinctively rebel against Jessie's bloody and violent end. However, Jessie's violent death is "the agent for transformation . . . to freedom, autonomy, and individualism" (Smith 279). We equate the loss of life with death. Jessie does not. In describing the mindset of the suicidal person, Perlin writes:

for most suicides the act does not really mean dying. Dying for them is something that is suffered and passively submitted to; when actively performed it becomes a triumph, as if the ego has proved itself to be almighty when it is strong enough to cast its own life aside. (150)

George Colt, in his book *The Enigma of Suicide*, details historical views of self-destruction. We may believe that suicide has always been universally repudiated as an evil. This study proves otherwise. Suggesting that Greek and Roman attitudes toward suicide were not monolithically negative, Colt tallies the number of Greek myths that mention suicide without judgment or shame—for example, the stories of Jocasta, Leukakas, Dido, and Erigone (144–45).

Indeed, the first Christian edict against suicide did not come until S.C. 452, when the Council of Artes declared suicide to be "caused by diabolical possession" (158). That edict, prompted by Augustine's earlier condemnation of suicide as a mortal sin, was an attempt to stem the tide of Christian martyrs, who were virtually throwing themselves into the mouths of lions in order to gain the title of martyr and the guarantee of heaven. The Catholic Church's actively firm stance against suicide stems from the days of the over-zealous Christian martyrs.

Undoubtedly, there has always been a horror of self-destruction, but the act of suicide has had its defenders for centuries. And the defenders come in surprising guises. In Thomas More's *Utopia*, the notion of euthanasia is set forth. More, whose own death is perceived by some to have been a suicide, argues for a person's right to end life:

But if the disease be not only uncurable, but also full of continual pain and anguish; then he will determine with himself no longer to cherish that painful and pestilent disease and . . . seeing that life is to him but a torment, that he will be not unwilling to die, but rather . . . dispatch himself out of that torment . . . or else suffer himself willingly to be rid out of it by another. (201)

More's firmly theocentric world view still held room for the possibility of self-inflicted death. John Donne, another deeply religious man, defended suicide in *Bianthanatos,* a work not published in his lifetime. And the Romantics, of course, were obsessed with the notion of premature death. Thomas Chatterton, the young writer who killed himself in 1770 because of his lack of financial and artistic success, became the symbol of a generation of poets who believed it was better to die young than wither into middle age.

The views of More and Donne notwithstanding, there can be no doubt, however, that suicide has often carried with it the potential connotations of insanity and moral disease. Well into the 1800s, suicides in England were buried under distinct rubrics:

Suicides had been buried at cross-roads because these were signs of the cross; because steady traffic over the suicide's grave could help keep the person's ghost down . . . and suicides had been staked to prevent their restless wanderings as lost souls. (Gates 6)

Our own technological century, with its Kevorkian possibilities, offers myriad opportunities to end life. Discussions about the quality of life and living wills often take as a given that we have the right to control our own destiny. And Jessie's premise that she can terminate her own existence, while horrifying to her mother, makes sense, because the gun, as Laura Morrow asserts, offers "Jessie power over her destiny" (29). What Edwin Shneidman says of all suicides is poignantly applicable to Jessie. "Every suicide makes this statement: This far and no farther" (*Definition* 135)

Jessie no longer believes that time is benevolent. Deprived of hope, she envisions life as an endless procession of days, bereft of meaning or joy. Her inability to view time as good is not peculiar to Jessie, of course. Or even the twentieth century. In his book, *Milton's Poetry: Its Development in Time*, Edward Tayler explains that the classical understanding of time involved a distinction between *chronos* and *kairos*—between temporality and eternity. Human beings need to seize the opportunities that are presented to them, because, like the unspoken word in David Copperfield's childhood home, once gone such occasions are "lost forever" (123). If a human being never recognizes those places where time (*chronos*) intersects with eternity (*kairos*), much opportunity is lost. But the distinction between temporality and eternity is a meaningless one for Jessie. Crucial to Tayler's discussion is the understanding that the fullness of time cannot be rushed. Human beings must wait, in hope, for fulfillment.

Jessie will not wait. Lynda Hart points out that "as the play opens, Jessie has exhausted all the images that might have sustained her . . . she has long awaited the arrival of a self to call her own; but she has forfeited all hope for its appearance" (75). Perhaps eternity has something good in store for Jessie Cates. But she's no longer interested. Psychiatrist Sidney M. Jourard explains:

A person lives as long as he experiences life as having meaning and value, and as long as he has something to live for—meaningful projects that will animate him and invite him into the future or entice him to pull himself into the future. He will continue to live as long as he has hope of fulfilling meanings and values. As soon as meaning, value, and hope vanish from a person's experience, he begins to stop living; that is he begins to die. (quoted in Shneidman, Nature 132)

The meaning, value, and hope to which Jourard refers have vanished for Jessie. Like those terminally ill patients who choose not to be resuscitated by extraordinary means, Jessie has decided to say, "Enough." She cannot bear the endless parade of nothingness that opens up before her. Her world view is not unique to her. In his work *From the Closed World to the Infinite Universe*, Alexandre Koyre discusses the "scientific and philosophical revolution" that brought forth the "destruction of the Cosmos." Koyre explains that the view of the world as hierarchic and theocentric gave way to an understanding that the universe was "indefinite." Concepts such as "perfection, harmony, meaning, and aim" faded away (2). As we've known for a long time, Didi and Gogo aren't the first two fellows to simultaneously question the meaning of existence and the wisdom of waiting for something that never materializes. Koyre's study makes clear that a benevolent world view disappeared a long time ago. Jessie inherits an empty place in the universe.

Jessie believes she is free to control her own existence. Frank Kermode, in *The Sense of an Ending: Studies in the Theory of Fiction*, recognizes the "freedom of persons" to change the relationship between "beginning, middle, and end" (30). Deprived of a sense of an ending, characters find ways to impose endings. Human beings cannot move endlessly throughout time. In a world where time is not benevolent and there is no ending in sight, suicide can become a triumph. Jessie's death is "the most creative thing she has done, at least as she sees it. She is taking hold of her life. She is making a decision, and that decision is 'no'" (Porter 56). For this woman, like many others, can "create a future only by killing [herself] . . . that is [she] can reawaken psychic action and imagine vital elements beyond the present only in deciding upon, and carrying through [her] suicide (Colt 227). In her discussion of her death, Jessie never refers to a cosmic ordering of life or her place in the overall scheme of the universe. She is a misfit in a world that never welcomed her anyway.

The word *time* is repeated with surprising regularity in *'night, Mother*. And the effects of living in a world where time offers no hope are everywhere evident. Marsha Norman's stage directions insist "The time is the present, with the action beginning about 8:15. Clocks onstage in the kitchen and on a table in the living room should run throughout the performance and be visible to the audience" (40). Thus, we are ever aware that time is running out. Norman's insistence on using real clocks flies in the face of the theatrical tradition that warns against using real clocks. "Something always goes wrong with real clocks onstage," Robert Torok at the Yale School of Drama once told his students. "Do anything to avoid having to fuss with real Time on the stage. It's always a mess." But in Norman's case the passing of time is crucial. The clocks dramatically remind us that life slips away. At play's end, when Jessie wills her watch to her son, Ricky, she acknowledges that her own hours and minutes are finished.

Norman's authorial insistence that "there will be no intermission" forces us to experience the unrelenting nature of Jessie's existence. Jessie never gets a break from her psyche-deadening existence, nor will we be granted a reprieve as we watch her suicide preparations.

Early on it is evident that time holds no hope for Jessie. Her upcoming dusting-powder birthday does not excite her. She's on a bus that's "hot and bumpy and crowded and too noisy and more than anything in the world [she] wants to get off" (33). Her decision is to get off now because there is nothing to look forward to.

Jessie's expectations are not outrageous ones. If there were any one thing she could look forward to, like "rice pudding or cornflakes for breakfast or something, that might be enough" (77). But the future holds more of the past's dreary sameness. As she says to her mother, "Mama . . . I'm just not having a very good time and I don't have any reason to think it'll get anything but worse" (28). Nothing she touches comes to life. Even her son is destined to become a murderer. It's "only a matter of time" (25). Should she muster the interest to stay alive, her conviction is that Dawson and Loretta and Agnes and Ricky would continue to be sources of lethal irritation.

Thelma's enjoyment of life brings Jessie's deep despair into sharp dramatic relief. Leslie Kane words it so well when she writes "that for Thelma the little she has sustains her; for Jessie the little she has indicates all she does not have" (267). Perhaps objectively, Thelma Cates does not have an enviable life, but she is happy with her existence. Needlework and television occupy her time. She looks forward all week to her Saturday night manicures. She has friends enough. The contrast between mother and daughter is nowhere more evident than in Thelma's furious outburst near the end of the play:

You make me feel like a fool for being alive, child, and you are so wrong! I like it here, and I will stay here until they make me go, until they drag me screaming and I mean screeching into my grave.

Thelma hangs on to life with both hands, and Jessie loads a gun and pulls a trigger.

Mama, not understanding Jessie's acute sadness, tells her daughter: "There's nothing really sad going on right now. If it was after your divorce or something, that would make sense" (29). In addressing the timing of Jessie's suicide, Raynette Smith contends that although "everything is wrong with [Jessie's] life . . . no one thing is all that unusual or traumatic" (285). Jessie, however, who has contemplated suicide for at least a decade, asserts that the past uneventful Christmas gave her an added reason to move toward death. Christmas, with its attendant wrong-sized slippers and wrongly intended calculators, depresses Jessie.

Nothing is worth staying alive for. Not Christmas. Not her son. Whereas Mama believes Ricky will improve with time ("He just needs some time, sugar" [11]), Jessie adamantly maintains that her son faces the same relentless psychic assault she does. Jessie explains that Ricky is a combination of her and Cecil "together for all time in too small a space. And we're tearing each other apart, like always, inside that boy . . ." (60). Thelma's response, "Give him time, Jess" (60), does not alter her daughter's view. Mama believes that in time Ricky will get better. Jessie believes that in time, he will only get worse.

Deprived of a carefree childhood herself, Jessie has grown to expect trouble. Her marriage to a man who didn't really love her confirmed her sense of hopelessness. Epilepsy, a wayward son, her inability to hold a job—all coalesce to make her feel worthless. And even her mother's frantic attempt to introduce the notion of hell and sin does not affect Jessie. "It's a sin. You'll go to hell," Thelma warns her daughter, to which Jessie curtly replies, "Jesus was a suicide if you ask me" (18). But the thought of hell holds no fear for Jessie. In discussing the cosmology of suicide, Schneidman asserts "the concept of hellfire has been discarded by most educated people today" (92). In planning for her funeral, Jessie doesn't even consider the maimed rites that attended Ophelia's death. Eternal damnation is not the question here.

We can wish for Jessie that her life view were different. We can wish that like the emotionally deprived David Copperfield, she triumphed over bleak existence. We can grieve that only in death was she free, but Norman's work moves us to an inexorable conclusion. In death, Jessie Cates finds life. "Although many argue that her death is merely an act of desperation, Jessie's decision to take her own life displays a new confidence in herself; she knows that it is the right decision for her . . . [she finds] her own meaning only in the rest afforded by death . . . and [she] does manage to find herself in the act of dying" (McDonnell 103). Given that some of us do not find ourselves in either life or death, Jessie's end is no small triumph.

Works Cited

Browder, Sally. "'I Thought You Were Mine': Marsha Norman's *'night, Mother.*" In *Mother Puzzles: Daughters and Mothers in Contemporary American Literature.* Edited by Mickey Pearlman. New York: Greenwood P, 1985.

Colt, George Howe. *The Enigma of Suicide.* New York: Summit, 1991.

Dickens, Charles. *David Copperfield.* New York: Signet Classic, 1980.

Donne, John. *Bianthanatos.* Edited by Ernest W. Sullivan, II. Newark: U of Delaware P; London: Associated UP, 1984.

Gates, Barbara T. *Victorian Suicide: Mad Crimes and Sad Histories.* Princeton: Princeton UP, 1988.

Hart, Lynda. "Doing Time: Hunger for Power in Marsha Norman's Plays." *Southern Quarterly* 25 (1987): 67–79.

Kane, Leslie. "The Way Out, The Way In: Paths to Self in the Plays of Marsha Norman." In *Feminine Focus: The New Women Playwrights.* Edited by Enoch Brater. New York: Oxford UP, 1989.

Kermode, Frank. *The Sense of an Ending: Studies in the Theory of Fiction.* London: Oxford UP, 1967.

Koyre, Alexandre. *From the Closed World to the Infinite Universe.* Baltimore: Johns Hopkins UP, 1957.

McDonnell, Lisa J. "Diverse Similitude: Beth Henley and Marsha Norman." *Southern Quarterly* 25 (1987): 95–104.

More, Thomas. *Utopia: Three Renaissance Classics.* New York: Scribner, 1953.

Morrow, Laura. "Orality and Identity in *'night, Mother* and *Crimes of the Heart.*" *Studies in American Drama* 3 (1988): 23–29.

Norman, Marsha. *'night ,Mother.* New York: Hill and Wang, 1983.

Perlin, Seymour, ed. *A Handbook for the Study of Suicide.* New York: Oxford UP, 1975.

Porter, Laurin. "Women Re-Conceived: Changing Perceptions of Women in Contemporary American Drama." In *Proceedings: Conference of College Teachers of English of Texas.* Lubbock: U of Texas P, 1989.

Shneidman, Edwin S. *Definition of Suicide.* New York: John Wiley, 1985.

———, ed. *On The Nature of Suicide.* San Francisco: Jossey-Bass, 1969.

Smith, Raynette Halvorsen. "*'night ,Mother* and *True West:* Mirror Images of Violence and Gender." In *Violence in Drama.* Edited by James Redmond. Cambridge: Cambridge UP, 1991.

Tayler, Edward W. *Milton's Poetry: Its Development in Time.* Pittsburgh: Duquesne UP, 1979.

Marsha Norman, 1991. Photograph © courtesy of Susan Johann.

Scene from Getting Out, *Actors Theatre of Louisville. Left to right: Susan Kingsley, Lynn Cohen. Photograph courtesy of David S. Talbott.*

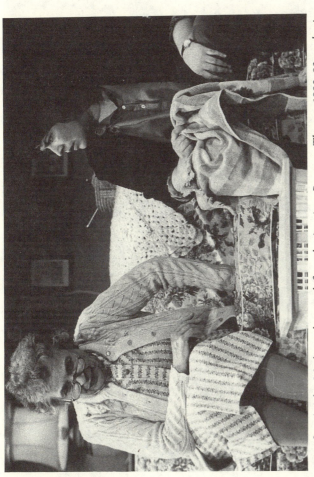

Scene from 'night, Mother; photograph from the American Repertory Theatre, 1982–83 production (supplied by A.R.T.); directed by Tom Moore. Left to right: Anne Pitoniak, Cathy Bates. Photograph courtesy of Richard Feldman.

Scene from D. Boone, *Actors Theatre of Louisville. Left to right: (above) Dave Florek, Skip Sudduth; (below) Catherine Christianson, Gladden Schrock. Photograph courtesy of Richard Trigg.*

Scene from Sarah and Abraham, *Actors Theatre of Louisville, 1988 Humana Festival of New American Plays. Left to right: Beth Dixon, Valarie Pettiford. Photograph courtesy of David S. Talbott.*

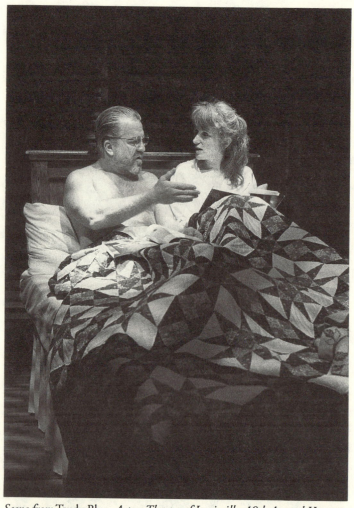

Scene from Trudy Blue, *Actors Theatre of Louisville, 19th Annual Humana Festival of New American Plays, 1995. Left to right: Leo Burmester, Joanne Camp. Photograph courtesy of Richard Trigg.*

"I Don't Know What's Going to Happen in the Morning"

Visions of the Past, Present, and Future in *The Holdup*

Robert Cooperman

Marsha Norman's *The Holdup* (1983) is a most ambitious play and, indeed, one that the playwright herself considers atypical of her work (Wattenberg 507). Its ambitiousness stems from Norman's use of American mythology, her development of symbolic characters, and her conscientious manipulation of history. The play manages to blend these ingredients to form a vision of the future (ironically, set in the past) that is both positive and negative, both exhilarating and horrifying, and both hostile to and thankful for the history (real and mythological) that shapes it. Indeed, it is a historical framework that dominates *The Holdup*. While its characters either cling to history or attempt to break free of its shackles, the force of history is omnipresent, shaping lives, the country, the world, and the play.

That Norman tackles the American frontier myth is in itself ambitious, for it is typically a masculine genre, originally defined by historian Frederick Jackson Turner in his famous 1893 essay, *The Significance of the Frontier in American History* (Wattenberg 507). Turner's thesis "shook the academic world to its foundations," for it dared to downplay European influences and to credit a purely American environment for the development of the frontier psyche (Billington 3). The American frontier, according to Turner, weakened class distinctions, encouraged political and social equality, and, most important for Norman's work, severed cultural ties with the past, creating a sense of individualistic and nationalistic pride: "the advance of the frontier has meant a steady movement away from the influence of Europe [and] a steady growth of independence on American lines" (Turner 201).

Although the spirit of Turner's myth permeates *The Holdup*, it is only one of a number of American myths implemented by Norman.

Wild West mythology, itself a descendant of the frontier myth, prominently figures in the action (Robertson 160). The central character of this myth is, of course, the cowboy, identified as the Outlaw in Norman's play. The American mythology of war—war as "an instrument of American progress"—is also at work in the play (Robertson 325). This blending of mythologies results in a staunchly American play, which uses national myths both for nostalgia and for the edification of the modern age.

The Holdup takes place in New Mexico in the fall of 1914, "miles from nowhere and long past sundown" (107). Two brothers, Henry and Archie Tucker, are working on a wheat-threshing crew, although the crew itself is in town and the Tuckers are alone at their cookshack. The Outlaw, "a worn, grizzled desperado," appears at the cookshack looking to eat and to meet up with Lily, his estranged girlfriend of twenty years, who soon arrives on the scene. Henry, a self-styled expert on the Old West, challenges the Outlaw to reveal his name, leading to a pathetic gun fight in which he is killed with one shot. After a funeral of sorts for Henry, the Outlaw proceeds to attempt suicide with an overdose of morphine, but he is nursed back to life by Lily and Archie. The play concludes with Archie going off to seek his fate and Lily and the Outlaw looking forward to their approaching marriage.

If the plot seems simple and sketchy it's because it is; Norman is working within the tradition of the Western holdup play, which Rudolf Erben defines as "obviously contrived and conducive more to thought and talk than action and plot" (311). (By "holdup," Erben means stagnation or entrapment rather than robbery at gunpoint.) An uncomplicated plot also furthers Norman's advancement of symbolism by allowing the historical components of time and place, and a mythological treatment of character, to remain at the forefront of her creation. For example, Norman is precise in her temporal specifications, either in stage directions ("the fall of 1914") or in dialogue: "Some Archduke Somebody-or-other got killed and it's all about to blow up!" (110). Of course, it is the outbreak of World War I to which Archie refers and the global impact of the war is immediately felt, even "miles from nowhere" in New Mexico. Although the script seems indifferent to the impending danger of the war—there are no extended discussions about either the glory or the horror of war, nor even the specific causes that led to the outbreak of hostilities—Norman wants World War I to figure prominently in *The Holdup*. Significantly, the play concludes with Archie's departure to the "faint strains of some World War I song" (157).

The fact that a war will take place in 1914 is of great importance as a device whereby Norman can examine the advance of civilization and the effect of progress. Indeed, it is progress that distinguishes 1914 from other eras of the past, and historians paint a dynamic portrait of it as a year of milestone advances in science, technology, and business. Page Smith's *America Enters the World*, for example, highlights the "explosion of technology" that characterized the first decade of the twentieth century (855). Norman does not ignore these facts: we learn, for example, that Henry and Archie's wheat-threshing crew owns a new separator that "threshes ten times as much wheat as the old one in half the time" (113). It is also through Archie that we learn that in 1914, humanity has more powerful and deadly means to wage combat: "They're gonna fly airplanes in this war, Henry!" (110–111). Lily, the businesswoman from the enterprising east, signals the steady march of progress just by her arrival: she "rushes onstage, wearing a Barney Oldfield-type duster," having just parked her Buick (115). The presence of an automobile in the uncivilized New Mexican "scrub country" is quite shocking to the others, especially Archie, who gasps, "Did you really come all the way out here in a car?" (116). As the embodiment of progress, Lily is delighted by the advance of civilization, especially since it has made her rich. She describes her hotel business in terms of the new inventions and improvements found in it: "There's actually trees growing in barrels all along that front hall. Oh . . . and Roy Luther hooked me up a waterfall, inside the dining room. And I'm about ready to go order another automobile . . . ," and she brags about the telephone she has added for all the "fancy eastern folks coming through" (120; 117). Although the Outlaw suggests that at one time Lily was a stereotypical saloon gal, progressive 1914 has made her an entrepreneur: "Do you know what year this is? I'm not a whore. It's not a whorehouse. It's a hotel now and I own it" (117).

However, not every character shares Lily's enthusiasm for the evolution of civilization. Indeed, it is their responses to this evolution and to the future that define each character, a typical Norman device, according to Leslie Kane, who argues that "for Norman the issues of past [and]

future . . . are inextricably linked to how a person perceives herself"
(258). Archie Tucker, seventeen and wide-eyed, is at first impressed with
the progress made in 1914, but from an immature perspective. To Archie,
World War I means a chance for him and Henry to save the world:

ARCHIE: . . . it's all about to blow up!

HENRY: What is?

ARCHIE: The world, Henry! Unless we get there in time! (110)

Archie is aware that airplanes will forever change the nature of
war, but he fails to recognize the ominous ramifications of that
change. Instead, he glorifies a war fought in the skies as an exciting
adventure: "You'd like that, zoomin' around in the sky. You could be
the Outlaw of the Air, Henry!" (111). Here Norman may be guilty
of forcing a World War II mentality on Archie; American response
to the outbreak of World War I was generally "horror and incredu-
lity" (Smith 435). Still, it is Archie's idealism that is the point, an
idealism further exemplified by his reaction to Lily's Buick. However, Archie loses his boyish idealism for progress when his brother
is gunned down by the Outlaw. The post–Henry Archie is less enthusiastic about the war and indifferent to his possible role in it:
"The war could need me, I guess," and he no longer equates the
development of the airplane solely with warfare (150). The mature
Archie clearly wants more than some fictitious military achievement,
as he recognizes that his isolation from civilization has been stifling
and his perspectives childlike. He now wants to make contact with
"crowds . . . things, people, cars . . . ," for he knows he cannot save
the world daydreaming in New Mexico (150). In addition, the
Outlaw's deadly gun has shown Archie the terrible price that society
pays when warfare progresses and when he asks Lily, "Do you believe there's airplanes?" his unstated query is, "Do you believe there's
airplanes that can kill so many so swiftly?" He realizes that the bullet
that ends his brother's life is to be multiplied a thousandfold by
progress and because "some Archduke Somebody-or-other got killed."

By contrast, Henry understands an evolving civilization and as
a result chooses not to accept the realities of the present. Instead, the

coarse and unlikable Henry absorbs himself in the study of the uncivilized Old West, the tales of gunfights and saloons where the heroes were villains like the Sundance Kid. The appearance of the
Outlaw is therefore of particular interest to Henry, for the old gunslinger represents the living embodiment of a past he relishes and
mythologizes. As Archie says, "Henry believes in outlaws," a fact
that Norman parallels with Archie's religious convictions to show
how deep a believer each brother is:

ARCHIE: *That stuff is made up, Henry . . .*

HENRY: *'Bout like the Bible, I guess.*

ARCHIE: *The Bible is the truth. (110)*

One can surmise that the Old West is for Henry what the Bible is
for Archie, and neither would relish thinking about his life without
his sacred beliefs.

Even more resistant to the future is the Outlaw himself, a
man mired in the past. The Outlaw wants no part of the march
of history and the advancement of civilization that inevitably
accompanies it. He is uneasy with Lily's Buick for two reasons:
He thinks it forward for a lady to drive a car, and it's not a horse.
The Outlaw dreams of traveling to Bolivia, which he believes
he'd prefer even to the isolation of the New Mexico he sees as
being threatened by civilization: "We'll have a wonderful time
[in Bolivia] and we won't think about . . . all the people like
you back here building houses and running for mayor" (119). In a
telling speech given after Henry has tied up Archie and plans to
ride off with the Outlaw, the desperado voices his disgust with
modern life:

*Nobody I know ever tied up his brother . . . I mean, we got rules out
here for this sort of thing, or used to. Is this how people do now? 'Cause if
it is, I don't want any part of it. I'm goin' right back where I been and
I'm stayin' put this time. I mean, you drop out of sight for a little while
and look what we got for boys now. And you're drivin' a car and talkin'
hard, girl. (126)*

The Outlaw is skeptical of the future even at the conclusion of the play, when he is to marry Lily and live on her farm: "I'm glad I'm not gonna be there for the future," he tells Archie just before he departs with his betrothed (153).

If *The Holdup* defines the characters in relation to the future, then it also places them in relation to the past, and specifically within a mythological framework. Each character either symbolizes a mythological icon himself, or defines his existence in terms of the mythology of the Old West. The most obvious mythological figure is the Outlaw, a man who embodies the Old West in appearance as well as in his aforementioned attitude toward civilization and the future. The Outlaw, resistant to give his rightful name (Tom McCarty), instead tries to say he's any number of famous bandits, although Henry, a student of the Old West, is not fooled:

HENRY: You tell me who you are!

OUTLAW (Grinning): *Kilpatrick.*

HENRY: Dead.

OUTLAW: Sundance.

HENRY: Bolivia.

OUTLAW (Laughing, mocking): *Nope. Dead. I'm Billy the Kid. I'm Jesse James. (126)*

By defining himself as Billy the Kid and Jesse James, and by using their names almost simultaneously as if he were both at once, the Outlaw proves himself to be a sort of "Platonic Outlaw," a man who embodies all the gunslingers of Old West lore and thus a mythic figure himself. Norman is careful, however, not to make the Outlaw completely a legendary figure (which would make her characters types rather than flesh-and-blood people). He is also a man with very human faults and frailties, such as his resistance to change.

There is no question as to where Henry fits in relation to the Old West and to the Outlaw. Henry is a true believer whose interest in the Outlaw stems from his concern that the aging gunslinger is not "the real thing" (that is, a mythological figure). At first Henry mocks the Outlaw as "just some old prospector lost track of the mother lode," but soon he comes around to believe that maybe the desperado is in fact a relic of a bygone age (120). Henry becomes so taken with the Outlaw as an embodiment of the past that he attempts to join his nonexistent gang: "He needs somebody to ride with him and I'm it!" (123). Finally, however, Henry despairs because he does not know who the Outlaw really is or what he may represent: "You tell me who you are," he challenges the Outlaw just before the gunfight that takes his life (126). By challenging the Outlaw, Henry is challenging the myth of the Old West, and because he thinks the Outlaw may not be the real thing—that is, the myth may be false—he realizes that his life, defined by the myth, may be meaningless. Thus, the deadly gunfight, brought about by his taunting of the Outlaw, is purposefully staged by Henry so that he may die:

HENRY: *Coward! Coward!*

OUTLAW (Turns around): *Why does it have to be you? Why couldn't it be somebody I—*

HENRY: *What are you waiting for, coward?*

OUTLAW: *You're asking me to kill you, boy.* (129)

His death a few moments later is no accident. It is a suicide brought about by the existential angst that accompanies a shattering of belief. Ironically, the act of a gunfight confirms the Old West myth, as the Outlaw reaffirms his position as a mythological icon.

Henry's death is significant, for it creates a feeling of remorse in the Outlaw that, in keeping with Norman's development of his character, is explainable on both human and mythological levels. He reveals himself as Tom McCarty, a man he claims to have "buried . . . alive," which demonstrates his conscious effort to bury his past and to put to rest the myth that he represents, a myth as old and worn out as he is. Act 2 of *The Holdup* is actually an enactment of a ritual in which the myth, and the mythic figure embodied by the Outlaw, die and are resurrected in a new form. Apparently, the Outlaw has attempted to self-destruct before: "Contrary to popular opinion and in spite of everything I've tried, I am still alive," and he expresses dismay that no one has attempted to do him in: "Yes sir . . . things are pretty bad when you can't count on somebody else to kill you" (135–136). The Outlaw implies that he is being kept alive despite his obvious death wish; as he remarks over Henry's dead body, "You got something I want, Henry." In this context, the Outlaw can be understood as Norman's mouthpiece, arguing that the myth cannot and should not be put to rest despite the fast-paced, changing world of 1914.

In an attempt to finish himself off, the Outlaw takes an overdose of morphine and it is up to Archie and Lily, the two characters for whom the future is eagerly anticipated, to keep him alive. In this scene, which takes up most of Act 2, Norman dramatizes the battle between the past and the present, a battle she prolongs so as to heighten audience concern about the outcome, which will determine America's direction and its attitude toward history. If the Outlaw has his way—death—then the past will cease to be of use to the present and the future, a position with which the playwright appears uncomfortable. Still, the Outlaw appears on the brink of death several times during the struggle, demonstrating that his death wish is nothing more than bravado, for he is quick to repent when he fears that he may actually perish: "I don't want to die. Don't let me die . . ." (141). However, the morphine proves powerful and he passes in and out of consciousness, waking sporadically to find himself completely enmeshed in the spirit of the Old West: "Keep firing . . . one at a time . . . slip through. Take Teapot north. (*Now slumping as quickly as he awoke before*) Brakeman . . . shoulda killed the brakeman" (143).

When he finally regains full consciousness, the Outlaw is disoriented but alive and a changed man. He now grudgingly accepts the future by agreeing to marry Lily and live on a farm, although he characteristically complains about it. Archie, too, is a changed man; indeed, he sounds more like the Outlaw of old complaining about the lack of discipline in uncivilized New Mexico:

We're so far away from everything, everybody acts like there's no rules at all and anybody can just do whatever they like—well they can't. Or if they can, I don't have to sit here and watch them, not anymore. I've got my own ideas about how people should live and this ain't it. No sir. (154)

The newly liberated Archie then burns "the newspaper articles, wanted posters and other bits of evidence of the Outlaw's exploits," thus destroying some of McCarty's personal belongings (154). Archie, however, refuses to burn the Outlaw's satchel, an act that symbolically preserves the past. The myth of the Old West has been retained into the present, symbolized by the satchel that McCarty passes to Archie, a gesture demonstrating a past which finds its way into the future. "I'm gonna need something like this," says Archie, a remark that underscores Norman's conviction that an appreciation for and an understanding of the past—even if that past is glorified as a myth—is vital in shaping the future of her characters and, by extension, the future of the country (155).

At the conclusion of the play, Archie and the Outlaw, the two characters who were most at odds concerning the past, present, and future, find common philosophical ground. The Outlaw now understands the present, Archie the past, and both begrudgingly accept the future after a maturation process involving death (the Outlaw's near-brush with mortality; Archie's witnessing of Henry's murder). Norman highlights their meeting of the minds through a technique whereby the Outlaw relates, almost verbatim, and takes as his own, a story Archie has told him about being nicknamed "Doc." While they still debate the nature of the human condition, their perspectives have radically changed; the Outlaw states his case without regard to the past, and Archie without regard to the present:

OUTLAW: This is how things are . . . here.

ARCHIE (Very Strong): *Were . . . here.*

OUTLAW (Stronger still): *Are! Everywhere!*

ARCHIE: No! Not anymore. Not everywhere! (153)

Their exchange underscores the fact that both now have the strength to define their future.

Norman also tinkers with theatrical spectacle when she has Lily and Archie emerging from the cookshack in the morning light after spending the entire night together. The dawn of a new era is ushered in with an appropriate light cue as Archie loses his innocence and virginity, and Lily performs her gender-specific roles as mother figure and lover. But Norman makes Lily much more than the embodiment of all traditional/symbolic female functions. Unlike Archie and the Outlaw, Lily has no need for a maturation process in order to accept the present. It is quite significant that when she is introduced, Norman specifies that her costume incorporate elements of both the civilized east and the uncivilized west, both the promise of the future and the truth of the past: "It all looks very expensive, but is clearly western and meant for hard use" (115). Here, clothes clearly make the woman, for Lily embodies the perfect balance of past and present. Although her reaction to the future is one of delight, she possesses a keen grasp of realism, which forces her to be cautious: "I don't know what's going to happen in the morning," she characteristically remarks (149). While she is very much a woman of the present, she also recognizes that the figure from the past—her beloved Outlaw—is a sorely missing element from her life: "I waited for you to come back, you know. I kept eggs in the house for two years for you" (119). Lily is modern enough to run a hotel and old-fashioned enough to play the role of a coquettish female in order to please her man: "A girl needs to hear a man talk a little" (120). Lily is, of course, an atypical hero in Norman's mythological/historical setting (a point well argued in Richard Wattenberg's "Feminizing the Frontier Myth: Marsha Norman's *The Holdup*"), but she is also the only character (significantly the only female character in the play) who is not restricted either by archaic or hopelessly idealistic conceptions of time. Consequently, she is the agent who links the past and the present and is therefore responsible for "linking" the minds of the Outlaw and Archie; it is through Lily (specifically through her sexuality, as her symbolically-laden night with Archie demonstrates) that these men are able to come to an agreement to accept the future.

While one may walk away from *The Holdup* with a positive view of the future, a view that Norman invites us to have through her neat solutions for the dilemmas of the remaining characters, the fact is that this rosy scenario may not be as straightforward as the play indicates. One of the difficulties inherent in writing a play that takes place far in the past is that the playwright must find a bridge to the past with contemporary concerns or run the risk of losing the import and timeliness of her message. Surely, the notion that the present and future are dependent on the past is not a new one and one that other playwrights have tackled in a more modern setting. What, then, is Norman's purpose for setting this play in 1914? Why the emphasis on World War I, a war in which the United States adopted an immediate policy of neutrality?—a fact that makes Archie's idealistic response to it even more questionable (or at least atypical)? Why does the play take place in New Mexico, a setting that the play's most idealistic character, Archie, calls "scrub country" (and this very late in the play, when he has matured spiritually and sexually)? Part of the reason, certainly, is utilitarian: Where else would one expect to find a "*worn, grizzled desperado*" like the Outlaw, and when else but at a time when America still contained a few unsettled frontiers (New Mexico had been a state for only two years in 1914)? Also, few American myths are as compelling as the Wild West or the frontier, so a setting was needed to accommodate that environment. An examination of Turner's work adds yet another layer to Norman's design: "Moving westward," he writes, "the frontier became more and more American" (201). Thus, the New Mexico of 1914 was the right choice for Norman to incorporate all the mythological, historical, and uniquely American elements of her tale.

But for her modern audience, Norman may have other, more compelling purposes, and this is where her use of mythological and factual history, as well as genre, may be at its craftiest. The frontier myth, the Wild West myth, the western holdup play, and the general worldwide *zeitgeist* at the onset of World War I all reveal a world at a crossroads. The myths show a new and unique America developing out of a discarded European past (this is the part of Turner's theory that caused such dissent among academics). The western holdup play, as defined by Rudolf Erben, "presents the American West in dramatic tension, between past and present" (312). Turner himself labeled the frontier as "the meeting point between savagery and civilization" (200). The world in 1914 "had reached one of those dramatic and essentially incomprehensible turning points," as well as a belief "that a new and better age was dawning" (Smith 436, 455). Norman seizes upon these inherently dramatic situations and applies them to the modern day with the hope that a perceptive audience will comprehend the implied link between past and present. She takes her source materials—the legends of great men on the frontier, in business, and on the battlefield—and twists them to conform to our contemporary notions of how the world really works. The past, even a mythological past, becomes a respected advisor, not a hindrance to be dismissed in the name of progress, and women become active as nurturers and nation-builders. And, as Lily proves, a man need not be present as a guiding force in order for a woman to make her mark in the world and to be a harbinger of progress in the untamed west. We accept these changes in our present, and this acceptance gives Norman license, essentially, to rewrite the past.

We must resist the idea that in *The Holdup* Marsha Norman is arguing for a return to the "good old days" before nuclear bombs and unchecked epidemics. The contagious excitement of likable characters such as Lily and Archie indicates that she genuinely favors the advances of an evolving civilization, be they scientific, technological, artistic, or military. But Norman seems to take Turner's warning to heart—that the frontier supported democracy "with all of its good and with all of its evil elements" (222). Norman's play begs for prudence on the part of the civilization (that is, the new democracy) that benefits from such "good" advances. It is this prudence that, if we are sensible, will force us to be as realistic and practical as Lily, and will allow us the intelligence to be as concerned with the present and how it evolved as we are with the future, if it is to evolve. It is only when we create a secure present that we can bravely face the fact that we "don't know what's going to happen in the morning."

Works Cited

Billington, Ray Allen. *The Genesis of the Frontier Thesis: A Study in Historical Creativity.* Calif.: Huntington Library, 1971.

Erben, Rudolf. "The Western Holdup Play: The Pilgrimage Continues." *Western American Literature* 23 (1989): 311–322.

Kane, Leslie. "The Way Out, the Way In: Paths to Self in the Plays of Marsha

Norman." *Feminine Focus: The New Women Playwrights*. Edited by Enoch Brater. New York: Oxford UP, 1989.

Norman, Marsha. *The Holdup*. In *Four Plays: Marsha Norman*. New York: Theatre Communications Group, 1988.

Robertson, James Oliver. *American Myth, American Reality*. New York: Hill and Wang, 1980.

Smith, Page. *America Enters the World: A People's History of the Progressive Era and World War I*. New York: McGraw-Hill, 1985.

Turner, Frederick J[ackson]. *The Significance of the Frontier in American History*. March of America Facsimile Series 100. Ann Arbor: UMI, 1966.

Wattenberg, Richard. "Feminizing the Frontier Myth: Marsha Norman's *The Holdup*." *Modern Drama* 33, no.4 (December 1990): 507–517.

The "Other Funeral"

Narcissism and Symbolic Substitution in
Marsha Norman's *Traveler in the Dark*

Scott Hinson

Marsha Norman's *Traveler in the Dark* is frequently damned with faint praise. Critics write that her play is contrived and that action does not grow directly out of character or situation, but out of Norman's need to dramatize a philosophical and theological debate.[1] The most frequently cited criticism comes from Jack Kroll, who complains that "the action [in *Traveler*] seems whipped up under the lash of Norman's urgent need to dramatize a crisis of faith" (quoted in *DLB Yearbook* 311). Yet the same critics who damn her offer backhanded praise, suggesting that while *Traveler* "is beset by a number of weaknesses . . . Norman has fashioned an intelligent play" (Kane 268). Though Leslie Kane claims the resolution of Norman's play is difficult to swallow, she nonetheless observes that "the play seeks to debate science and faith, love and self-knowledge, the rage to grow and the resistance to change" (Kane 272; quoted in *DLB* 311). Though much of current criticism rightfully points out many of *Traveler*'s weaknesses, it dismisses Norman's accomplishment too easily and fails to explore the depth and psychological realism with which Norman depicts her characters.

Marsha Norman's *Traveler in the Dark* presents stark truths about how human beings continue in the face of mystery and powerlessness. *Traveler* also explores how our sense of loss can transform us into "inhuman" monsters, willing to annihilate those around us in an effort to diffuse or escape the unbearable pain of living in the world. In part, this truth seems to return Norman to one of her earliest attempts at writing, a prizewinning high school essay, and one of the most persistent themes in her work: "Why Do Good Men Suffer?" Most important, however, Norman's greatest achievement in this play is the depiction of the psychology of the narcissist and the protagonist's struggle to come to terms with his grief and guilt over his dead mother.

On the surface, *Traveler*'s tension resides in Sam's particularly modern crisis of faith: his existential loss of faith in God, science, and his own intellectual powers. After losing his mother as a child, Sam loses his Christian faith. Even after having preached soul-saving sermons, Sam feels God has betrayed him and he turns away from religion. His faith in God destroyed or lost, Sam has turned to science, medicine, and an unflagging faith in his "mind" to bolster him in the world (*Traveler* 176). However, despite his international reputation as a miracle-working surgeon, he is unable to save his long-time nurse and childhood sweetheart. Her death and his inability to save her destroy Sam's faith in medicine and himself: "I believed in everything. I even believed in you—or love, I guess. Didn't I? Yes. And in God, and fairy tales, and medicine and the power of my own mind and none of it works!" (197). Sam's confusion and pain are translated into vengeful attacks on his wife, whom he threatens to leave; his son, whom he swears he will take with him; and his father, who decides to follow Sam's career in the newspapers, but does not want to see him anymore.

Stripped of all faith, the anguish Sam experiences is quintessentially existential—faith cannot save him, since existence, according to Sam, is "absolute submission to accident, to the arbitrary assignment of unbearable pain, and the everyday occurrence of meaningless death" (198). The loss of his companion, nurse, and childhood sweetheart, whose funeral Sam has traveled home to attend, engenders in Sam a devastating and bitter existential emptiness. However, it is only when Sam realizes that he is driving away everyone who cares about him, and confronts his own isolation and powerlessness, that he can accept, on faith, the mystery and glory of life on the planet. "I have nothing for you," Sam tells his twelve-year-old son, Stephen, yet what he hands him is a "nothing" that equalizes and binds, a "nothing" full of the mystery of life (201). Sam hands Stephen the geode that his mother had so loved and had refused to crack open, telling him "it's . . . your mystery now" (201). Sam's crisis of faith finds resolution in his acceptance of his human condition as a "traveler in the dark" (204).

However, as Sam's crisis of faith moves toward resolution, we learn that he is plagued by guilt, deeply narcissistic, and ensnared in a bitter Oedipal rivalry with his father. Freud's investigations into narcissism are useful for understanding Sam's complex pathology and the tension that gives depth and realism to Norman's travelers in the dark. Here I will examine the psychology underlying Norman's complex protagonist, his attempts to come to terms with the death of his mother, and his struggle to shape an illusion that will keep him alive.

Marsha Norman describes the play's protagonist, Sam, a world-famous surgeon, as "a brilliant loner . . . [and] preoccupied, impatient, and condescending" (161). However, Norman's description of Sam hardly prepares us for the Sam that we meet—a distant, arrogant, and selfish man with a penchant for psychologically torturing his wife, Glory, and his son, Stephen. Sam's devaluation of his wife and his insistence on treating his twelve-year-old son, Stephen, as an adult regardless of the damage it might do to him, appear at first to be the result of the grief he feels over the death of his long-time nurse and childhood sweetheart, Mavis. In fact, Sam exhibits many of the traits that Freud identified in the mourner, including "a profoundly painful dejection, abrogation of interest in the outside world, loss of the capacity to love, [and] inhibition of all activity" (125).

However, we soon learn that Sam is grieving as much for his mother as he is for Mavis. Moreover, it becomes apparent that Mavis' death triggers Sam's unresolved feelings over the death of his mother. Both Sam's nostalgia for his mother's memory and his bitterness toward her can be explained as elements of his grief. In "Mourning and Melancholia," Freud refers to the ambivalence that the bereaved feels toward the lost love object (127, 130–131). According to Freud, the love object is at once highly valued, yet, as the object cathexis and reality testing gradually take place, the object becomes devalued, and is eventually rejected as no longer belonging to reality (127).

At one point, Sam describes his mother using images taken wholly from fairy tales; she is, in Sam's memory, "the gingerbread lady," with "curly red hair and shiny round eyes and big checked apron. Fat pink fingers, a sweet vanilla smell, and all the time in the world" (171). However, despite these rosy memories of her, Sam's bitterness toward his mother emerges in his interpretation of Humpty

Dumpty, in which Sam is cast as Humpty Dumpty. In Sam's reading of the nursery rhyme, as Humpty Dumpty he is betrayed by his mother, falls off the wall, and cannot put himself back together again. When Stephen asks how Humpty Dumpty got on the wall, Sam replies, "His . . . mother . . . laid him there" (Norman's ellipses; 164). Further, Sam suggests that Humpty Dumpty's mother deceived him when she told him that he was a man: "She told him he was a man. See?" (164). In fact, Sam seems especially bitter because he feels that his mother led him to believe that he, too, was a man, and therefore worthy of her affection and attention. Her death is a betrayal in Sam's eyes and both metaphorically and literally deprives Sam of his mother's affection. Moreover, because her death led him to reject the fairy tales and magic he shared with her, it is his mother who sets him up for his current crisis of faith.

Sam's unresolved feelings of guilt and excessive grief border on psychosis. Sam is hardly aware that he is grieving for more than his friend, and this lack of awareness and unconscious grief suggest a more profound pathology. For example, he expresses extreme dissatisfaction with himself on a moral level that also suggests melancholia ("Mourning" 129). Freud writes that "the melancholiac displays something which is lacking in grief—an extraordinary fall in his self-esteem, an impoverishment of his ego on a grand scale . . . . In melancholia it is the ego itself [which becomes poor and empty]" (129). Moreover, according to Freud, the melancholiac represents himself as "worthless, incapable of any effort, and morally despicable" and extends his self-abasement back over the past (129–130). In melancholia, then, Sam's tremendous ego has a longer way to fall than most since he assumes the blame for the death of Mavis and his mother.

However, despite his grief, borderline melancholia, and his self-criticism, Sam persistently overestimates his own ego. According to Freud, the narcissist, like the infant, believes that "he is really to be the center and heart of creation, 'His Majesty, the Baby'" ("Narcissism" 113–115). The narcissist directs libidinal energies onto the ego, choosing the self as love object rather than someone or something outside the self. Freud's theory of narcissism turns on the notion that human beings possess an inherent narcissism and that the choice to love something or someone other than oneself involves an object choice and a subsequent redirecting of one's libidinal energies away from the self and toward an outside object choice. Norman's infantile protagonist frequently displays traits characteristic of narcissism. Longing to be at the center of everything, when his mother died he acted "like it happened to me instead of her. I wouldn't eat. I broke things" (171). Similarly, when Mavis dies, he attempts to break up his marriage and destroy all illusions for his child, caring little for their feelings or how much he might hurt them (171). In addition, his reaction in both cases also suggests that he believes he should be beyond the touch of death.

Sam's narcissism also surfaces in frequent biblical allusions. For example, the comparisons between Sam and the arrogant, anthropologist-novelist God of his imagination; this is the God who, according to Sam, "sets it up, we live through it, and He writes it down. What we think of as life, Stephen, is just God gathering material for another book" (182). Sam had believed that his mother was his and is bitter when he learns that, according to his father, she belonged to God (182). Also, Sam projects his own arrogance and malevolence onto God when he describes him as "bored" and "lonely": "He's lonely, Stephen. He sits and waits for someone to notice Him, and then, when they don't, or when they don't notice Him enough, well, He plays His little tricks. He gives His little tests" (182). It is Sam who is bored and lonely, Sam whose excessive grief screams for attention, and finally, it is Sam who "plays his little tricks" when he isn't noticed enough. Sam goes on to compare himself with Job, the sufferer who finally triumphs over God, showing God where he had sinned: "And in that moment, God found God, and it was man" (183). Similarly, when God failed Sam as a youth, Sam found Sam. Sam's analogies with God and Job belie his belief in himself as a "supreme being".

Sam's overestimation of his ego can be seen in the allusions to fairy tales. In his version of the story of Sleeping Beauty, the king, according to Sam, "just forgot" about the evil thirteenth fairy—death—and when his kingdom awakens after a hundred-year-long sleep, "some prince is upstairs kissing his daughter" (170). This story and Sam's interpretation align Sam and the king. Like the king, Sam attributes his own carelessness and thoughtlessness to a bad memory and then to repression: "He forgot because he didn't want to re-

member!" (170). Fairy tales provide the text for Sam's interpretation
of his marriage as well as his own fate. Sam borrows from the story
of the frog and the prince, which he reinvents to describe his perceptions of his marriage: "The princess got old and the frog croaked"
(166). Sam depicts the narcissistic child, "His Majesty the Baby,"
who is not to be touched by "illness, death, renunciation of pleasure, restrictions on his own will" ("Narcissism" 115). His narcissism grows out of having been "abandoned" by his mother's death,
and his response to being rejected a second time, this time by Mavis,
is to behave just like a child. He wants to leave his wife, Glory, before she has a chance to reject and abandon him as his mother and
Mavis have. Wanting a divorce, Sam believes that "it just doesn't
make sense, this marriage. It never has. Ask your mother" (167).

In phrases evocative of Norman's *Traveler*, Freud suggests that
the narcissist will "fulfill those dreams and wishes of his parents which
they never carried out, to become a great man and a hero in his
father's stead, or to marry a prince as a tardy compensation to the
mother" (115). Sam perceives himself as having fulfilled the dream
to save lives more fully than his father. As a surgeon, Sam is able to
extend his patients' lives, even though, as he recognizes, he "can't
save lives . . . Death always wins" (191).

Sam's arrogance and narcissism are also apparent in his attitudes toward those around him. He admits that he feels he is better than the other hometown folks (194). Moreover, a more appropriate choice for Sam's love object is Mavis, who embodies the
intellect and self-confidence that Sam admires in himself; who is,
in Sam's words, "as smart as they come" (194) and "someone exactly like me" (195). Similarly, Sam believes that he would have
been good for Mavis as well, and that Mavis settled for a relationship with Sam's father since she couldn't have Sam. He is probably
right, for, as Glory says, Mavis "worshiped" him (195). Finally,
Sam's feelings of superiority are also apparent when Sam tells his
father, Everett, that he "didn't deserve" or love his mother (191).
The suggestion is, according to Sam's pathology, that Sam might
have been better for her, that he might have provided her with a
shining prince. Ultimately, Sam wants Everett to leave his "Mother's
house," to leave him there, alone with her garden, as if he alone is
worthy of her (192).

Finally, as narcissist, Sam perceives himself as almighty and believes that he possesses, or should possess, the power to create or destroy his family: "I thought I could save Mavis. I thought I could protect you. I can't do any of those things. I don't know what I *can* do" (Norman's italics; 201). Glory finally calls Sam out on his desire to be almighty. When he suggests that he can "save them," Glory responds with, "I don't need you to save me! . . . I've already got a God, Sam" (196). The realization that Sam is not all powerful, that he can be defeated by the powers of death, strikes a crushing blow to his ego.

In fact, Sam finds that death is the ultimate threat to his own ego (ego-ideal). Confronted by death and his inability to surmount it, Sam faces a crisis unlike any he has faced before. As he says, "Other people die, Glory—not me, not my family, not my friend" (197). Freud writes that "at the weakest point of all in the narcissistic pattern, the immortality of the ego, which is so relentlessly assailed by reality, security is achieved by fleeing to the child. Parental love, which is so touching and at bottom so childish, is nothing but parental narcissism born again, and, transformed though it be into object-love, it reveals its former character infallibly" (115). According to Freudian theory, then, the egoist and narcissist Sam retreats from death by transferring his own narcissism onto his child, Stephen, and what appears to be his only tenderness and unselfish emotion and attachment to Stephen is, in fact, Sam's own narcissism.

Sam's deplorable treatment of his family can be explained in part by the threat to his ego posed by his mother's death, yet this does little to explain the bitter rivalry between Sam and his father. To understand this rivalry, it is important to look more closely at their relationship and the Oedipal dynamics that shape it. For example, the death of Sam's mother is tied up with the loss of Mavis, as both were objects of Sam's affection. Yet Norman makes both women objects of Everett's affections as well. Sam's ambivalence toward his mother demonstrates that he has experienced her death as a rejection of him, and we might well expect that Mavis' death would be experienced similarly, though the play offers no direct evidence for such a reading. Nonetheless, he still struggles to overcome her loss and the sparks of the battle for her affection still fly between his father and himself. Sam's belief that he is better suited than Everett for both Mavis and his dead mother places him and his father in the position of rivals for their affection. According to Sam, if his mother hadn't died, he would have been the "biggest momma's boy you ever saw" (171). Also, Sam displays his jealousy and bitterness toward his father for not having loved his mother the way he should have. Sam tells Everett that he "didn't deserve her" or love her (191).

Similarly, Sam's father shared a special relationship with Mavis, one based on a respect for mystery and magic, a respect that Sam did not share. Indeed, he reveals that he is jealous of his father's close relationship with Mavis. When Glory states that Mavis loved Josie Barnett, Sam jealously retorts, "Mavis loved dad" (163). Sam's insistence on pointing out Mavis' love for his father belies an undue interest in her choice of love object. As Mavis stands in the position of symbolic substitute for his dead mother, these reminders of Mavis' love for Sam's father rekindle in him an Oedipal rivalry for the mother's affections. For example, Sam flatly denies that he and Mavis were involved—much to the chagrin of Sam's father, who in interesting Sam in Mavis sought to redirect his libidinal energies away from the mother. Even though Sam recants later, he tells Glory that he married her "to spite [his] father" (177).

Despite the tension between father and son, Sam seems trapped in a pre-Oedipal stage, in which he is less interested in battling with the father than in merging completely with the mother, in identifying with her completely, perhaps as a means of restoring his childhood image of himself. Glory refuses to allow him to wallow in total mother identification, although, in part, Sam's acceptance of nursery rhymes and "mystery," restores to him his own narcissistic and childlike ego.

Tied to his struggles with the father, Sam's struggle in *Traveler in the Dark* is to reconstruct the chain of the symbolic substitutions for his lost mother, of which Mavis had been the most satisfying and suitable link. It is this vital chain of symbolic substitutions for the mother that Mavis' death shatters and that Sam attempts to put back together again. The occasion for Norman's play and for Sam's crisis is the death of his close friend and nurse, Mavis. Yet Sam spends very little time grieving for her. Sam's preoccupation with his mother appears in the frequent references to her, her things, and Sam's memories of her. Moreover, Norman devotes considerable energy to depicting her character, though she is not present. Sam's first words are a reference to his mother and her garden: "There she is. Mother." (162). We learn as well that Sam had attempted to save his mother and failed, just as he had attempted, and failed, to save Mavis. Sam had begun to try to keep his mother alive symbolically even as he sat on her deathbed; according to Everett, "there was my little boy, Samuel, sitting on his dear mother's bed, and he didn't know she was dead, he was just sitting there, reading as loud as he could, as fast as he could, but he was shaking like a young tree in a driving rain" (192). We can believe that, just as Sam wants to "save" everyone in his life, he feels considerable responsibility for his mother's death. In fact, as Everett tells Stephen, "Your daddy is a doctor today because his mother died when he was so young" (183).

Finally, Sam's devotion to his mother is echoed in his double, Stephen, who, like Sam, is being shaped by his father into a mirror image of himself and who chooses to reject the father and cling to the mother. When Sam threatens to take Stephen away from his mother, Stephen reacts violently: "I'm living with Mom. . . . Don't call us! Don't come see us! . . . Don't come get your things!" (190). Thus, Sam's search in this play is not only for a way back to some kind of faith. Instead, he must also find some way to reconcile himself with the guilt he feels for his mother's death. He must symbolically erase her loss, of which Mavis' death is a reminder.

While Sam does not attend his friend's funeral, he presides over the "other funeral" in this play, the funeral for his mother. In order to absolve himself of the guilt he feels for her death, Sam must find an object that is suitable as a substitution for her. As a female friend completely devoted to him, Mavis resembles very closely the mother that Sam lost at such an early age. Like his mother, Mavis "worshiped him" and was always there for him (195–96). Because of the sexual element in their relationship, Glory is less well-suited as a substitute for Sam's original love object. Equally as likely, however, is that Glory occupied a position in the chain of substitutions primarily because of his sexual relationship with her. If so, his rejection of her is comparable to the ambivalence he displays toward the memory of his mother. However, because Sam seems more interested in merging with his mother, rather than possessing her sexually, either of the two women serves as a suitable substitute for her.

Faced with the destruction of his most satisfying substitution for his mother, Mavis, Sam returns home, only to begin resurrecting other symbolic substitutes for her. Just as Mavis has suggested to Glory that Sam's "illusions [concerning Glory] must be preserved," Sam works throughout the play to restore his mother's garden and the illusion that he has not lost her (202). He devotes his energy to restoring his mother's garden, and thus his childhood relationship with her, as a means of absolving himself of his guilt for her death. He sweeps and cleans the wall wherein his toys and other symbols of his childhood are enshrined in an effort to create a suitable symbolic substitute for his missing mother. He cleans and replaces the stone rabbit, the loose stones, and the stone Mother Goose as a way of preserving his own illusions.

Like the fallen angel, Sam reaches his most poetic moment in his own "private hell" (198). Here he faces the harshness of the world stripped of illusions, the world without magic tricks or symbols: Only when we face the "everyday occurrence of meaningless death, Sam says, "can we believe that . . . love blazes across the black sky like a comet but never returns" (198). The restoration of the garden does help Sam to restore his mother symbolically; however, ultimately the geode discovered by Stephen provides Sam with the symbol that will restore the memory of his mother, which can no longer reside in Mavis. They discuss cutting open the geode, but Sam refuses, in contrast to his surgery on Mavis. Nonetheless, it was in cutting Mavis open, examining her more closely that Sam found "forgiveness": "It was . . . (And suddenly, the words come from him the way "it" came from Mavis in that moment) it was forgiveness" (Norman's ellipsis; 202).

The close identification in Sam's mind between Mavis and his mother allows Sam to find forgiveness through Mavis for his mother's death as well. Moreover, the decision not to cut the geode open simultaneously allows Sam to reverse his decision to operate on Mavis and preserves the symbol of his mother. Sam is highly protective of the geode as an object (symbol) that, first, belonged to his mother and is closely associated with her, and second, is a symbol whose meaning must not be investigated. When Stephen suggests that they get the hammer to crack open the geode, Sam responds: "(Sudden alarm): No! (Then more quietly) Once you crack them . . . she didn't like to crack them" (201).

With the discovery of the geode, an apt symbol of the mother, Sam is able to admit his weaknesses, his human fallibility. With the restoration of the garden and the stone Mother Goose, and the preservation of the geode, Sam's mother is symbolically restored and his grief abates. Freud helps to explain Sam when he suggests that once the narcissist has been "partially freed from his repressions, we are frequently confronted by the unintended result that he withdraws from further treatment in order to choose a love object, hoping that life with the beloved person[s] will complete his recovery" (123). Sam is able, then, to redirect his feelings/energy toward things outside of himself, such as his wife, son, and father.

Again, as the surface conflicts in this play are fairly easily resolved, this essay seeks to focus on the play's underlying tensions. *Traveler in the Dark* is a play that presents itself as a philosophical and theological debate, yet it is driven by deeper psychological conflicts. Norman presents us with a portrait of a narcissistic character, searching desperately for symbols that will restore his beloved mother. Given Sam's pathology, Norman's resolution seems somehow too tidy and quick, and not entirely convincing. At times, it seems as if Norman is anticipating the magical restoration that takes place in *The Secret Garden* and neglects the magnitude of the crisis for the characters she has created in *Traveler*. Still, the realism with which Norman paints this subtle psychological portrait moves her play beyond the merely philosophical into a personal realm. If we do not see ourselves in Sam's philosophical debate, then certainly his deeper psychological dilemmas resonate for us on a personal level. Because Sam accepts that he will continue in the dark, his philosophical crisis is resolved. Similarly, Sam prefers to continue in the dark created by symbols of his mother, rather than face the truth of her death. Like Sam, if we look at all, we look only with reluctance into the dark through which we must travel.

Notes

1.   See Esther Harriot's *American Voices: Five Contemporary Playwrights in Essays and Interviews,* 142–147, and Leslie Kane's "The Way Out, the Way In: Paths to Self in the Plays of Marsha Norman," in *Feminine Focus: The New Women Playwrights,* ed. Enoch Brater, pp. 268–273. Leslie Kane devotes considerable space to pointing out the deficiencies of *Traveler in the Dark.*

Works Cited

Bruccoli, Mary, ed. *Dictionary of Literary Biography.* Detroit: Gale, 1984.

Freud, Sigmund. "Mourning and Melancholia." In *A General Selection from the Works of Sigmund Freud.* Edited by John Rickman. New York: Doubleday, 1989. 124–140.

———. "On Narcissism." In *A General Selection from the Works of Sigmund Freud.* Edited by John Rickman. New York: Doubleday, 1989. 104–123.

Harriot, Esther. *American Voices: Five Contemporary Playwrights in Essays and Interviews.* Jefferson, NC: McFarland, 1988.

Kane, Leslie. "The Way Out, the Way In: Paths to Self in the Plays of Marsha Norman." In *Feminine Focus: The New Women Playwrights.* Edited by Enoch Brater. New York: Oxford UP, 1989. 268–273.

Norman, Marsha. *Traveler in the Dark.* In *Four Plays: Marsha Norman.* New York: Theatre Communications Group, 1988. 161–204.

Marsha Norman's
Sarah and Abraham
"The Moon Is Teaching Bible"

Katherine H. Burkman and Claire R. Fried

In her play *Sarah and Abraham* (1992), Marsha Norman depicts a group of actors who have come together as a company to improvise and then play the biblical story of Sarah and Abraham. Weaving the personal lives of these actors and actresses into the imagined lives of Sarah and Abraham, Norman gives mythic resonance to the contemporary characters. At the same time, she reinterprets the drama of the biblical story through the light shed on it by its characters' contemporary counterparts.

Although at first reading or viewing, one might find the play to be about a traditional triangle in which Sarah/Kitty and Hagar/Monica fight over the protagonist Abraham/Cliff, at closer examination, one may perceive that Norman has reshaped biblical myth to focus on the women in fresh ways. Savina Teubal postulates in *Sarah the Priestess* that through the male narration of Genesis, we can read between the lines that the matriarch Sarah was a priestess of a nonpatriarchal tradition in her time, her life presenting a struggle between her nonpatriarchal culture and the budding patriarchal culture of Abraham (xv). If the biblical writers made Abraham the patriarchal center of the tale, Marsha Norman further revises the original myths to reclaim the women's roles. In her treatment she does not neglect the Hagar figure, but her emphasis is on reclaiming Sarah as a contemporary feminist—with a difference.[1]

The situation is that Jack, the company's director, has imported Monica, a former member of the company who has become a successful movie actress, to play Hagar to Kitty's Sarah. Kitty's husband, Cliff, is receiving his big chance when he is given the role of Abraham. He has apparently spent his career playing minor roles, as his wife has been the prime actress and mainstay of the group. "So

yes," Jack informs Cliff in the opening scene, "Kitty's going to get
the billing, and Monica's gonna help us sell some tickets, but (*a
moment*) this is going to be *your* show, Cliff. You're the real star. Or
you will be when it's over. I want *you* to play Abraham" (5). Jack's
words turn out to be prophetic. Cliff is successful in the role and
will play it when the group opens in New York. Displacing Kitty as
star, who plans to stay home to have a baby, Cliff's ascendancy in
the dramatic action reflects the ascendancy of Abraham over the
priestess to whom he is married, the taking of biblical stage center.
Jack reads the critic's review aloud: "Cliff Well's transformation from
tribal house husband to noble patriarch is nothing short of miracu-
lous. Before our very eyes, the pagan age of mystery and moon worship ends, and the sun rises on the world as we know it" (106).

Not so. The ironies of the play lie not in a subtext that subverts
this overt movement of plot but in the intertextual interplay of the
relationships of the actors as they create their roles and the plot. Because Kitty/Sarah opts to give up her dramatic career and her husband
to focus on her soon-to-arrive baby, one might conclude that the play
is antifeminist. But Norman has made it abundantly clear in the drama
that more real strength comes from the pagan, moon-worshiping Sa-
rah/Kitty than from the newly emerging, sun-worshiping Abraham/
Cliff.[2] The treatment of gender is complex and becomes even more so
with the introduction of Virginia Mason, a scholar imported from
the University of Wisconsin, who is to contribute her knowledge to
rehearsals and to create a script out of the improvisations of the troupe.
Her name is suggestive both of virginity (Virginia)—she is in a sense
the novice in the group but also a source of wisdom—and of building
(Mason)—she is helping to construct a new fiction that is built on
what may be hidden in the biblical tale. That she is drawn into the
play as actress/Scribe gives another feminist dimension to Norman's
dramatization of the biblical tale.

Virginia's research evokes biblical scholarship on Sarah as a high
priest of "the old Mesopotamia Moon Worship" (11), which was apparently prevalent in the society that is being portrayed in Genesis.[3]
Despite the Jewish distrust of the moon, and its forbidden air, the
moon has remained an important idea in Western culture. The Jewish
calendar is a lunar one, the first of every month being the day of the
new moon, most Gregorian or solar calendars depict the moon and its

phases, and farmers today depend on the moon to determine harvest times. By endowing her "scribe" with an awareness of the power of such moon worship, which the Bible takes such pains to suppress (biblical narrative generally constructing the moon as a symbol of submission[4]), Marsha Norman plays upon these natural associations with the moon and reworks its image in her play, using its positive connotations, which have survived biblical negativity. The moon, it would seem, has something to teach, something to offer us.[5]

Cliff's associations with the sun and Kitty's with the moon begin to take shape with the first improvisations on the biblical story in scene 2. As Cliff worries about who and where he is, Kitty encourages relaxation: "Just rest, Cliff. It's the first time you've been in the shade all day" (12), she quips, diagnosing his problem as a sun worshiper from the very start. Cliff's efforts to understand Abraham's movement to a new land in terms of a move to California offer further amusing definition of him as a sun worshiper. Kitty sees this move to the "coast" as one in which he can buy a new wife, suggesting in her improvisation the subtext of their relationship and her desires: "I want our life to stay the way it is" (17). When Cliff/Abraham insists that he is not leaving her by moving to the coast, she adds, "Where everybody leaves everybody and nobody gives a shit" (17). When Cliff narcissistically follows Jack off, wondering, "Will they see why God picked me?" Virginia and Kitty collude on their understanding of Sarah's role. Virginia further defines the coast to which Abraham/Cliff wants to move as a heathen, sun-worshiping area that would interest Sarah only as a priestess of the moon in search of converts.

SARAH: *Actually, I can see worshipping the moon.*

VIRGINIA: *I know. I can too. Fertility, crops . . .*

SARAH: *Mystery, romance . . . (18)*

Although Jack as director has been having an affair with Kitty and is also attracted to the imported Virginia, he is in a sense the "God" who has cast Cliff as Abraham, and he is invested in an amusingly clichéd vision of how the drama should work itself out in traditional patriarchal terms on stage. His first stage direction to Kitty/ Sarah is "O.K. Now Sarah, darling. There he is [Abraham]. The Love of your life" (14). When Kitty asks Virginia how Sarah spent her days and is informed that evidence points to her role outside the pages of the Bible as a high priestess of moon worship, Jack interrupts Virginia to address Kitty: "Kitty, who Sarah *really* was is not part of our story here. It's the Bible version we're after. How marriage used to be. You loved this man (*indicating Cliff*). You stood behind him, all the way. When God told him to move, you started packing" (12). When Sarah rebels against Jack's stereotyping of her as wife ("Jack, maybe it would be fun if I played the maid this time, and Monica played Sarah" [9]), Jack reveals more of his autocratic bias; casting is not negotiable. "You're perfect for Sarah. You're just exactly who she must have been. Or so Virginia tells me. And if you hate being Sarah, well, then, (*a moment*) we'll know she hated it too" (9).

That is indeed what the audience comes to know, although this knowledge escapes Jack entirely. The stereotypes that Jack harbors are played upon by Norman as well, as she introduces Monica, who will play Hagar, as little more than a "Hollywood babe" of whom Kitty, as wife stuck in a role she doesn't want to play, is properly jealous. Still, Kitty initially does play her "traditional" role, apologizing to her husband for the less than perfect coffee she has given him for breakfast. Improvising the biblical tale allows for exploration of these stereotypes, which break down in the process.

As they continue to work on the play-within-the-play, the text develops not only in terms of God's calling of Abraham to a new land and new role as patriarch, but also in terms of the subtext of Kitty and Cliff's power struggle. Feeling uncomfortable with his written script, Cliff improvises his own inner conflicts while commenting on the writing. Speaking of Sarah's relationship with Abraham, he says, "This is *her* town and he knows it. That's why he wants to get away. They worship her here" (21). Since this is Kitty's town, where she plays the leading roles, the conversation about the play is clearly about their own relationship. When Kitty/Sarah explains that "It's not her fault she's a priestess," and that the entire tribe is depending on her, Cliff's response, "If she doesn't want to be a Priestess, why doesn't she quit?" is met with his wife and Sarah's very real question: "Would that make him happy?" (21).

By exploring in further dialogue what happened to Sarah when she did follow Abraham to the "coast" to make him happy, Kitty begins to see the future of her own relationship with Cliff as he gets involved with Monica. The biblical tale (and its continued rehearsal) becomes a cautionary tale leading to her own decision not to follow her husband to New York.

We see Sarah's decision to remain, which is counter to the biblical plot and its patriarchal thrust, taking shape early in the play. When Virginia improvisationally advises Sarah as scribe, in the play-within-the-play, to send Hagar away rather than let her produce an heir, what is at stake is both the entire issue of a people's survival, in terms of the play-within-the-play, and the issue of Sarah/Kitty's and Abraham/Cliff's relationship. Here we learn through Norman/Virginia/Scribe that in her role as a high priest, Sarah cannot bear a child (38). Although in Genesis Sarah is barren, the interpretation of Genesis that Norman employs suggests that the real reason for her childlessness is that her position as moon priestess precludes childbearing (Teubal 37). At this point in the play, Sarah/Kitty is still too involved with her feelings for Abraham/Cliff simply to let him go, and hence she enlists Hagar as surrogate mother. This is also the proper role of the moon priestess, who enlists another to have her child. Still, the possibility of losing Abraham to Hagar or even of relinquishing Cliff to Monica, which is Kitty's final choice, is in the air in this early scene in Sarah's exchange with the scribe.

VIRGINIA: (looks up from her writing) *Send her away, my Lord. She is not respectful of our ways.*

SARAH: *I cannot. I fear that Abraham would follow her.*

VIRGINIA: *Then you must let him go. (38)*

At this point, Sarah/Kitty can't do this, but it is what she will do. When she plays the scene out, bringing Hagar to Abraham, all of the actors are impressed with her acting. Jack exclaims, "There's not another actress in this whole country with that kind of power, Kitty" (41), and even Cliff and Monica are in awe of this "power." The power that Kitty is displaying as an actress, which is so enmeshed with what she is learning as a person, emerges from Virginia's insights about Sarah as a moon goddess. Just as Virginia and Kitty colluded earlier (Act 1, scene 2) in an appreciation of moon worship, now Monica joins them in beginning to intuit the power of Kitty/Sarah's moon-teaching; Kitty is beginning to separate from Cliff, to develop her independence.

Although Monica retains more of her initial stereotypical "Hollywood babe" role than Kitty retains her long-suffering wife stereotype, she is enough infected by Kitty to emerge as more of a character herself. By exploring her role as Hagar, she is able to examine, as well, her new role as Cliff's mistress. "As far as I can tell," she complains to Cliff, "You're the only one who's looking at me and seeing a real person" (23). As a Hollywood outsider, Monica can understand Hagar's feelings of victimization and alienation. Improvising the playlet, she subtextually pleads for herself, telling Jack she wants to leave camp before her baby, fathered by Abraham, is born.

HAGAR: *Don't you know what's going to happen to this baby when I have it? Sarah is going to take him away! Here she stands, everybody treating her like some kind of goddess, and all the time, she's planning to steal my child.* (tearing off her pregnant padding) *Now when in this goddamn play do* I *get* anything *except screwed?* (51)

What Monica begins to grasp, however, which gives some feminist spice to Hagar/Monica's suffering, is that she is not particularly interested in the patriarchal emphasis on legitimate heirs. Jack insists that what is at stake is legitimacy. He explains that if Sarah doesn't adopt Hagar's baby, it won't have that legitimacy, but Monica resists what Hagar accepted just as Kitty resists Sarah's role in the tale. She does not care if the baby is legitimate, she protests, nor if he is the founder of Islam: "I don't care who he grows up to be," she insists. "I can't say these lines" (51). The only way the others can lure Monica into continuing is by giving her a sense of a space that is not dominated by Kitty/Sarah. Her son will not have to worship the moon, God will speak to her, and her Egyptian practice of circumcision will become established with Abraham's people.

Monica confesses to Kitty, further deepening her use of the play-within-the-play as a way of talking about their relationship, that she had left the company in the first place because she felt like a mere entertainer to Kitty's real abilities as an actor—"You've got all this wisdom and power, and all I've got is good legs" (55). Kitty's response, however, is just as revealing about how Sarah/Kitty feels about the "other woman." "You're O.K.," she assures Monica. "You're better than you know. You're what everybody wants. Even me. I would give just about anything for a little entertainment right now" (55).

This discussion causes some bonding between the rival women in the play, each of whom begins to understand a bit more of how the other feels. Monica has complained that "Virginia hasn't got a clue how hard it is to be a slut" (49), and after Monica's tantrum over her treatment (inside and outside the play-within-the-play), Virginia notices that she has been neglecting the Hagar-figure, who, after all, "is the only woman in the Bible that God ever talked to directly" (56). The moon, teaching Bible, involves this bonding of the women in an effort to work out their values apart from those imposed by the men.

The bonding of the three women is further developed at the drama's climax, which neatly coincides with the climax of the play-within-the-play, when Hagar warns Sarah in improvisation that the sacrifice of Isaac is about to take place and should be resisted. Jack's insight, that Abraham/Cliff really feels murderous toward the child, doubtless stems from his own fury at the unborn child that will keep Kitty from joining the company and him in New York. He sets up the improvisation for the sacrifice of Isaac as a kind of test of whether Cliff will go with them to New York, creating yet another parallel to God's test of Abraham's allegiance. Emboldened by Jack's own resentment of the child, Cliff has hardened as well, so that he finally requests a real knife for the scene. Such a prop, it turns out, would have been fatal since Cliff gets so carried away that despite Kitty's protests, Virginia's physical interference, and Monica's observation that "This is sick," he actually plunges the cardboard knife down onto the child playing his son. Perhaps what the three women share is Kitty's insight at this climax: "He's a child. You're not mad at him. . . . You're mad at me" (93). Such an interpretation seems justified, since Cliff is annoyed when Kitty tries to interfere with the scene—"What is it with you?" he exclaims. "Can't I have one scene in this play?" (93).

If the sacrifice of Isaac is the culminating action of the play-within-the-play, Kitty's decision to devote herself to the child she expects is the culminating action of the entire drama. Kitty's pregnancy surfaces as subject at the opening of Act 2 when Cliff complains to Jack that Kitty has not discussed it with him; what ensues is a subtextual discussion of that pregnancy in terms of Sarah's discussion of her pregnancy with Abraham. The ambiguity of the child's paternity, since Kitty is not sure whether the father is Jack/God or Cliff/Abraham, is further evidence of Norman's focus on Sarah's role as moon goddess. Teubal's scholarship points out that crucial to the goddess paradigm is the supernatural conception of a child (99). What we see working itself out under and through the multiple conflicts that emerge over Sarah/Kitty's pregnancy is the independence that this moon child gives to Kitty, if she will just have the courage to claim it.

Cliff as Abraham is aghast at the pregnancy, feeling betrayed by Kitty, who refuses to assure him he is the father. "I thought you loved me," he complains, denying that he knew she wished for a child (62). "Does Sarah want a divorce?" he inquires, noting that "She can't marry God" (62). Kitty as Sarah assures Cliff/Abraham that she does love him but does not need to simply watch his infidelities. Unable to be upstaged by his wife, Cliff explores the possibility of doing "Sodom and Gomorrah," but is brought back to the issue as Jack tells him they are only doing what involves Sarah—"You can do Sodom when you do the movie" (65), he adds, punningly, further debasing Cliff/Abraham's coastal ambitions.

Kitty/Sarah, however, moves into an exploration of Sarah's biblical laughter at the miracle of her pregnancy as the laughter of fulfillment. "I am happy," she informs Tom, the stage manager. "Finally, I'm doing something that has to do with me" (66). Confiding in Tom that she does not plan to work after the birth, she merges with Sarah as moon goddess: "I like this lady. Whenever she has a choice to make, she does the right thing" (66). Virginia now fittingly becomes the midwife to a birth that is strangely moving even to the objecting Cliff/Abraham.

What enriches the play here is not a single-minded rejection of Cliff/Abraham by a superwoman-goddess figure, but a complexity of reaction to this "birth" that seems to symbolize more than Sarah/Kitty's assertion of power in her relationship with her husband and his lover. Kitty does not stop being jealous of Monica, as becomes clear in the further playing out of the biblical story. And despite his climactic, murderous rage at his wife, displaced onto Isaac, whose sacrifice becomes his temptation, Cliff continues to feel confused, both before and after, and needy. When he seeks help and advice from Virginia, who is so basically aligned with Sarah/Kitty, she nevertheless helps him: "Well. I think . . . what Abraham does right now, is solve the problems he, Abraham, can solve, and not try too hard to understand what God is doing. He makes his own decisions, I mean. He protects the ones he loves and keeps working to provide for his people" (80).

In other words, although Norman's drama is one in which Sarah/Kitty moves toward a finding of her own power as moon goddess/woman, and although this involves quite a bit of humor at the expense of the male characters, the playwright is not insensitive to the dilemmas of the male caught in the middle, living in the shadow of his wife's success and seeking to "have it all."

Cliff cannot understand Kitty's decision to remain behind when the play goes to New York. Infidelity is such a part of their relationship that he apparently felt his relationship with Monica was but another episode rather than a fatal rupture. Sarah explains to him that she is not going "because Jack is a tyrannical bastard and you are his blind slave. . . . " (98), which comes out as a thinly disguised judgment of the biblical God and Abraham. On a more personal note, she explains that "if you really don't want something to break, you have to force yourself to stop dropping it" (100).

The entire play, however, contributes to and is about Kitty's decision to stay home. As the play-within-the-play ends on a note of reconciliation, Sarah speaking from her grave to the still-living Abraham, the Scribe/Virginia tells us of their final burial together. Sarah/Kitty had asked Virginia at the outset of the drama if Sarah dies, and the scholar had responded, "Night after night" (10). It is Cliff, however, who is exiting to the nightly dying that will take place in New York, while Sarah remains "on stage," home, alive.

SARAH: *I'm not dying, Cliff. I'm just . . .*

ABRAHAM: *I know. You're just. . .*

SARAH: *Staying home. (107)*

Lest this "staying home" be narrowly construed as caving in to traditional unempowering roles for women, Sarah has also made it clear to Jack that her decision is not locking her into a single role. "Who says this is my one shot at the big time," she informs him. "Who says I can't go to New York later if I need to. If this is my one shot at anything it's being a mother, and I'm going to take it" (81).

Earlier in the play, Cliff had mentioned coming by to pick up some of his things, and Kitty showed concern that he might want the cat. It turns out that he never liked the animal and he is mystified that this is what she chooses to keep. One must remember, however, that we are dealing with Sarah/Kitty. The name becomes suggestive here of what Kitty will retain—herself. [6]

Perhaps the least convincing part of Norman's *Sarah and Abraham* is the play-within-the-play itself. Since this is finally shaped more by Jack/God than anybody else, the final scene (played out without interruption as a performance) seems too narrated, too conventional, and too humorless. Why the audience is applauding madly and the critic reports his enthusiasm is hard to imagine. As a foil, however, for Norman's nonnarrative, unconventional, and humorous treatment of the biblical tale, it serves its purpose. Norman's play becomes something of a feminist midrash; that is, a feminist exegesis of the biblical tale of Sarah and Abraham. Norman draws on the tradition of involving the Hebrew Bible, as the ancient Jewish sages did, in explaining/defending/justifying their own views of life. At the same time that the rabbis drew on the Bible, using its language and its teachings to illuminate their own writings, their own interpretations of what may not be explicit in the Bible provide new texts. Like these ancient rabbis, Marsha Norman employs biblical language and motifs in her feminist midrash to reclaim the lunar power that the ancients repressed.

The men in Norman's play are concerned, as were their biblical counterparts and the biblical women, with paternity. God assured Hagar that despite her sufferings, her son Ishmael would be the father of a great people. Sarah, too, is assured of her son's importance in the future of the Jewish people. Elie Weisel, who is critical of Sarah in her treatment of Hagar, suggests that emphasis on the importance of the male heir has resulted in division between peoples of the Western world (249). In Marsha Norman's play, neither woman is concerned about paternity. Kitty does not care who has fathered *her* child. She seems to be experiencing, as she assures Cliff that she is not dying but merely staying home, a sense of generation that gives her and her unborn child a renewed sense of a less divisive kind of life. Whereas the play's internal critic is enthusiastic about the drama's depiction of the decline of pagan moon worship with the rise of the patriarchal Abraham, Norman's play ends with a single light that holds on Sarah/Kitty—surely a light that is lunar.

Notes

1. Norman draws upon a tradition of revising myth that is explored by Jo Ann Hackett in her article "Rehabilitating Hagar: Fragments of an Epic Pattern." Hackett says that in the Near Eastern myth upon which the writers of Genesis drew, there is a male mortal protagonist who as an underling stands up to the god and goddess figures and engages the sympathy of the audience. What the biblical writers do is shift the emphasis to the male authority figure, Abraham, who takes the underling's place in this retelling of the god figure. In other words, in Genesis, when Sarah finds herself childless and persuades Abraham to bear a child for her through her handmaid, Hagar, and then turns on Hagar when she has her own child in a competitive rage, Abraham navigates the rivalry between the women to become the story's protagonist. Because Abraham negotiates the rivalry between Sarah and the now-female underling, Hagar, our sympathy is now supposed to rest with him. Hackett, however, proposes that by replacing the male mortal with the female Hagar, the biblical writers are now really focusing our sympathies on her as victim (22).

2. This struggle between the sun and moon is echoed in Jewish biblical scholarship. Although the sun and moon "were originally equal . . . jealousy between them caused dissensions, so God decided to make one of them smaller. The moon was chosen to be degraded because it had unlawfully intruded into the sphere of the sun, and hence the difference between the sun, 'the greater light,' and the moon, 'the lesser light'" (*Encyclopaedia Judaica*, "Moon"). Does this midrash, perhaps, echo woman's intrusion on the male domain?

3. This controversial approach to Sarah is supported in some biblical scholarship. Myra Siff, one of *Enclyclopaedia Judaica*'s contributors, gives us a hint of how Sarah might be linked to the moon by suggesting that Sarah's name points to a connection between her and the moon: "The usual interpretation of the name Sarah is 'princess' or 'chieftainess,' although it may also be connected with the Akkadian Sarrat, one of the designations of the moon-goddess Ishtar" ("Sarah").

4. Canaanite civilizations existing before and at the same time as early Judaism worshiped the moon as a god. Indeed, the moon has often been associated with femininity and with paganism in Western civilization, one important connection between the two being that a woman's menstrual cycle is approximately the same length as the orbit of the moon, twenty-eight days. The tendency in our time is to view the moon with suspicion, attributing strange behavior to the full moon and using it as a symbol for pagan festivals like Halloween. Our culture's distrust of the moon reflects its similar distrust of and revulsion for the functions of the female body.

    The sun, too, in much biblical imagery, must submit to God, but the moon in particular as a female symbol must submit to a male god. In Psalm 136, the moon and stars "rule by night" (Ps. 136:9) but God has power over all. Perhaps this forced obedience of the moon reflects the Judeo-Christian cultural fear of female sexuality and female perceptions. The Bible forbids the worship of the moon as just one way of setting the Jewish people apart from its Semitic neighbors, in the process stigmatizing the worship of female gods and femaleness. "I will show portents in the sky and on earth, blood and fire and columns of smoke; the sun shall be turned into darkness and the moon into blood before the great and terrible day of the Lord comes," (JL 2:30–31). As the moon turns to blood, it calls to mind its association with the menstrual cycle.

5.   The Moon Is Teaching Bible

> *The moon is teaching Bible.*
> *Cyclamen, poppy, and mountain*
> *listen with joy.*
> *Only the girl cries.*
> *The poppy can't hear her crying—*
> *the poppy is blazing in Torah,*
> *burning like the verse.*
> *The cyclamen doesn't listen*
> *to the crying—*
> *the cyclamen swoons*
> *from the sweet secrets.*
> *The mountain is sunk in thought.*
> *But here comes the wind,*
> *soft and fragrant,*
> *to honor hope*
> *and sing—*
> *each heart*
> *is a flying horseman,*
> *an ardent hunter*
> *swept to the ends of the sea. (Zelda 124)*

6.   One is reminded here of Harold Pinter's play *The Collection*, in which Stella, somewhat victimized by the three men in the drama, remains enigmatically strong as she is aligned with her cat.

Works Cited

Hackett, Jo Ann. "Rehabilitating Hagar: Fragments of an Epic Pattern." In *Gender and Difference in Ancient Israel*. Edited by Peggy L. Day. Minneapolis: Fortress P, 1989. 12–27.

"Moon." *Encyclopaedia Judaica*. Edited by Cecil Roth. Jerusalem: Keter Publishing House, 1971.

Norman, Marsha. *Sarah and Abraham*. Unpublished manuscript, Tantleff Agency, New York. January 1993.

Pinter, Harold. *The Collection*. In *Complete Works: Two*. New York: Grove Weidenfeld, 1977. 119–157.

"Sarah." *Encyclopaedia Judaica*. Edited by Cecil Roth. Jerusalem: Keter Publishing House, 1971.

Sandmel, Samuel J., et al., eds. *The New English Bible with the Apocrypha: Oxford Study Edition*. New York: Oxford UP, 1976.

Teubal, Savina J. *Sarah the Priestess: The First Matriarch of Genesis*. Athens, OH: Swallow Press, 1984.

Weisel, Elie. "Ishmael and Hagar." In *The Life of the Covenant: The Challenge of Contemporary Judaism; Essays in Honor of Herman E. Schaalman*. Edited by Joseph A. Edelheit. Chicago: Spertus College of Judaica Press, 1986. 235–249.

Zelda. "The Moon is Teaching Bible." In *Burning Air and a Clear Mind: Contemporary Israeli Woman Poets*. Athens, OH: Ohio UP, 1981. 124.

"This Haunted Girl"

Marsha Norman's Adaptation of *The Secret Garden*

Lisa Tyler

In Frances Hodgson Burnett's classic children's novel *The Secret Garden*, a contrary young girl named Mary loses her parents in a cholera epidemic and comes to England to live with her uncle, Archibald Craven, and her cousin, Colin. Through her discovery of and experiences in the hidden, walled garden of the story's title, Mary overcomes her contrariness and brings herself back to life. In her relationships with the motherless family that has taken her in, she also learns how to foster the growth and health of another human being—in short, how to mother.[1]

Pulitzer Prize–winning playwright Marsha Norman, who had never before read the novel,[2] wrote the libretto and lyrics for a musical version of *The Secret Garden* that opened on Broadway in May 1991 and ran until January 1993.[3] Norman seems an unlikely choice, given her penchant for dark subjects (including suicide, sexual abuse, and despair), as Norman herself has acknowledged. "It was very difficult for people to believe that I really wanted to do a musical or had it in me to do one," she asserts. "But in fact, at the same time I was working on *'night, Mother*, I was working on a musical about the Shakers" (quoted in Evett). She had once considered becoming a composer (Betsko and Koenig 334), and even before she wrote *Getting Out*, she had written "a children's musical, *Edison*, based on the life of the inventor Thomas Alva Edison" (Stanley H5). She was particularly attracted by the possibility that musicals offer of exploring her characters' psyches in language, specifically through song lyrics—a possibility not as readily available to a playwright using nonmusical, realistic forms (Evett; Barbour G11). Norman evidently found her successful experience pleasurable: "I would like to spend the rest of my theatrical life in the musical theater" (Barbour G12).

While Norman's adaptation of *The Secret Garden* is less overtly sentimental than the Edwardian original; it is also, in many respects, startlingly faithful to the original novel. In many instances, Norman chose to use Burnett's dialogue with few or no alterations. Her play, like Burnett's book, is "preoccupied with death" (Gohlke 896);[4] in fact, Norman prides herself on the play's honesty:

[Norman] has noticed that children are curious about death, which they encounter in everything from Saturday morning cartoons to "Bambi."

"It's one of those great, powerful subjects that children want to see because it's part of the world," Norman said. "They don't want to be lied to about it."

"Most [adults] won't talk to them about it," she added. "Well, we do." (Miller E11)

Despite the faithfulness of the adaptation, however, Norman has altered the original material in her work. In this essay I examine Norman's changes and discuss their implications for an interpretation of the work. Those changes include an expanded role for Archibald Craven, a reconfiguring of Mary's relationship with her parents, a diminished role for both Colin's mother and the secret garden itself, the elimination of Mrs. Sowerby as a character, and, of course, the presence of the controversial and sometimes confusing ghosts. The net effect of Norman's changes is to focus the plot on a man exorcising the ghost of his dead wife, rather than on the children who have been damaged by emotional neglect resurrecting themselves and each other through their nurturing of an apparently dead garden.

Several of these changes were developed and refined during the musical's evolution from a draft into a Broadway production. According to the play's program, producer and set designer Heidi Landesman first came up with the idea of doing a musical version of the novel after a friend sent her a soundtrack album of a British musical based on the book. She didn't care for the British version but was nonetheless prompted to reread Burnett's novel (Landesman 7). Having worked on productions of two of Norman's earlier plays—*'night, Mother* and *Traveler in the Dark*—Landesman invited Norman to draft a libretto (Dolen, "*The Secret Garden* in Full Bloom" A9).

Composer Lucy Simon (sister of pop singer Carly Simon) joined the team soon after, and the play then went through several stages of development, beginning with a staged reading in the summer of 1989 at the Skidmore College Arts Center in Saratoga Springs, New York. After revision by Norman and Simon, the play was given a trial production at the Virginia Stage Company in Norfolk, Virginia. Director Susan Schulman signed on at that point and helped revise the play further (Landesman 7; Evett). The play was then produced in one more workshop, where it garnered sufficient backing for a Broadway production (Barbour G11). The play was believed to be the first Broadway production generated by an all-female creative team.[5] Despite mixed reviews, that 1991 production won three Tony Awards, including one for Norman's book and lyrics.

Perhaps in part because so many talented women were involved in the creation of the musical, Norman made several changes in her adaptation that would probably strike modern-day feminist readers as salutary. Colin does not take over the play as he does the novel (Adams 54 n11), and in the play's final spoken lines, it is Mary's achievement that is recognized, not Colin's as in the book.[6] Moreover, in Norman's version, it is Mary, and not Colin (Burnett 134, 158, and 215), who has Lily's eyes, as Archibald and Neville Craven note in one of the loveliest songs in the play (Norman, *SG* 54–55). This change was evidently the result of a conscious refocusing of the play on Mary:

In the Norfolk production, this song originally referred to Colin's resemblance to Lily—i.e. "the boy has Lily's hazel eyes," and was sung by Ben the Gardener in response to his question "Why does my father hate me?" . . . The new draft focused as much as possible on Mary and her effect on the household. Hence "the girl has Lily's hazel eyes"! (Landesman 7)

Although the shift in emphasis from Colin's character to Mary's now seems justified, the shift in emphasis from the children to the adults is more troubling.[7] In the novel, it is "the behaviour of the children" that is "the proper focus of our interest" (Marquis 168). Archibald Craven, Mary's uncle, appears only briefly near the beginning of the novel and then again at the end. In the play, however, he appears throughout—possibly, it has been suggested, to attract adult audiences to the play or to make the role attractive to such stars as Mandy Patinkin, who played the role in the original Broadway cast (Ridley, *"Secret Garden* in New York"; Rich).[8] According to Simon, "The desire was not to do a children's musical" (quoted in Barbour G11). Landesman has acknowledged that the Norfolk, Virginia, production was even more focused on the adults. It seems to have been Landesman who encouraged Norman to revise her very adult-centered original version to focus a bit more on the children. Norman herself has admitted that it has been difficult "to find the balance between the adult characters and the children's story. I think the big victory came when Heidi [Landesman] said, 'We must see this from Mary's point of view'" (quoted in Barbour G11). Norman seems initially at least to have been less interested in Mary than she was in the grief-stricken father, who resembles Sam in her play *Traveler in the Dark*, a work that oddly prefigures this one in its concern with father-child relationships, the loss of nurturing maternal figures, fairy tale motifs, and the dead garden.[9]

"What Marsha has done is find the adult story that's there between the lines," [composer Lucy] Simon says. "Mary is definitely the leading role, but Archie, Archie's dead wife, all of the adult world is very present and powerful. The power of the story is not just Mary finding the garden and bringing everything back to life, but helping Archie out of his mourning state, helping him to accept and find his son again." (Evett H8)

Norman herself has cited artistic reasons for enlarging Archibald Craven's role. "The children need him," she told one interviewer (Miller E11).

Norman is right, of course; the children do need him. But that's precisely Burnett's point. It is Archibald's neglect, and not Lilias's death, that has left Colin a bedridden hysterical child given to tantrums and unreasonable whims. Norman has tried unsuccessfully to present Archibald as a loving father: "[H]e visits his son only when the boy is asleep, a quirk that never makes psychological sense" (Henry 75). Norman seems to have similarly misunderstood—or, at best, deliberately but inexplicably altered—the reasons for Mary's bad behavior. In a scene invented for the play, Neville Craven (who has been transformed from Archibald's relatively unimportant, vaguely villainous cousin into an openly malevolent brother) threatens to send Mary to school, and she throws a tantrum. Burnett disapproves of tantrums and seems to believe that happy, healthy children will automatically prefer more civilized forms of behavior; once he has begun to recover through his experiences, Colin isn't even sure he can *pretend* to have a tantrum (Burnett 243). Norman seems, on the other hand, to be advocating the judicious use of tantrums as a means to an end.[10]

More seriously, Norman presents Mary's loss of her parents as traumatic and painful, and certainly that makes psychological sense. But that interpretation of her experience nonetheless represents a dramatic departure from Burnett's novel, in which Mary's psychological problem is not grief but apathy, an affectlessness generated by her neglectful parents:

Her father held a position under the English government and had always been busy and ill himself, and her mother had been a great beauty who cared only to go to parties and amuse herself with gay people. She had not wanted a little girl at all, and when Mary was born she handed her over to the care of an Ayah, who was made to understand that if she wished to please the Mem Sahib she must keep the child out of sight as much as possible. (Burnett 9)

It is apparent from the text that Mary barely even knows her parents: "She never remembered seeing familiarly anything but the dark faces of her Ayah and the other native servants . . . " (Burnett 10). Mary thus responds rather atypically to her parents' deaths: "Mary had liked to look at her mother from a distance and she had thought her very pretty, but as she knew very little of her she could scarcely have been expected to love her or to miss her very much when she was gone. She did not miss her at all, in fact . . . " (Burnett 16).

In Norman's adaptation, on the contrary, Mary misses her parents very much. When she hears someone crying, she imagines it might be her parents calling for her (*SG* 15). She asks her uncle what happens to dead people and during the course of the ensuing conversation mentions both of her parents (*SG* 27–28). She is apparently so traumatized by her loss that she has repressed her memories of the cholera epidemic; when she is scolded by Mrs. Medlock and Dr. Craven for speaking to Colin, "Mary *begins to remember* exactly what happened at that dinner party" (*SG* 64; emphasis added). As she remembers, she runs out into the maze in a hysterical terror. She sees the ghost of her father, "the last person alive to think of her," and "runs into his arms" (*SG* 68); he leads her to Lily (Norman's adaptation of the name Lilias), who in turn leads her to the door to the garden (*SG* 69). And even there Mary is haunted: "Everyone is there, Archibald, Lily, Rose, Albert, Dickon, Martha and the other Dreamers, the living and the dead, exactly the way Mary would like to see them" (*SG* 73).

It is the presence—or omnipresence, as some critics have charged[11]—of these ghosts that constitutes the most obvious difference between Burnett's novel and Norman's adaptation. The play has a chorus, identified in the roster of characters as "Dreamers," that consists entirely of dead people: Mary's parents, Rose and Albert Lennox; Rose's friend Alice; Lieutenants Wright and Shaw, officers in her father's unit; Major Holmes and his wife Claire; a fakir; and an ayah, Mary's Indian nanny. According to Norman's own note, "The characters referred to collectively as the Dreamers are people from Mary's life in India, who haunt her until she finds her new life in the course of this story. They are free to sing directly to us, appearing and disappearing at will" (*SG* xii).[12]

It is these characters who, after a brief bit of song from Lily Craven, open the play with their stylized dance of death, a game of "Drop the Handkerchief" played to a macabre version of the nursery rhyme "Mistress Mary, Quite Contrary," to symbolize their abrupt deaths from a cholera epidemic (*SG* 4–5). But they do not disappear in death; rather they remain present as a chorus until the final scene of the play. It is the Dreamers who establish the eerie gothic atmosphere of Misselthwaite Manor (*SG* 11–13, 74) and seem to haunt it themselves (*SG* 17–18, 57–58).[13] At least one critic has suggested that the play's "big budget" (which he further characterized as "$6.2 million demons shrieking for gewgaws") prompted the inclusion of the ghosts (Kroll 69). The play's director, Susan Schulman, has been credited with the original idea of adding the Dreamers (Dolen, *The Secret Garden* in Full Bloom"); they were added after the Norfolk, Virginia, trial production (Evett). Daryl H. Miller of the Los Angeles *Daily News* notes the presence of one ghost in the novel—Lilias

Craven, Colin's mother—when Mrs. Sowerby, the mother of Martha and Dickon, tells Colin, "Thy own mother's in this 'ere very garden, I do believe. She couldna' keep out of it" (Burnett 268). He goes on to add, "Because such passages exist, Norman felt justified in adding the spirits" (Miller E11).

But in the novel, it is only Colin's mother who appears as a ghost, and her one act is to call Archibald home from Europe to rediscover his newly healthy son (Burnett 274–75). And even then, Archibald also receives a non ghostly request to come home, this one in a letter not from Mary, as in the play, but from the archetypally maternal Susan Sowerby. Mrs. Sowerby, the oracular mother of twelve (including Dickon and Martha), is an important minor character in the novel; she never appears in the play. The multitude of ghosts rather dilutes the effect of Colin's mother, and the absence of Mrs. Sowerby confirms that, in this play at least, Norman is no longer interested in the issue of motherhood, an issue central to Burnett's novel (Marquis 179, Tyler 27–28). Moreover, by giving Mary's mother (unnamed in the novel) the name Rose, Norman implies that she is as connected to the garden as Lily (or Lilias) Craven and thus severs the novel's direct correspondence between mother and garden.

The garden, too, is given relatively short shrift.[14] Few scenes take place there: "Of the eighteen scenes in this *Secret Garden*, only four involve the children in activities out of doors—two before the garden is discovered, which occurs one-fourth of the way through the book but halfway through the musical, and two afterward" (Ridley, "*The Secret Garden* Is Exorcised"). More than one critic has described the resulting atmosphere as "claustrophobic" (Richards, "Only"; Ridley, *The Secret Garden* Is Exorcised"). Moreover, Mary and Colin do virtually no actual gardening onstage (Richards, "Only"), whereas in the book gardening restores both of them to health and well-being. Complains Richards: "[N]ature has an incidental role. Ghosts are doing the instructing" ("Only"). Thus the garden loses much of its importance as a symbol of rebirth and renewal.[15]

"When you have a garden, you have a future," Burnett once wrote (quoted in Thwaite 243). But Norman's play is not about the future so much as it is about the past; as Edwin Wilson observes in his review of the Broadway production, "*The Secret Garden* becomes a musical about ghosts rather than living people, about exorcising the past rather than dealing with the present, about magic and the supernatural rather than the human dimension of Mary's life."

Richards suggests, "Ms. Norman's is not a joyful temperament, and she ends up convoluting a simple story, without necessarily improving upon it" ("Only"). "I'm certainly not a person who goes around thinking gloomy things all the time," Norman has countered. "The stories I like are the ones where people are trying to solve their problems, and that is what's happening in *The Secret Garden*" (quoted in Watts 25).

But the difficulty lies in defining the problem that Mary, as the protagonist of the play, is trying to solve. In the musical, Mary is perpetually surrounded by spirits, in a staging that belies her emotional isolation (Wilson; Weales 406). Neville Craven describes her as "this haunted girl" (*SG* 76). Thus Mary's trauma becomes *not* isolation, but ordinary bereavement. Burnett's implicit point is that it is infinitely worse to be ignored and forgotten than to suffer a loss; Norman's changes are at odds with that point—even though it was principally Mary's "isolation" with which Norman herself identified (Stanley H5).

As Esther Harriott observed in 1988, "Marsha Norman called her first play *Getting Out*, and that could be the subtitle of each of her plays since" (129). Norman writes most often about freeing oneself from the shackles of one's personal past, specifically through acceptance and reintegration: "Put another way, we live a relationship to loss through our active recognition of the past within the present" (Cline 301). In such plays as *Getting Out*, *The Laundromat*, and *'night, Mother*, each of her female characters struggles successfully to come to terms with her past (Brown 77; Cline 298; Stone 58), so it is perhaps hardly surprising that Mary must do so as well.

Yet ultimately, in Burnett's novel, Mary's task is *not* to free herself from her past. On the contrary, if we accept the familiar line that "Freedom's just another word for nothing left to lose," then Mary's problem is *too much* freedom, an excess of freedom that leaves her bereft of human ties. It is not her past that Mary must face; it is her future.

The product of Norman's first successful venture into musical theater is a pleasant and likable work, but it lacks the rich humor, harrowing impact, and heartfelt quality of *Getting Out*, *The Laundromat*, and *'night, Mother*. Even her language in this adaptation is bland compared to that in her previous work, and she occasionally lapses into clumsy clichés (e.g., when Archibald sings that Mary "needs to . . . learn to work her girlish charms" [*SG* 48] or in the final scene when he abruptly asks Colin, "Can you ever forgive me?" [*SG* 125]).[16]

Perhaps in creating this work Norman concentrated on mastering the technical aspects of musical theater at the expense of the play's language; perhaps, too, the collaborative process by which *The Secret Garden* came into being had the unintended effect of diluting the power of Norman's considerable talent. Bruce Weber has analyzed how this process, which the medium of the Broadway musical inevitably demands, contributed to the dramatic failure of *The Red Shoes*, Norman's most recent venture into musical theater.

But in judging *The Secret Garden* against her own earlier work, we are indulging in a failure for which Norman has previously castigated her critics. For it is perhaps unfair to expect Norman to sustain the brilliance of *'night, Mother* throughout her entire *oeuvre*. More importantly, perhaps, the musical when considered by itself, apart from Burnett's novel and Norman's other work, merits the attention of both theatergoers and scholars. Despite its flaws, Marsha Norman's *The Secret Garden* is as charming as the Edwardian valentine that its lavish and beautifully detailed sets suggest.

Notes

1. The story essentially retells the ancient Greek myth of Demeter and Persephone, which centers on the daughter's successful achievement of identification with her mother. For the myth, see Athanassakis (1–16). For this interpretation of the myth, see Arthur. Finally, for a more comprehensive explanation of the way in which Burnett draws on the myth, see Tyler.

2. See Henry and Stanley.

3. Norman's adaptation is one of the latest in a surprisingly long series of dramatizations of the novel; other versions include a 1993 film; a 1949 Hollywood version starring Margaret O'Brien, Herbert Marshall, and a young Dean Stockwell; a much more recent Hallmark Hall of Fame movie made for television; a thirteen–part BBC series (Dolen, "*The Secret Garden* in Full Bloom"); at least two different non musical American-produced stage plays (Ridley, "*The Secret Garden* Is Exorcised"; Dolen, "*Garden* Enchants Children"); an opera (Weales); and finally, the 1985 British musical version that first prompted Heidi Landesman, producer and set designer of Norman's Broadway version, to reread Burnett's novel and consider making her own musical version (Evett; Barbour).

   "Lots of people have tried to adapt it and all have failed," Norman is quoted as saying (Watts 24). "All the versions are boring."

   For a comparison of the filmed versions of the story, see Louisa Smith.

4. As Jerome Weeks observes of the musical, "In *The Secret Garden*, people sicken and die. Children are unhappy and intolerable. The music is often minor-key and imploring" ("Secret").

5. Virtually every reviewer comments on this fact, but Mimi Kramer of the *New Yorker* offers the most entertaining assessment of its impact on the production: "Watching [*The Secret Garden*], you find yourself wondering how anything produced on the commercial stage could be so tasteful, so utterly on the mark, and thinking, Well, of course, they're women" (84).

    In "*The Secret Garden* 'Misread': The Broadway Musical as Creative Interpretation," Phyllis Bixler, who has written extensively on Burnett's work, shares Kramer's opinion: "Reminding myself that the playwright, composer, set designer, and director were all women, I affirmed my intuition that on some issues in some books we can indeed speak of communal female responses" (102).

6. See Miller for a similar observation (E11). The play ends with Archibald Craven telling Mary, "Mary Lennox, for as long as you will have us, . . . we are yours, Colin and I, . . . and this is your home, and this, my lovely child . . . is your garden" (*SG* 127). The novel, by contrast, excludes Mary completely: "Across the lawn came the Master of Misselthwaite and he looked as many of them had never seen him. And by his side with his head up in the air and his eyes full of laughter walked as strongly and steadily as any boy in Yorkshire—Master Colin!" (Burnett 284).

    Bixler also discusses this change at length ("*The Secret Garden* 'Misread'" 110–111).

7. Clifford A. Ridley remarks, "A yucky thing happens to the spunky children in *The Secret Garden* . . . : All the adults keep getting in the way" ("*Secret Garden* in New York"). Weeks comments, more favorably, "*The Secret Garden* is a remarkably adult musical" ("Secret"). See also Hulbert and Gooding.

    See Bixler ("*The Secret Garden* 'Misread'" 113) for a more positive discussion of this change of emphasis.

8. Kramer notes, however, of the original Broadway cast, that "Mandy Patinkin, Alison Fraser, and Robert Westenberg appear[ed] without billing, as part of an ensemble" (85)—a fact which would seem to contradict the supposed catering to stars that Ridley and Rich have proposed as a reason for Archibald Craven's expanded role.

9. Bixler also notes the "uncanny resemblance" ("*The Secret Garden* 'Misread'" 117).

10. See Bixler ("*The Secret Garden* 'Misread'" 117), who sees Mary's use of the tantrum in much more positive terms.

11. Frank Rich rather sneeringly calls them "a strolling chorus of ghosts." Jerome Weeks complains that the ghosts "often clog the scenes and make several songs nearly indecipherable" ("Secret"). Dan Hulbert observes that "the guardian-spirit ghosts are given too much to sing for their minimal involvement in the story." Christine Dolen adds, "One quibble: The ghosts of Lily, Mary's parents and others, used as almost an omnipresent chorus, are a little *too* omnipresent" ("*Secret Garden* Blooms").

    There were apparently even more ghosts in the earlier, pre-Broadway productions (Miller E11; Witchel).

12. Norman favors this expressionistic mode of dramatizing the past; she similarly dramatized Arlene's memories of her past self in *Getting Out*.

13. Of the show's gothic atmosphere, Jerome Weeks remarks, "It's a musical theatre equivalent to *The Turn of the Screw* or *Wuthering Heights*" ("Secret"). Composer Simon has also commented on the work's ties to *Wuthering Heights* (Weeks, "How" C6), which reflect Burnett's allusions to it in her novel (Bixler, *Frances Hodgson Burnett* 100; Tyler 24–26). Bixler attributes the musical's gothic and spiritualist elements to Norman (106–107).

14. See Hulbert.

15. Bixler vigorously disputes this reading, arguing that: Music is used to create the

illusion of not just gardening but the garden itself, especially by evoking the characters' feelings for it. To those who have found too little of the garden in the musical (Rich; Richards), I have wanted to reply, "Did you listen as well as look?" ("*The Secret Garden* 'Misread'" 118)

16. In his review of *The Red Shoes*, Richards has more recently criticized the lyrics Norman contributed as clichéd ("Ambition").

Works Cited

Adams, Gillian. "Secrets and Healing Magic in *The Secret Garden*." In *Triumphs of the Spirit in Children's Literature*. Edited by Francelia Butler and Richard Rotert. Hamden, CT: Shoe String Press, 1986. 42–54.

Arthur, Marilyn. "Politics and Pomegranates: An Interpretaion of the Homeric Hymn to Demeter." *Arethusa* 10. (1977): 7–47.

Athanassakis, Apostolos N. *The Homeric Hymn*. Baltimore: Johns Hopkins University P, 1976. 1–16.

Barbour, David. "Women of the House." (Hackensack) *Record,* 21 April 1991. NewsBank, 1991, PER 61:G10–G12.

Betsko, Kathleen, and Rachel Koenig. "Marsha Norman." In *Interviews with Contemporary Women Playwrights*. New York: Morrow, 1987. 324–342.

Bixler, Phyllis. *Frances Hodgson Burnett*. Boston: Twayne, 1984.

———. "*The Secret Garden* 'Misread': The Broadway Musical as Creative Interpretation." *Children's Literature* 22 (1994): 101–123.

Brown, Linda Ginter. *Toward a More Cohesive Self: Women in the Works of Lillian Hellman and Marsha Norman*. Ph.D. diss., Ohio State University, 1991. Ann Arbor,MI: UMI, 1991.

Burnett, Frances Hodgson. *The Secret Garden*. 1911. New York: Dell, 1986.

Cline, Gretchen Sarah. *The Psychodrama of the "Dysfunctional" Family: Desire, Subjectivity, and Regression in Twentieth-Century American Drama*. Ph.D. diss., Ohio State University, 1991. Ann Arbor, MI: UMI, 1991.

Dolen, Christine. "*Garden* Enchants Children." *Miami Herald,* 15 October 1991. NewsBank, 1991, PER 138:A8.

———. "*Secret Garden* Blooms on Beach." *Miami Herald,* 15 May 1992. NewsBank, 1992, PER 74:A12.

———. "*The Secret Garden* in Full Bloom." *Miami Herald,* 10 May 1992. NewsBank, 1992, PER 74:A8–10.

Evett, Marianne. "Seeds from Playhouse Burst Brightly on Broadway in *The Secret Garden*." The (Cleveland) *Plain Dealer,* 28 April 1991.

Gohlke, Madelon S. "Re-reading *The Secret Garden*." *College English* 41 (1980): 894–902.

Gooding, Miranda. "*Garden* Doesn't Grow on this Kid." (New York) *Daily News ,* 29 May 1991. NewsBank, 1991, PER 75:B14.

Harriott, Esther. *American Voices: Five Contemporary Playwrights in Essays and Interviews*. Jefferson, NC: McFarland, 1988.

Henry, William A., III. "A Children's Haven of Healing." *Time,* 6 May 1991, 75.

Hulbert, Dan. "Though Beautiful, 'The Secret Garden' Lacks Youthful Allure." (Atlanta) *Journal,* 6 May 1991. NewsBank 1991, PER 75:B12.

Kramer, Mimi. "The Key to the Garden." *New Yorker,* 13 May 1991, 84–85.

Kroll, Jack. "Broadway Hot-house." *Newsweek* 6 May 1991, 69.

Landesman, Heidi. "Behind the Scenes." *The Secret Garden* [theater program]. New York: Heidi Landesman, Jujamcyn Theaters/TV ASAHI, and Dodger Productions, 1991. 7.

Marquis, Claudia. "The Power of Speech: Life in *The Secret Garden*." *AUMLA: Journal of the Australasian Universities Language and Literature Association* 68 (November 1989): 163–187.

Miller, Daryl H. "Center Stage." (Los Angeles) *Daily News ,* 15 July 1992. NewsBank, 1992, PER 97:E11–12.

Norman, Marsha. *Getting Out*. In *Four Plays*. New York: Theatre Communications Group, 1988. 1–56.

———. *The Laundromat*. In *Four Plays*. New York: Theatre Communications Group, 1988. 60–81.

———. *The Secret Garden*. New York: Theatre Communications Group, 1992.

———. *Traveler in the Dark*. New York: Dramatists Play Service, 1988.

Rich, Frank. "'Garden': The Secret of Death and Birth." *New York Times*, 26 April 1991.

Richards, David. "Ambition vs. Romance in a Pas de Trois." *New York Times*, 17 December 1993.

———. "Only the Wind Should Sigh in this *Garden*." *New York Times*, 5 May 1991.

Ridley, Clifford A. "*The Secret Garden* in New York." *Philadelphia Inquirer*, 26 April 1991. NewsBank, 1991, PER 62:A3.

———. "*The Secret Garden* Is Exorcised." *Philadelphia Inquirer*, 13 May 1991. NewsBank, 1991, PER 75:C1.

Smith, Louisa. "Reviewing *The Secret Garden*: Differences between British and American Presentations." Paper presented at the Thirty-second Annual Meeting of the Midwest Modern Language Association, Kansas City, Missouri, 1–3 November 1990.

Stanley, Alessandra. "Marsha Norman Finds Her Lost Key to Broadway." *New York Times*, 21 April 1991.

Stone, Elizabeth. "Playwright Marsha Norman: An Optimist Writes about Suicide, Confinement, and Despair." *Ms*, July 1983, 56–59.

Thwaite, Ann. *Waiting for the Party: The Life of Frances Hodgson Burnett 1849–1924*. London: Secker and Warburg, 1974.

Tyler, Lisa. *Our Mothers' Gardens: Mother-Daughter Relationships and Myth in Twentieth-Century British Women's Literature*. Ph.D. diss., Ohio State University, 1991. Ann Arbor, MI: UMI, 1992.

Watts, Patti. "Staged for Success." *Executive Female*, March/April 1991, 24+.

Weales, Gerald. "Lost in Translation: *The Secret Garden(s)*." *Commonweal*, 14 June 1991, 405–406.

Weber, Bruce. "What Went So Very Wrong with *Red Shoes*." *New York Times*, 30 December 1993.

Weeks, Jerome. "How the Garden Grew." *Dallas Morning News* 15 June 1992. NewsBank, 1992, PER 86:C6–7.

———. "A 'Secret' Revealed." *Dallas Morning News*, 17 June 1992. NewsBank, 1992, PER 86:C9.

Wilson, Edwin. "Bold Girl, Pale Ghosts." *New York Times*, 3 May 1991, Eastern edition.

Witchel, Alex. "A *Garden* with Fewer Ghosts." *New York Times*, 3 May 1991.

Writing the Other

Marya Bednerik

D. Boone marks the return of playwright Marsha Norman to her point of origin and to the theater that encouraged and produced her initial work. Produced by the Actors Theatre of Louisville, Kentucky in 1992, this play was a commission made possible by a grant from the Honorable Order of Kentucky Colonels to the theater in celebration of the state's bicentennial.[1] As part of the sixteenth annual Humana Festival of New American Plays, its surface ostensibly honors those early trailblazers who pushed back the wilderness and settled Kentucky while also providing the audience with a warm evening of romantic fun.

The plot of *D. Boone*, retitled *Loving Daniel Boone*, focuses on Florence, a contemporary woman, who has fallen in love with Daniel Boone. Flo forsakes the present, with its unsatisfactory contemporary male prospects, and time-travels to the past to assist in saving the premiere frontiersman. Boone's capture by the Indians means the destruction of the Boonesborough settlement is imminent.

The critics reviewed the production as an "amiable" evening of gentle humor and romance. Dale Sandusky, reviewing for the *New Albany Tribune*, questioned whether good history makes bad plays or bad history, good plays. However, the audience greeted this play enthusiastically amid programming that the visiting producers, academics, stage directors, and out-of-town critics jokingly labeled for the somber content of its dramatic offerings "the festival of death." Two blue-haired subscribers were overheard expressing great relief at *D. Boone's* inclusion and offering hearty applause for a play that was funny and familiar in romantic content if not exactly in form and in staging. They thought Actors Theatre had presented some very strange plays lately; they spoke with nostalgia for those past productions of

Broadway revisited or classic plays.

Stephen Greenblatt, in his article "Culture," points out that texts are performances that are produced in "social, historical, cultural moments." He argues

the world is full of texts, most of which are virtually incomprehensible when they are removed from their immediate surroundings. To recover the meaning of such texts, to make any sense of them at all, we need to reconstruct the situation in which they were first produced. Works of art by contrast contain directly or by implication much of this initial situation within themselves, and it is this sustained absorption that enables many literary works to survive the collapse of the conditions that led to their production. (227)

Greenblatt suggests a number of cultural questions that focus the work as an act of "praise or blame." (226) He investigates the "kinds of behaviors" and "models of practice" that the work enforces. When looking at the production context, the production itself, and the representations of the other in the text, *Loving Daniel Boone* provides an interesting critique of current culture and "the links between text and values, institutions and practices" (226) that produce the playwright as well as refer to the world beyond the play (227). Which cultural boundaries are widened and which are maintained?

In "writing the other," Marsha Norman accomplishes a number of interesting acts: She reclaims history for herself and other women; she transmits her culture and its energy through reforming the oral tradition of the folktale; she heals breaches between both the theater and herself and the theater and its audience, and she explicates and critiques the historic gender categories produced by the traditionally binary thinking that separates the manly man and the womanly woman. In refashioning history, indigenous Americans, and the categories of masculinity, she no doubt rewrites the self.

Working from generally remembered events, the playwright personalizes and dramatizes selected moments from Boone's captivity to the chance arrival of a rain storm which terminates the siege. The Indians' capture of Daniel Boone and his long absence from his settlement lead historically and dramatically to the attack on the fort by the British and the Indians. The destruction of Boonesborough means the destruction of three cultures: British ownership, the Indian way of life, and the pioneers' civilizing of this wilderness. In historical record, these events culminate in the signing of a treaty setting boundaries north and south of the Ohio River to separate settlers from native Americans. In Marsha Norman's play, the events result in a verbal social contract between Hilly, the new man, and the metaphorically baptized Florence. Norman changes boundaries.

The Louisville production—the enactment of the dramatic and theatrical texts—encodes many social and political meanings, as Marsha Norman adds her fabrication to those of other historians who are also storytellers. Early in the text, Hilly, who is Flo's contemporary pursuer and eventual savior, sets up the play's essential question as he makes this demand: "I want to know what you want in a man" (20). The representation of Daniel Boone—both myth and man—makes an initial answer, one that is discarded by the end of the play.

In a special exhibition of Daniel Boone paintings and drawings mounted at the Washington University Gallery of Art, J. Gray Sweeney's catalogue summarizes Boone's history in the visual arts and literature, those double fictions. Sweeney aptly titles his work "The Columbus of the Woods: Daniel Boone and the Typology of Manifest Destiny." He demonstrates both the popularity and the paradox of this prototype pathfinder. Daniel Boone in paintings and drawings is often likened to a Moses leading his people to a promised land. He is shown as the prime developer of the civilized social order that will follow him. His romanticized figure as frontier hero eventually is refigured under the demands of Jacksonian democracy into more "realist" representations. Sweeney writes:

The underlying reason for Daniel Boone's disappearance in the visual arts is that at the heart of the Boone legend there was a paradox. Depending on the artist and the audience in question, the Boone hero was expected to symbolize all things about the American experience of the frontier. He was to be a freespirited hunter-wanderer or the upstanding bringer of civilization, the exemplar of white, Anglo-Saxon, Christian family values or a potential renegade white Indian. He was ordained by Providence to accomplish his mission, but having served his purpose he was relegated to the margins as a venerated prophet of the new order, his place in the pantheon of art usurped by new, more universal masculine heroes like the cowboy. (69)

Dialogue and the presence of a specific actor in *D. Boone* create a contemporary Daniel Boone. The tall, broad-shouldered actor (Gladden Schrock) wearing a fringed, suede jacket, generates a complex historical, social, aesthetic, and gendered sign. His look supports audience expectations, formed partially by Sweeney's compilation of those conventions of art and literature. (In actuality Boone was short and small.) Marsha Norman, in her selection of rival male figures (today's Hilly and the dead Daniel Boone), follows the pattern in her heroine's choice of man. Florence gives up the dream pathfinder for the metaphoric cowboy.

Boone as a theatrical character is a refashioning of both old and new gender categories, a man made for the 1990s. A recent conversation with Diana Dixon, Harlequin romance writer, reveals that the current publishers' tip sheets require the male hero to return to the figure of the "alpha male" or "the alpha male plus." The alpha male is part hero, part villain; he is hard-edged, an old-fashioned primitive prime progenitor. The plus can be a sense of humor or the sensitive qualities in masculine characters acceptable to liberation fiction. These requirements take readers back to a patriarchy of strong decision-makers who place women under their care or who escape from women to the wilderness in mythopoetic movements and male bonding rituals. Marsha Norman both makes use of and rejects these attributes.

While the titular character Daniel Boone in the dramatic text is incomplete, the performance text adds the actor. Ultimately, the casting of the role completes the written text and makes its strongest statement. Gladden Schrock as Daniel Boone looks the part. He fills out the buckskin-fringed jacket. He sits carving his initials on the tree stump, a perfect first picture from history books. He appears as the romantic hunter of female dreams who can protect her from bears, make peace with the Indians, and do battle for her heart. However, this particular actor lacks passion and energy; he is tired and middle-aged. He makes a world-weary Daniel Boone, one whose energy is drained by the burden of others' myths and the reality of responsibility for the safety of his followers. Past his prime and wheezing a bit in the obligatory fight with Hilly over Florence, this actor completes the demythologizing act of the playwright.

The casting of the role ironically supports and subverts the dramatic script. Louisville's Boone earns these adjectives in the *Bardstown*

Standard review: "bland," "laid back," and "lacking even ordinary passions." The reviewer wonders, "Is Norman showing us that ordinary people sometimes do extraordinary tasks? And that history subdues the ordinary to be replaced by the legend?"

Women are frequently the conveyors of culture. With the energy of the oral storyteller, Marsha Norman spins the paradoxical Daniel Boone into the tradition of the trickster figure. Her Boone manipulates situations, misleading the participants and disarming his audiences. He calls for a bucket of water to be poured on the ground so that the Indians will believe the settlers have an abundance. He keeps a few men walking the barricades to make the Indians believe there are many men within the fort. He misleads his daughter with a tale that Flo is a lost white woman whom he found wandering around after the Indians killed her husband. In response Jemima, the disbelieving daughter, intensely questions Flo about this lie; in turn she forces Flo to invent a tall tale. The stage directions indicate Flo is not "a practiced liar." Flo is vague about whether the men were dragged off by Indians or bears and finds herself telling Jemima that all that were left were their hats (62). She gives Jemima a romance novel's image of the first encounter with Daniel Boone: "the next thing I knew, your Dad was giving me a drink of water and asking me who I was"(62). To Jemima's continued pursuit of truth, Flo finally says in exasperation, "What do you think this is, a story I made up?" (63). In this self-reflexive moment, there is recognition that the playwright is the ultimate trickster.

Folklore depends on the audience's prior knowledge of the broad outlines of events. The delight lies in the filling out of details and the bonding that occurs in the listener-participants. This sharing of laughter, knowledge, and events reinforces the sense of community. Politically, the folktale lays out its materials; it is the listeners' task to believe or not believe. And it is the quality of faithful acceptance in Florence (a surrogate for the audience?) that connects Hilly to her. He says, "You're a believer, Florence. A man needs a woman like that"(92).

The trickster character is common to festival and carnival. To promote joyous fellowship, participants often wear elaborate costumes and engage in physical antics that symbolically displace power. Mikhail Bakhtin shows how the activities are designed to invert hierarchies; to stand authority on its head. The low are made high; the high, low. True holders of power play the fool. The Humana Festival, too, is marked by feasting, drinking, and face-to-face telling of theatrical tall tales. Appropriately sponsored by a healthgiving agency, Marsha Norman's play leads to renewal and life-prolonging laughter. However, it also indicts its dominant culture.

Marsha Norman represents the gamut of historical categories in her depiction of various masculinities. She also pushes against the boundaries of these socially constructed categories as she make them risible objects. Kevin White, in *The First Sexual Revolution*, describes the emergence of male heterosexuality from the nineteenth to the twentieth centuries.

In the seventies and eighties, men divided up between "masculinists" and "feminists": the masculinists emphasized the perpetration of male culture as defense against women's criticisms; the "feminists" advocated acceptance of the demands of the women's movement, whatever they happened to be at any given time. More satisfyingly, by the mid 1980's, the "Changing Men" appeared. They accepted the desirability of equality with women. They actively tried to think out how to change in response to women's requests, but also utilized their own observations of what might work for men. (187)

In her doubling and rejection of the unsuitable mates, Marsha Norman presents several masculine categories. The contemporary suitors come in sizes too small. Hilly is assisting Mr. Wilson, who is photographing an icon, freezing a moment in time. Hilly, holding the knife, poses like the statue of Boone, displacing him.

HILLY: Guess who?

MR. WILSON: (laughs) *That's good.* (he snaps a picture)

HILLY: What about the hunting shirt? Was that his?

MR. WILSON: Heavens, no. Boone was big. That shirt would be snug on (he looks at Hilly) *either one of us.(29)*

There are no suitable marriage partners. Flo's domineering lover Rick (played by Skipp Sudduth in the Louisville production), a mechanic, is married and slow to divorce his wife; Mr. Wilson (Mark Shannon), her effete boss, who seems at first so intelligent and suave, though he fails to notice her, turns out to be gay. Mr. Wilson does not know what women want. He offers financial stability and states, "I'm a decent, responsible man. I just want to know if that will be enough"(39). Flo's silence makes it clear that indeed the historic category of male achiever and provider is not enough.

The playwright does not take the opportunity of integrating homosexual desire into these characters' lives or into the play. The play clearly praises heterosexual marriage. Mr. Wilson, while portrayed as the historian and boss, the one who knows, is often made the object of laughter. Marsha Norman is seeing straight. Upon getting his orders from Boone, Wilson exclaims, "Lord God. A real man"(67). His initiation in the past is to walk endlessly around the barricades pretending to be an army of men. Kevin White, in his chapter on male ideology, notes that historically, "the homosexual was specifically presented as the antithesis of the heterosexual, the male ideal"(65). William Mootz, in *The Courier-Journal* review, describes the actor in this role: "Mark Shannon's gay curator is too campily mannered in museum surroundings, but settles down to spark some of the evening's funniest scenes as he bravely faces Indian warriors."

The category of the red man is presented in the delineation of Chief Blackfish. In the text, Blackfish, having adopted Boone, becomes the ultimate father who knows the ways of forest and folk. He speaks in short, simple sentences, gathers information, and provides the feed lines for Boone's humorous ripostes. His portrait hasn't progressed beyond beads and feathers, the sympathetic stereotype of the white oppressors. Occasionally, his language is Hollywood poetic:

Tell them what Dragging Canoe has said, "that a dark cloud hangs over this land." That no Indians have lived here for many years because of this cloud. That the bones of the ancient men rise up in the night and kill him who sets his lodge poles in this place. (60)

Chekoth Miskenack in this role plays the stoic manner and measured rhythms of the media Indian. The *New Albany Tribune* reviewer describes Chief Blackfish as "an accommodating straight man who would be better suited as a borscht-belt comedian." The actor seems to have based his characterization on old fictions. He serves as the male who commodifies women. He is comic stereotype of ethnic characters in the pattern presented by commercial theater before the type is assimilated fully into the culture and gains more fully human dimensions in its staging. It is still the early days for the portrayal of Indians on the American stage.

Rick, Flo's contemporary suitor who joins somewhat reluctantly in bringing Flo back from the past, is given the comic ordeal of killing a buffalo (punishment perhaps for his failure to tell Flo that he is already married). Successful as the hunter of animals if not women, this act causes him to compare present-day tests with those of the past.

RICK: Look, Flo. You want a hero. You deserve a hero. Now, I'm a nice enough guy and all, but I'm the first one to say it. Fixin' a guy's transmission isn't exactly a heroic act.

FLO: It is if it's really fixed.

RICK: Thanks.

(She looks at him a moment. Then down at the buffalo.)

FLO: They owe you the tongue for killing it.

RICK: That's O.K. They can have it.

FLO: No. You eat it. Or dry it, if you want to. Doubled over, a dried buffalo tongue would make a nice pouch for a wrench, or something. (84)

While she validates Rick's present deeds, the playwright places them in a pale and comic juxtaposition.

Flo tells Hilly, "Being in love was something people used to do—when they had more time." Hilly makes an unconventional hero, tested in conventional ways. He must fight past fiction. Flo thinks he wins her in a fight with Daniel Boone; Hilly confesses that the truth is, he lost. Played in Louisville by Dave Florek, a first-rate character actor who is not the usual casting choice for a romantic lead, he not only gains Flo's heart but also wins that of the audience. Hilly is willing to risk everything—there is the possibility, in entering another timespace, of no return. To do battle with a dead hero in another timespace makes literal the metaphor of following a woman to ends of the earth. Hilly, who is part Indian, must battle with death: This is the stuff of Grail romance and love stories throughout musical and literary history. Yet it also makes a perfect trope for the present revision of gender roles.

His action and attributes answer the essential question of the evening: What do contemporary women want in a man? Florence chooses the best actor. Hilly's final words claim Boone's title as "the best man in Kentucky." He has been an excellent contender. Hilly gets Florence because he knows her. To know someone is to recognize and to accept the selfhood of another. Hilly both literally and metaphorically knows Flo's name. In the culminating moments of the play, Florence accuses Hilly of thinking he should have anything he wants—a childish state of being. She, however, does not know him and misunderstands his answer.

HILLY: *It's not just because I want it. It's because I'm willing to pay for it.*

FLO: *What do you mean, pay for it? Are you buying me now? What do I cost, Hilly?*

HILLY: *I don't know, Florence. Maybe everything I've got. Maybe my job. Maybe my whole way of lookin' at things. Maybe you're gonna drive me crazy. Maybe Linda [his daughter] won't like you and I'll lose this thing I have with her. Or maybe she'll like you better than me, and I'll feel like a jerk for bringing you in there. Or maybe it'll be wonderful and I'll love you to the end of the earth and you'll have a heart attack and die. Or you'll run off with somebody else and I'll have a heart attack and die. I don't know what you'll cost me, Florence. And I don't care. (102)*

Unsure, Florence answers with a litany of her own faults. Hilly asks her to marry him and offers her this freedom: "Be whatever you want." And he adds, now that he has learned her whole name, "Florence Adams. I love you." Flo accepts for an important 1990s reason: "I think you are the first man I ever knew who actually just heard what I said."

The text praises and invents yet another new man for the nineties, one who goes beyond the sensitive male or the mythopoetic wildman; a man who takes action; not a romantic hero of past fictions (or history), but a manly man whose central signifier is not "someone to watch over her." He is someone who can hear a woman's voice. He not only lets her talk, but what she says makes a difference. This act lobbies for a politics of recognition.

The characters negotiate a relationship and agree to an old social contract (marriage), but with a clear sense of its formation in a world operating by chance. Joseph Campbell, in *The Power of Myth* says, "Marriage is not a love affair. A love affair is a totally different thing. A marriage is a commitment to that which you are. That person is literally your other half. And you and the other are one" (200). He goes on to define marriage as "the symbolic recognition of our identity—two aspects of the same being"(201). The conclusion of the play renews the values of the society and its basis in heterosexual marriage, but it cites clearly the failure of the patriarchy to allow women's voices to be heard and to acknowledge women's places in history and, by extension, in the theater. The play adds a dimension to those issues, which were the attack of early feminists. To tell women's stories is not enough. Women's words must be accepted and known.

Florence, whose literal as well as symbolic employment is to clean the museum, is quitting her job to go in search of Daniel Boone. This work trope suggests revitalizing and humanizing history; it also implies correcting the record. By her actions, women are put back into the historical event. Flo thus must instruct her replacement, the new man (another metaphor), Hilly, in the care and preservation of the artifacts. Most of them, while authentic to the time period, are, in their connection to Daniel Boone, fake. The curator, Mr. Wilson, explains to Hilly: "false views of historical personages nevertheless, interesting to historians"(30).

Florence wonders why she is angry all the time. To make a total commitment to the path of selfhood but to make it to a dead hero is to seek death. Questioned about this choice by Hilly, Florence points out the people she knows in life are metaphorically dead.

By time travel, Flo goes back and reclaims women's places in the event. She helps Boone bury the dead; she brings Boone food, weapons and information; she pours bullets in preparation for the siege; and Boone identifies her as the one who keeps him on the right path. Florence knows the way, and she serves as translator. Prophetically, Flo deciphers the difficult handwriting on a document in the museum. She indirectly admonishes the audience as she reads: "Necessary to notice political events" (36).

One such event is clearly the reclamation of women's roles in historical events. Flo's nurturing and caring for others lurk somewhat hidden by the romance of tracking with Daniel Boone. Crossing the threshold to the past, Florence moves out of "museum" space into the wilderness, where male adventures happen. Wives are absent, but daughters are present. Jemima Boone suspects Flo of being her father's Indian wife. She is a voice of reality when she reminds Flo that Mrs. Boone is at home; that place is taken. Flo as the other woman can't go there. Similarly, Flo discovers Hilly also has a daughter. Present in dialogue but absent on stage, Linda doubles Jemima, and shows a single working parent who must deal with the problems of child care. This time the parent is male. Flo accuses Hilly of talking too much, another switch of gendered descriptors.

By forming her play in parallel universes, ruptured by crossing a literal but significant threshold, the playwright gives both audience and characters space in which to participate in the challenges presented by simultaneously existing representations of history. The audience is asked to examine both past and present and to interrogate that relationship. In order to do this, the audience will have to reconsider, perhaps, the values held.

This frequent alternation of scenes past with scenes present causes the audience to examine and, perhaps, reformulate some of their assumptions about the historical event, the formation of gender categories, the act of marriage, and the value of family. For example, Flo questions Boone about his marriage. While he has been idealized in many visual representations, here he is demythologized as the husband/father who prefers the unknown wilderness to the known hearth. Boone says, "It's better to really be gone. Better than

sittin' there with 'em [the family] wishin' you were gone" (33).
Jemima, his daughter, gives yet another view, painting her father as a
Jiggs cartoon character who is afraid of the domineering wife who
holds the frying pan. She suggests Boone took to the forest because
he was afraid of his wife. Mrs. Boone had Daniel's number. Jemima
counters Flo's assertion that Daniel Boone is the bravest man in this
country.

*JEMIMA: He is not. He's afraid of Mother. He's afraid of Colonel
Calloway. He's afraid of the British. He's afraid of the whole state of
North Carolina. And most of all, he's afraid of honest work.*

FLO: Is that what your mother says?

JEMIMA: Well, she ought to know. (65)

In the next scene, Flo questions Hilly methodically to investi-
gate his marital relationship. She finds Hilly was faithful until death
did part his wife from him. Because Flo and the museum are keeping Daniel Boone alive, Hilly states "You think the dead are still
alive. Well, I'm here to tell you they aren't" (35).

Marsha Norman, through her writing and like her central female character, places herself in Kentucky's history and in doing so
is also placed in the history of Actors Theatre, an indigenous regional theatre. In *Black Folktales*, Julius Lester points out that

*folktales are stories that give people a way of communicating with each
other about each other—their fears, their hopes, their dreams, their fantasies, giving their explanation of why the world is the way it is. It is in
stories like these that a child learns who his parents are and who he will
become. (vii)*

Face-to-face or mediated in shared forms of communication, the
folktale is offered to a homogenous audience. It is didactic and offers, in its teaching, information about the origins of the group. It
also enforces certain behaviors and practices: Transmission of values
and the promotion of a social and collective self are a part of its
functions.

The commissioning of this folkloric play by the Kentucky Colonels (an organization for the male warrior, a group that excludes female membership) is delightfully ironic: The male military hierarchy sponsors a play that asks for a new equity in male/female relationships. An interesting negotiation has taken place between Florence and Hilly. He connects to her because she is a "true believer." Florence is willing to replace the old culturally determined categories outlined in White's history of heterosexuality. As the play narrows the boundaries that separate the sexes, the freedom of androgyny is offered. Marsha Norman refuses dualism and the role of the other, the objectification that places the burden for social problems on women. Ynestra King, quoted in *Women and Nature*, asserts:

No person should be made into an "other" to despise, dehumanize, and exploit. As women we have been an "other," but we are refusing to be the "other" any longer and we will not make anyone else into an "other." Sexism, racism, class divisions, homophobia, and the rape of nature depend on this process of objectification. (45)

The new deal prizes consolidation. From those polarities from which cultures can be defined are the boundaries delimiting a social group (masculine/feminine; young/old; separate/communal; creative/destructive). From these, Marsha Norman refashions the world of the play. Instead of celebrating youth, individualism, creation, and masculinity—those all-American values—Marsha Norman renews the culture by redefining it. The play by its final curtain no longer supports binary thinking but praises these cultural polarities: middle age, togetherness, creation, and androgyny. In the comic inversion of beliefs, values, and practices, Marsha Norman produces a utopia and, in doing so, probably also produces herself.

Thus the play frames a historical event that celebrates local origins (no doubt there were audience members in Louisville who could trace their own ancestry back to Boonesborough). Within it, the playwright gives birth symbolically not to Eve but to Florence Adams. In the flow, the stream of history and dramatic creation, all persons can be celebrated. Another frame signals make-believe, and the request of the playwright for believers. While the frames are indigenous to the community where they originate, they reflect outward

to other cultural behavioral practices and social understandings.
Through the fabulist skill of playwright Marsha Norman, the outcomes are a purchasable commodity, a political act of patriotism,
and an irresistible act of subversion.

Notes

1.   The performance of *D. Boone* referred to was staged by the Actors Theater of
      Louisville, Kentucky, in Louisville, in March 1992. Gloria Muzio directed, and the
      cast included Catherine Christianson, Gladden Schrock, Rod McLachlan, Dave
      Florek, Skipp Sudduth, Mark Shannon, and Chekoth Miskenack.

Works Cited

Bakhtin, Mikhail. *Rabelais and His World.* Translated by Helene Iswolsky. Bloomington:
       Indiana UP, 1984.
Campbell, Joseph, with Bill Moyers. *The Power of Myth.* Edited by Betty Sue Flowers.
       New York: Doubleday, 1988.
"*D. Boone* Is Skewed Look at History at Actors Theatre." *Bardstown Standard,* 29
       February 1992.
Degh, Linda, and Andrew Vazsonyi. "Legend and Belief." In *Folklore Genres.* Edited by
       Dan Ben-Amos. Austin: U of Texas P, 1976: 93–123.
Devine, Maureen. *Women and Nature.* Metuchen, NJ: Scarecrow Press, 1992.
Dolan, Jill. "Gender Impersonation Onstage: Destroying or Maintaining the Mirror of
       Gender Roles?" In *Gender in Performance.* Edited by Laurence Senelick. New
       York: UP of New England, 1992: 3–13.
Gennep, Arnold van. *The Rites of Passage.* 1909. London: Routledge, 1960.
Greenblatt, Stephen. "Culture." *Critical Terms for Literary Study.* Edited by Frank
       Lentricchia and Thomas McLaughlin. Chicago: U of Chicago P, 1990, 225–232.
Greiner, Donald J. *Women Enter the Wilderness.* Columbia: U of South Carolina P,
       1991.
Lester, Julius. "Keep on Stepping." In *Black Folktales.* New York: Grove Weidenfeld,
       1969. 153–157.
Mootz, Willliam. "Theatre Review *(D. Boone).*" *The Courier Journal,* 28 February 1992.
Norman, Marsha. *Loving Daniel Boone.* Unpublished manuscript (1992). The Tantleff
       Office, New York, NY.
Sandusky, Dale. "Historical Goofs Aside, Play Is Fun." *New Albany Tribune,* 28 Febru-
       ary 1992.
Sweeney, J. Gray. *The Columbus of the Woods: Daniel Boone and the Typology of
       Manifest Destiny.* St. Louis: Washington U Gallery of Art, 1992.
Turner, Victor. *Ritual Process: Structure and Anti-Structure.* Chicago: Aldine, 1969.
White, Kevin. *The First Sexual Revolution.* New York: New York UP, 1993.

Don't Read This Review!
'night, Mother by Marsha Norman*

Robert Brustein

Since the theater with which I am associated originated this production of Marsha Norman's 'night, Mother (Golden), I should disqualify myself from writing a review. Well, I'm going to commit an unethical journalistic act, and submit one anyway. I have two excuses for this totally self-serving decision, neither very exculpatory. One is that ever since I first read 'night, Mother , it has filled me with the kind of exultation I experience only in the presence of a major dramatic work, and how many new plays can you say that about in the course of a reviewing career? The other is that since my judgments have little influence on Broadway theatergoers, it is unlikely that anything I say will start a box office stampede. Still, there's no question I'm involved in a conflict of interest however I proceed. I can't very well pretend to be objective about the production, so I will forgo comment on it, but I simply can't resist writing about the play.

The play occupies about eighty-five minutes of stage time without intermission, as measured by three or four clocks that tick away remorselessly on the surfaces of the set. Scrupulously realistic, 'night, Mother is also chastely classical in its observance of the unities, especially the unity of time. However, it not only measures its own time (like the movie High Noon, for example), but also the time of the audience. Matinees excepted, the clocks on stage display the same hour as the watches on the wrists of the spectators. This sounds like a gimmick, but it gives the play the density and compression of an explosive device, and accounts in part for its remorseless power (it also helps explain the enduring strength and validity of the Poetics).

*Reprinted, with permission, from The New Republic, May 2, 1983.

The clock collection belongs to Thelma Cates, the aging mother of Jessie Cates; the two have been living together in a tackily decorated country house somewhere in the New South. In the brief course of the play, these two women will share a profound life crisis, a catalytic experience designed to reorder the chemistry of a familiar relationship, and expose both character and destiny. The crisis is initiated by Jessie. Having retrieved her dead father's rusty revolver from a shoe box in the attic, she announces calmly to her mother that she has decided that very night to use it on herself.

At first, Thelma is disbelieving, but Jessie's determination is unmistakable: the play is actually an extended death scene, preceding an inevitable, inexorable act. Jessie says she has informed her mother of her suicide plans in order to prepare her, both emotionally and domestically, for life without her. But even as she is outlining the shopping routine and inventorying the kitchen utensils (*'night, Mother* is a minutely detailed mosaic of the commonplaces of everyday modern life), Jessie is also trying to justify and explain the root causes of her extreme decision. Her passion for the quiet and darkness of death is fed by real misfortunes—her husband has left her, her son is a petty thief—but more incurably by a free-floating despair: "I'm just not having a very good time and I don't have any reason to think it'll get anything but worse. I'm tired. I'm hurt. I'm sad. I feel used." When her mother presses her further about the sources of her misery, Jessie answers: "Oh, everything from you and me to Red China."

The Red China issue we share with Jessie, but the "you and me" is personal, and, having made her decision, Jessie wants to use her last moments to explore her relationship with her mother and recall their past. She is full of recrimination, particularly about Thelma's failure to inform her fully about her epileptic condition, but underneath the bitterness and complaint lies a curious form of symbiotic love. Her suicide is perhaps meant partly to punish her mother, but it is also a means of reaching out to her, and in the agony of their parting there develops a deeper understanding between the two women than they could ever have achieved in life. But it is not enough. Jessie feels like someone who just failed to arrive. She waited and waited to fulfill the promise of her childhood, but it never happened: "I'm what was worth waiting for and I didn't make it. ME . . . who might have made a difference to me . . . I'm not going to show up, so there's no reason to stay, except to keep you company, and that's . . . not reason enough because I'm not . . . very good company . . . . Am I?" To which Thelma must truthfully answer no.

But Thelma is not simply trying to understand her daughter's suicide, she is also trying to stop it, and she uses all the strategies and arguments in her possession to stay the course of necessity. Thelma is a salty, shrewd, good-natured country woman who represents a strong force for survival. Having allowed her damaged daughter to take care of her in order to give her a purpose, she is now being brought to realize that nobody can organize or possess another's life; but she still thinks she can prevent another's death. In an incessant stream of chatter, she tries to distract Jessie's attention with jokes and anecdotes, resorting then to tantrums, exhortations, derision, pitiful pleas, even physical threats. Nothing works for her—not even her poignant effort to prepare hot chocolate "the old way," Marsha Norman's version of J.D. Salinger's "consecrated chicken soup" (both women discover they never liked it, since both hate milk). For Jessie has no real appetites, which is another symptom of her anomie. Wondering what might keep her alive, Jessie muses: "If there was something I really liked, like maybe if I really liked rice pudding or cornbread for breakfast or something, that might be enough," to which Thelma replies softly, "Rice pudding is good." "Not to me," answers Jessie.

In the climax of the play, Thelma's positive force finds expression in a resounding affirmation of life, as she screams her refusal to die until they drag her screeching and screaming to her grave. But it is not enough to counteract Jessie's pitiless and terrifying No. Realizing that Jessie is already dead—"I'm looking right through you. I can't stop you because you're already gone"—Thelma crumples into helpless resignation, weakly absorbing her daughter's instructions about how to behave after she hears the shot. And when, following Thelma's final desperate attempt to restrain her daughter, Jessie says goodnight, closes her door, and fulfills her destiny, Mama is left forlorn on stage, her left hand gripping the hot chocolate pan, as she picks up the phone to inform the rest of the family and confront the wreckage of her life.

It is a moment that must happen; yet we continue to believe that it won't, as in the highest tragedy. *'night, Mother* proceeds with the relentless force of a juggernaut, displaying not a single moment of artifice or contrivance or self-consciousness. In the absolute truthfulness of her treatment and dialogue, in the unforced poetry of her modern speech, and in her capacity to create major climaxes out of petty quotidian affairs, Miss Norman has followed the path of Chekhov, who believed that the great stakes of modern drama must emerge from under the trivial course of the daily routine: "Let the things that happen on stage," he wrote, "be just as complex and yet just as simple as they are in life. For instance, people are having a meal at a table, just having a meal, but at the same time their happiness is being created, or their lives are being smashed up." But the playwright to whom she is bound to be compared in future, in power, style, and intention, is Eugene O'Neill, for in the way it exhumes buried family secrets, exposes the symbiotic links among parents and children, and alternates between bitter recriminations and expressions of love, 'night, Mother is a compressed, more economical version of A Long Day's Journey into Night.

I am invoking some great names in describing this play because I believe Miss Norman, consciously or not, is writing in a great dramatic tradition, and, young as she is, has the potential to preserve and revitalize it. Nothing reinforces one's faith in the power and importance of the theater more than the emergence of an authentic universal playwright—not a woman playwright, mind you, not a regional playwright, not an ethnic playwright, but one who speaks to the concerns and experiences of all humankind. Implicated as I am, I have grown convinced that Marsha Norman is the genuine article—an American writer with the courage to look unflinchingly into the black holes from which we normally turn our faces. I hope you will, therefore, forgive me my ethical trespasses as I try to welcome her with all the awe and humility and gratitude that I think her work deserves.

Update with Marsha Norman

Linda Ginter Brown

Editor's Note The following interview between the author (LGB) and Marsha Norman (MN) took place at the Gershwin Theater on October 25, 1993.

LGB: I really appreciate your taking the time to talk with me, Marsha. What I want to do is focus mostly on related works, *Sarah and Abraham*, *Loving Daniel Boone*, and *The Red Shoes*, if you care to talk about it, and some general questions, but I did want to ask you one question about *'night, Mother* that I've always wondered about. You've been quoted in various interviews as saying that you were very angry when you wrote *'night, Mother*. What were you so angry about?

MN: Well, I was angry that the theater didn't seem to want my work. After *Getting Out*, there was *Third and Oak*, which was well-received, but unproduceable for the most part. I got a bad piece of advice from someone who told me to split them apart into two plays, and the result was that they were seen as one-acts and not as a whole play. So then after that came *Circus Valentine*, which people hated more than they ever imagined they would hate anything. They hated that play. It's only been produced that one time. The reviews say it was a disappointment, but I mean, really and truly, it just. . . . So the play after that was *The Holdup*, which was funny and a lark, and a traumatic experience for me because Gordon Davidson had commissioned it under a Rockefeller grant; when he actually saw the play he didn't like it. He thought it was silly and too funny.

LGB: My students loved it. I taught it in one of my classes and they really loved it.

MN: Thanks. Then I finally did kind of a workshop of it in Louisville; then it had two other productions that I know of, one in Saratoga with the Circle Rep and then it was done at ACT in San Francisco. It was just creamed in the press for being too funny. Who does she think she is? Neil Simon? That kind of thing.

LGB: Ridiculous.

MN: So I arrived at that moment feeling that I was going to be a flash in the pan. *Getting Out* was the only play I was ever going to write that people were going to like.

LGB: Were you almost beginning to internalize that yourself?

MN: Well, I was just very angry that I saw a lot of plays that I thought were not significant, not interesting, not well done, not anything.

LGB: I understand.

MN: And I didn't understand why those plays were being done and my work was sitting in the drawer. You know you will hear me say the same thing again about *Sarah and Abraham* and *Loving Daniel Boone*. People think that once you have a successful play all the doors open, and then you can just see your work whenever you like—those people are crazy. It's not true.

LGB: Actually, it's harder, isn't it?

MN: Well, it is harder. So I was just furious at the world of the theater. I had also just been fired, which was a good thing, in retrospect. I came to New York that summer. This would be the summer of '81. I had a job doing book and lyrics to a musical called *Orphan Train.* I was *thrilled* to have this job! It was all I ever wanted to do, to write musicals. Musicals are very tricky creatures. On that particular musical, Wilford Leach, the director, had his own idea of how the musical should go. The producers had quite a different idea, but I didn't know about the producers' different idea. I only knew what Will Leach was telling me. So I wrote the book and subsequent drafts to suit him, only to finally be fired by the producer and replaced by her eighteen-year-old son "who had had some good ideas—

LGB: (interrupting) How awful!

MN: —while he was mowing the grass." This is exactly what she said to me on the phone. That her son was cutting the grass and had some thoughts about it and she thought they would hire him instead. So I was just totally done in by Will Leach because he led me down the wrong path. He said, "Write this," but it wasn't what they wanted. He hoped that what I would do is convince them that his vision was right.

LGB: So, you would do his dirty work for him in a way?

MN: Exactly. This is the place that you are always in musicals. It's not a form where the writer has the kind of power that you have in plays. In any event, I was fired. So there I am in New York. I know no one. I have nothing to do, and I am furious. So there was this great big empty time. I had been thinking for a while about doing it, but suddenly being fired and hav-ing the whole summer free and not knowing anyone—the phone wasn't ringing, no was one was inviting me to lunch—that was what did it. So I thought, all right. I will write this play. I don't care if anybody ever sees this play. I don't care if anybody ever produces this play.

LGB: Yes, I know I read that you said that.

MN: Yeah, I'm going to write it the way *I* see it; nobody's going to have anything to say about it. I'm going to do it just for me, and if it goes in the drawer, fine. . . . I have a piece of paper with a little note that I wrote to myself at the end of writing it, and the note says, "Have I written something that anyone will ever want to produce, and have I written something that will humiliate me?"

LGB: Yes, yes, I see.

MN: I mean, that was *exactly* how I felt. I now espouse this "nature abhors a vacuum theory" of loss, you know? But when you are fired, as actually I quite often am now . . . I was fired three times this year (laughs).

LGB: (incredulous) Really?

MN: (nods) You can just count on it! Something's going to come in, something's going to rush in, something unexpected, unpredicted, not, not. . . .

LGB: You mean?

MN: Well, you know, if somehow you are not able to write what is in their head, then they don't make it into a drama. I will *never* be able to write what is in someone else's head. This is not a skill that I have. It's even more difficult now in the world of straight plays than it ever was. Bob Brustein told me two weeks ago, "Straight theater's dead. Regional theater's dead."

LGB: I hope he's wrong about that!

MN: Well, I do too, but I'm just saying that this is what he said. And he said to me, "You're so modest to go through commercial theater."

LGB: Well, that feeds into the next question, because I've been kind of scared that you aren't going to write anymore straight plays. You've been quoted as saying that you've felt that you've come to the end of what you can do in a play, and yet you've said that you felt like you could spend the rest of your life in the musical theater. You talk about how you grew up with the piano and that you've loved music all your life, that it's always been a big part of your life. And if you could've had your way, I think you even said that you had considered going to Juilliard. . .

MN: (interjects) But. . . .

LGB: But then, last spring I came across an interview where you were one of twelve women playwrights who were interviewed about sexism in the theater. In that interview you were quoted as saying that if you could get an institutional theater that would believe in you it would make your life easier. You said, "I would write fewer musicals. Currently, the only way I can ever write straight plays is when Jon Jory commissions them."

To me, there's a little contradiction here. If you really could do what you wanted, would you write the straight plays if you had a place to see them produced? I guess I have a little problem . . . .

MN: It's both. It's both things.

LGB: I mean, maybe it's presumptuous on my part. . . .

MN: No, but you know. . . .

LGB: . . . but I'm saying to myself, "I'm not quite sure I believe her because I think. . . ." But go ahead.

MN: Right. I have to make a living, you know? I cannot make a living in America writing straight plays. And I don't think anybody can. Not if they have two children in a private school. You know?

LGB: Yes, I can understand.

MN: And I don't want to have to work until I *absolutely* die. I would really like to be able to quit altogether in fifteen years or so. You know what I mean? And just read and quilt.

LGB: Yes, I do. I'm thinking of doing the same thing. I just want to save up enough money from teaching so I'll have time to write, and do some other things.

MN: Right! So that's *not* possible. I don't think that's possible in the world of straight plays. On the other hand, musicals really do produce an income for you. *Secret Garden* will probably be producing an income for me for ten years. This is very good! The other thing about musicals that make them necessary in my life is that they are high drama, and they are an opportunity for me to play with people that I love. I would work with Heidi Landesman on a musical of *Moby Dick*, for goodness sake! I like them. I like being in these pitched battles. That's what a musical is. It's an assault on Everest.

LGB: (laughs) On Everest. Yes, I know that job requirement!

MN: Just this afternoon I was convinced. . . (pauses). I have been really worried about the opening of *Red Shoes* because our director wanted it to be a way that I thought was guaranteed disaster. Now, this doesn't mean the whole thing would be a disaster, but you know? I just thought, "This won't work, what he wants. And so, I've been trying to figure out how to get something that will work, something that he agrees with, that he's behind. And you know just this afternoon I take part in a meeting with him and he says, "Well, okay, you're right. You're right. Go. Do. We'll do it your way. Which is great. It's fun to live, and it's fun to win. Right?

LGB: Right.

MN: So, it may not be so much the battle. It's both. It's fun to be with your friends, you know, in a collaborative environment, whereas the straight play world tends to be so lonely. Not as lonely as novelists have it. I mean I did that once when I was *really* lonely. Then I wrote a novel.

LGB: Ah! You were mad again when you did *Fortune Teller?*

MN: (nods vigorously) I was mad again. I was mad again. Well, I don't think you can help it. A lot of people, we all get very angry and feel very used by the theater, discarded by the theater. And, um, we're so . . . some people go off and drink, some people go off to Hollywood. You know, people have their various strategies for dealing with this.

LGB: Yes, I think this is some of the same thing that Lillian Hellman experienced.

MN: Exactly.

LGB: You know when you interviewed her, and you were talking about all the anger? You know she had said this. Instead of her works, in her writing, she talks about how the theater treats people. You know, you have to be a survivor.

MN: The theater does still treat people that way. I'm on the Council of the Dramatists Guild, and I find that a very valuable thing to do. I'm very committed to that work. But it's not just out of a spirit of good deeds. It's good to go see all those writers and to remember that the great challenge is not to end up my life in the theater bitter and angry.

So, you see (laughs), this is how I work out my anger. I go and try some other thing. I put all the anger, use it to sort of drive some new piece of machinery.

LGB: Does that mean we won't get another novel from you unless you're just really angry at something that has occurred? I liked *Fortune Teller*. I thought it was a very good novel. Of course, it had the "mother/daughter thing," which I love.

MN: Right. I can't say what I will do.

LGB: Yes.

MN: Because it's not as though I'm sitting with a stack of ideas that
      I want to write. There are some things I want to write, but, for
      me, writing, the actual sitting down to write them, . . . that
      writing happens when the situation is right for me. And the
      time is there when I can write in that form at that moment,
      and when I feel that I know exactly how to handle that content.
      I think you've probably read me saying that a play is a con-
      junction of form and content, and I know that I want to write
      about this motel that my aunt had when I was growing up.

LGB: Is this Aunt Bubbie?

MN: No, this is a different aunt. This is Aunt Iva, and she had a
      motel at Jamestown, Kentucky.

LGB: Oh, I know exactly where that is.

MN: You know where Jamestown is?

LGB: Well, sure, that's where Lake Cumberland is.

MN: Yes, well, the highway passed them by. You know the high-
      way went through about four miles away from where the
      motel was. There were two roads where the highway could've
      gone, and the highway went down the other road. Conse-
      quently, the Jamestown motel was a struggle. But we would
      go there every other week. We would get in the car and go
      and get sick in the car every other week on the way to the
      Jamestown motel.

      For some reason my uncle had this collection of French mu-
      sic. So anyway, I may write about that. But again, it would
      really be writing about my mother and her sister. And that
      life that they had, which was extraordinary. But I don't know.

I can tell you right now that Jon wants another play from me, and I told him that I would do it for the opening of the new theater, and then Heidi and I are going to do a musical next year.

LGB: Is it going to be an adaptation?

MN: We're going to work on the life of Aimee Semple McPherson.

LGB: Oh, yes, the evangelist. There have been some articles.

MN: Yes, and there's a new biography out.

LGB: Right, and there's a writer for the *Dayton Daily News* who did a couple of pieces in the paper about her visit to Dayton to hold a revival.

MN: Oh, really? Would you send those to me?

LGB: Yes, I'll look them up and send them to you.

MN: Great.

LGB: Well, talking about evangelists (laughs), this is kind of flowing into this next question also. I wondered about this, and I was talking it over with Katherine Burkman, who coauthored a piece for the book on *Sarah and Abraham*. There seems to be a shift in your work. Maybe you would like to talk about this. There seems to be more of a mythic approach or some fairy tale quality to some of the plays you've been doing. I'm thinking of *Sarah and Abraham* and, of course, *Secret Garden*, although that's an adaptation. *Loving Daniel Boone*, the fantasy of going back in time and having a relationship with Daniel Boone. Is that a conscious effort on your part?

MN: Well, I think it's because I am not interested in domestic dramas right now. I don't want to see kitchens onstage anymore. I don't want to think about that. I think that one of the reasons we, in the theater, have to move to this, to a more overtly theatrical [style], is that television and film have really taken all of that domestic dispute territory. They do it better—those social issue dramas. *'night, Mother,* you know, I mean, when I wrote *'night, Mother,* people weren't doing shows about suicide on T.V. Nobody was even saying the word. That's why I wrote it. But now it's said all the time. I think even the AIDS plays seem to me quite. . . , they don't need to be done in the theater. We see the abuse. Why would you write a play about any social subject? Because chances are the people who would be interested in that couldn't afford the tickets to the theater. Television has really taken all that over. On the other hand, television *cannot* do things like *Sarah and Abraham,* things like *Boone.* Television can't do musicals. Movies can't do musicals. I think that if we are to survive in the theater, this is just kind of a practical view, all right? If we are to have a living, thriving theater we have to do things that only we can do. Because nobody's going to pay sixty-five dollars to come and see a T.V. show.

LGB: Right.

MN: But it also coincides with my own interests.

LGB: You mean back to the musical theater?

MN: Well, no, I mean I'm just not interested in doing them.

LGB: You've done them.

MN: I've done them.

LGB: OK, well, let's just talk about *Sarah and Abraham,* since I brought them up. Can you give me a little background? Do you remember what your sources were? You've retold the myth of Sarah and Abraham, and you've given Sarah the larger part. She's the one that takes over instead of the patriarchal view that we get from the Bible. What were you thinking at the time you put that together, and how did you come to that focus or that approach?

MN: I had always been curious about the story ever since I was a girl. I did not understand this story as told by the Bible. What, what was she doing? Saying to her husband, "Go in unto my maid or it may be that I may bear children through her," whatever the Bible says, or seems to be saying. And, so I was wanting to write my marriage play. We all of us do. We write a marriage play; we write a theater play, we write theater. So this was my marriage play that I wanted to write, and I just started thinking about that. I began to read some of the feminist theologians and scholars on this subject and discovered that, in fact, the Bible was simply one version. There was great evidence that Sarah was a personification of strong matriarchal culture under siege. Whether she actually herself lived or not, she certainly represented what the world thought of as religion until about 600 B.C. And then I became really interested because I felt (sighs), well, it just made a lot of things I was confused about suddenly clear up—the idea that I was living, that we are living today in a world that worships the known, whereas the world of the patriarchal cultures was the worship of the unknown. The unknown makes much more sense to me in terms of things to worship and seems much more like the way we live. I don't think *for a minute* that my life's a linear path, that I know what's going to happen next, that by thinking very clearly I can determine the outcome of *anything!* I think you might as well dance around in a circle and pour hot oil on stones and breathe the fumes and see what happens. You know what I mean? I've just really found that the story of *Sarah and Abraham* was a kind of way at looking at what had happened to the world—that the world had been taken over by a patriarchal view, and the power had shifted to the patriarchs. That explained a lot of what made me uncomfortable. So, it was fun to write.

LGB: Do you believe in God?

MN: The one of the *Bible?* (firmly) No.

LGB: I read that you came from a very fundamentalist background, that your parents were very strict fundamentalists. So you've gone completely the other way? Maybe it's part of the myth or the fairy tale images I see coming out in your work, and it doesn't mean anything at all, but I sense a certain spirituality emerging.

MN: Absolutely! Absolutely! I feel that spirituality is at the very center of me, but it has nothing to do with a vengeful, restrictive, oppressive God as presented by the Old Testament, as created, as written by that group of people who wrote the Bible. I no more think that those people have a claim on what's the spiritual force. I find that the God that ignores women, that kills babies, that vicious, violent creature is somebody I don't want to have anything to do with.

I think that, on the other hand, there is this extraordinary power that we all feel that is best embodied in our care for each other, in our love for our children, and in our desire to see our society grow. I think that kind of force for good and force for help, that vision of a spiritual power that is accepting and helpful, defines what it is that we feel as opposed to saying, "I am God and you will have no other gods before Me; however, I'm not going to say whether I'm really a Baptist, or Mohammed, or a Muslim. I'll let you fight that out." Do you know what I mean?

LBG: I think so. But you know, in my own life, I know that I get really angry when I read St. Paul and his view of what women should be. You know, "Be silent; don't say anything." I argue this a lot at church (laughs). You know, I take the woman's point of view. (Pauses). But then, on the other hand, I look at Christ, who I think was a great feminist. He thought men and women were equal. It was the other people, many times, who put that approach on it. And, of course, the Old Testament is, in many ways, different from the New Testament.

MN: I think that the God, the notion of God, sort of small "g" god, this is a notion that has existed from the dawn of time. Everybody needs someone, some group of beings who are more powerful than you because you can't help but feel small. And this is good. We are small; we're tiny things. On the other hand, I feel that this religion that I grew up with, which was very respected, very, like I said, very oppressive—that is *not* good. I don't want to have anything to do with it. I can't get behind any kind of system which says "I'm going to kill my son" for *whatever* reason! You know? I *cannot* think of a reason; I cannot imagine!

LGB: That's always troubled me, too, and I've heard various explanations.

MN: It's not God who did that, you know? The Bible is written. It's a piece of writing. The people who wanted the kind of power they wanted, who desired to shape the society in the way they wanted to shape it, put that stuff in there—those notions of sacrifice, those notions that you can just casually kill children. No! You can't do that. I think that if you have to draw a real clear line, whatever your view is of God, that's one thing. Whatever your view is of the church as it's been created—it's an institution. This is the whole thing.

LGB: I'm just sitting here thinking, Marsha. Has your mother seen *Sarah and Abraham*? Is this another thing she's going to have to answer to St. Peter for? Besides *Getting Out*?

MN: She's dead.

LGB: I didn't know. I'm so sorry.

MN: She died four years ago, but she would've been terribly upset because she was very literal-minded about the Bible. She had a stroke. She reached up, felt her neck and said, "My neck is killing me," and died.

LGB: Oh, my. I do want to talk more about the biblical approach in a moment, but could we talk about the mother/daughter relationships? I'm always seeing mother/daughter relationships in almost all your works. Even when I was sitting there in the theater in Louisville watching Flo in *Loving Daniel Boone*, when she goes into the teepee there. To me, she was searching for her mother, going back to the womb. It seems so clear to me. Do you think you would consider retelling another biblical story? I know when I first went to graduate school—you were talking about this restrictive view—I gave a paper at the University of Florida comparing the biblical Ruth and Ruth in Pinter's *The Homecoming*, the prostitute. I can remember talking to my minister about some sources. He thought my paper was really sacrilegious, and he was quite upset about it. So I can identify with what you're saying.

What about Job's wife? Now there's a woman who needs her story told. You could get a wonderful play out of that. I've always been so angry, and have said this on occasion, about all the focus that's been put on Job, but look what his wife went through! Losing all their children, you know? It's just an idea to toss out.

MN: Yeah, I think there's an interest in those stories. I want to look at those stories. I will *not* take on faith what we have been told about how things are, you know? I want to know. In *Sarah and Abraham*, what I was really looking at was what she was doing. Who was she? In fact, she turns out to have this *enormous* life. One of the things I discovered was that at the time the Bible was written the most common image that appeared on coins was this image of this Mesopotamian woman—the high priestess.

LGB: I read that.

MN: Clearly, women in our culture feel invisible. I feel invisible. I felt invisible as a girl. That's why I have said so often, you know, I write about people you would never see, like *me*. This has got to change! We have got to have our stories told!

LGB: Like Ann [Pitoniak] said, you take common people, every-day people and make them heroes. They're survivors. They're doing the best that they can with what they have.

MN: Right.

LGB: Like I said in my dissertation, they go further along.

MN: But women do that. We do that. We are a group of heroes. Now, for example, last year I read the *Pioneer Diaries.* Here's another area practically like the Bible. Here is a tale—the American frontier was won by men, you were either a cow-boy or an Indian man, and they fought it out. For all we know, even all the buffaloes were men.

LGB: (laughs loudly) Hah!

MN: Do you know what I mean? And who actually made it pos-sible to go? The women. The women who literally kept ev-erybody fed, kept everybody well. You read the story of the Donner Pass. Who lived from the Donner Pass? Not one woman died. Not one child died. Sixty percent of the men died, but the women managed to stay alive and get those children through that winter. We are brave and powerful and wonderful. I am doing my part (laughs) to make sure.

LGB: (emphatically) Yes, you are.

MN: But we all forget that. People like Aimee Semple McPherson. Here's another great example. Here's a woman who possessed an incredible gift. This woman had the power to heal on such a level that the world has not seen since.

LGB: Yes, a writer, Roz Young, in the *Dayton Daily News,* talked about that. McPherson had a meeting at Memorial Hall in Dayton and had a healing service.

MN: Right. She had this talent, and she was preaching a religion of joy and a religion of health. During the Depression in Los Angeles, the Foursquare Gospel, the temple, fed more people than the City of Los Angeles did during that time. And yet preachers, men, became so suspicious of her that she abandoned her life in this fight to keep from being thought of as a slut.

LGB: It was so radical for her.

MN: Yes. But that whole business of the disappearance. This whole question of how Aimee Semple McPherson disappeared for a couple of weeks and couldn't really explain where she was. She said she was kidnapped. They said she was out with a man. So what if she was out with a man? Maybe she was kidnapped, you know? But that event—that she was not pure as the driven snow—and wasn't always right exactly where she could be found, was enough. You know there was a trial where she was accused of conspiring to create false evidence. This was nothing but a witch hunt all over again. Look at the inquisition. There has been this attempt all throughout history to eliminate the contributions of women, to keep women in a place of complete insignificance and silence.

LGB: The barefoot and pregnant bit?

MN: The complete invisibility. So, we just have to fight this, and the stories of women are wonderful ways, the stories I love best. Somebody just asked me to do the real true story of Annie Oakley, another person. So I think that what I can do, in looking at this, is to see that women's stories survive. If those stories don't survive, then we don't have a chance.

LBG: Our voices are silenced forever if we don't tell our stories, and if we don't have writers who will tell them for us.

MN: Right. So I can do that, and that's what I intend to do. That seems to me, at this moment, more important to do than to simply be a writer. You know what I mean? I don't have that kind of youthful, "Oh, I just want to write." I have a kind of, "I want to write for a very specific purpose which happens to coincide with what really interests me. "It isn't *just* a political act. It's a political act through and through. I have a little girl, Katherine.

LGB: How old is she?

MN: She's a year and a half. If Katherine is to grow up into a world that has a place for her and that is interested in her, then I have to keep clearing the path, because the weeds grow back really fast, as we can see with people like Aimee Semple McPherson. She clears the path, and what happens? The weeds grow back; for history she's erased.

LGB: That's true. You bring up a really good point. I remember starting graduate school in 1980, studying Charlotte Perkins Gilman. It was amazing to me to learn of all these feminist movements throughout American history. It wasn't just Gloria Steinem in the seventies and Betty Friedan earlier with *The Feminine Mystique*. Women have been scrambling and trying ever since the beginning of our country to find their places. Sometimes it seems to me that we take two steps forward and then one step back.

MN: Well, I think that whenever any single woman achieves any kind of prominence, there tends to be a conservative attempt to destroy her reputation or erase her memory—whatever it is.

LGB: Why do you think that's the case, Marsha? Do you think men are really that afraid of giving women their voice?

MN: Yes.

LGB: You do?

MN: Yes. I think they have a memory of the time when women were seen as the primary creators. You know Barbara Walker

talks about this. Do you know her work? There's a book called
The Skeptical Feminist, in which she reminds us that for a
very very long time in history the man's role in conception
was not known. So women were seen as these creative beings
who mysteriously produced new life. When it became known
that men did have a role in conception, there began to be a
struggle. There's was anger about, "Gee, you've been using us
for all this time, and now you find out that we're really useful. Now maybe what we would like to do is be seen as the
primary creators after all."

LGB: That's interesting.

MN: To the point that now the prohibition against having a child
out of wedlock without the permission, the legality of a man,
you know that's very much how the culture sees it. You really
have to have a father around in order to "begat." We all know
that it's not the fertilization of the egg that gets the child
born. It's a lot harder than that. It's a lifetime of involvement
for mothers.

LGB: This is the whole Nancy Chodorow theory that I talked about
in my dissertation. Even now, with two people working,
women are still the primary nurturers and are taking a lot of
the responsibility.

MN: Yes. I feel that I'm so glad that I'm a woman. I like that. I like
that I get to be that. It's the most profound experience in my
life—my children. I just don't want to be beat up for it. It's
not that I don't want to do it; I don't want to be attacked for
doing it. So I think that that's it. It's a struggle over who's the
creator, you know? Men as a group seem to have a kind of
inability to share creative power with someone.

LGB: They feel threatened.

MN: Yes. We have all this. You know women would be happy to
say, "We don't need to be the only creators. You want to come

and be cocreators with us? Great!" But most men have the view that there has to be only one—me.

LGB: I know I read in interviews you gave about *The Secret Garden* that it was an all-woman team who put that show together. Did you find that it was much easier working in that situation?

MN: (emphatically) Lots. It was grand.

LGB: Because it was more of a collaboration than a competition?

MN: Right. Right. And *Red Shoes* is difficult precisely for that same reason. There is a need to control and mandate that the men in this project feel. It isn't just toward us, but to watch them battling it out between themselves. . . . There are lots of these battles that I don't have anything to do with. I just watch them beat up on each other. I just find this so curious.

LGB: This is the way the men communicate. You know there's this whole theory of male/female communication. Men and women listen differently.

MN: Totally.

LGB: They speak a different language.

MN: I think the whole idea is that what men talk about is status. They're always negotiating status. We *never* do that. We don't know how. What is the point anyway? Who cares?

LGB: Right.

MN: What's to be cared about is how, "Well, how's it going? Is it as good as it could be? Does anybody need help?" Or, "Are we having a good time? Are we all working at the level that we could be?" Not, "Am I getting my way?"

LGB: Yes. I have one other question about *Sarah and Abraham*. It seems to me that even though Jack brings in Monica, that between Kitty, Monica, and Virginia there's a community of women, even if Kitty is jealous. Was that a conscious effort on your part? Were you trying to show a community of women working together?

MN: Well, I didn't start out knowing that. But I watched it evolve over the course of the piece. So, I quite often find in writing that I know things that I don't know that I know. In my mind I have the idea that there are these certain people at the back of my mind, and they know a lot of things, and they can talk to themselves. I proceed to look out the front windows and figure things out, and, suddenly, I will realize that I have on some level, I have perceived this. I will know it, but it just hasn't got into the front desk—that some of these folks in the background have been aware that those women had something in common. They couldn't recognize what they had in common while they were competing for the man.

LGB: Right.

MN: But once they stopped that, and there was something else more significant at stake, like the welfare of this little boy, suddenly all those women were on the same team.

LGB: Yes. That's what really came out to me, the community of women. All right, I'd like to talk just a little about *Loving Daniel Boone*. You said that this was a play where you had a cast of almost all men. You talked about how different it was writing that play. One reviewer, I don't remember his name, said that, "Flo is both a feminist's bad dream and a royal pain in the ass." I didn't get that from watching the play. But how do you look at Flo? What was going through your mind when you were shaping her as a character? How do you feel about her as a woman?

MN: She wants to find someone that she can really love and someone that she can really believe in. She doesn't understand why the men in the contemporary world seem kind of beat up. But they do. They seem to not have a lot of self-esteem; they seem to be kind of lost. They seem to be unhappy with themselves. This is where Flo and I agree wildly—that contemporary men seem to suffer by comparison to the heroes of old. I think the men suffer, too. In other words, it's hard for men not to be in an age of heroes, and it's hard for women to welcome them when they are not heroes because we've all bought this thing about the heroes. And what I was looking for in the piece was, what was so damn attractive about those old guys? Is it really true that they're gone and dead? I think it's not true. I think what we have to do in order to love the men that are around now is to redefine heroism.

LGB: Yes. I think so, too.

MN: I think we have to redefine it both now and in the past. I think we have to look at characters like Boone and see what was great about him and what was also really crummy about him.

LGB: That he was really human?

MN: Right. That he was really a guy that didn't want to be at home, that struck off. It would've been nice to meet him on the path, but you wouldn't have wanted to be involved in anything long-term with him. You know, I see a lot of women who are either still in love with someone from their past, who are not able to forget the past and look and see who's here now. You know, when Hilly has that line, "Can't count somebody out just because they're available," it's something that I really feel.

LGB: That's a great line.

MN: I wish more men knew now that they're terrific. I don't think they know it. I don't think they know what's really good about them. I'm actually quite encouraged about the number of men who have turned happily and lovingly to their families as a source of pride.

LGB: They seem to be able to do that more than our fathers did, don't you think?

MN: Absolutely. I think it's entirely possible. When Flo recognizes that Hilly is fighting a tough battle, and when he can tell her about it, this is a great victory for her and for us. We can't live in a world without romance. I don't want to live in a world without romance.

LGB: I don't either.

MN: So I was just kind of trying to figure out, well what does it look like then? You know that until this generation in America, there were always heroes from the war because there were lots of wars.

LGB: Yes, John Wayne.

MN: Right. Men always had this kind of aura that they could be one of those guys that comes back a hero. Now, I think we have lost all faith in the idea of war, which is good. We can't have any more wars. The ones that we've had lately haven't worked out; they haven't sent us home a crop of heroes. So, I think it's good that we get rid of this war idea as the only way to make heroes. But now what we need is another idea of what's an heroic act.

LGB: So we're back to redefining heroism.

MN: Right, because we need to. We need to make sure that it isn't extended exclusively to men. We all need very much to be heroic, bold, courageous, and able to stand and fight whatever it is. If we're fighting to save the whales, or save our children, or save ourselves, or save the daffodils, it doesn't matter. We have a need to do that, to feel heroic. I don't think we can live without it, quite frankly. I mean, it seems to me that America was quite in a fit of despair after Vietnam, in particular. You know, the idea, "Oh, my God, what are we going to do? We're worthless."

LGB: Yes, that's true.

MN: It's not surprising that as a writer for the theater, I would think about the subject of heroism because, clearly, the central character in any play is going to have some heroic or antiheroic qualities. This is why we're looking at that one person instead of all the secondary characters in the piece.

But I also feel that Boone is my most personal play on the level of "Marsha Norman looks at the world of 19–, whenever I wrote that play, and has some thoughts." (laughs) You know?

LGB: Yes, I do. When I was sitting there in the theater in Louisville watching it, I was so glad that it ended the way it did. I was so satisfied.

MN: Right.

LGB: I liked what Hilly said to Flo, "You're a believer, Florence. A man needs a woman like that."

MN: You know, I think men suffer from our lack of faith in them. I think that lack of faith happened because their use was almost exclusively defined, was too narrowly defined. It was that men are good for war and business.

LGB: So both of the sexes have suffered over the years by this way that we define the roles that we can take. I know that my son is much more involved with the raising of his children than his father ever was with him—the nurturing, it's good to see.

MN: (emphatically) It's great. I read a fascinating statistic the other day. In the days of caves, 75 percent of the food eaten by the family was provided by the woman.

LGB: I've read that too.

MN: Now, you know, hunting never worked as a way of feeding the family. Never worked. Yet, somehow, that was taken on as their thing to do and it was glorified like it worked.

LGB: Right. I can see what you mean. Marsha, before we wrap things up, I would like to talk with you just a little bit about your writing process. As far as writing a play, do you still work through the same type of process that you talked about when you gave an interview to Lois Rosenthal at *Writer's Digest* four or five years ago? I couldn't get it in my mind, Marsha, how you could read four or five hours a day *and* write. (laughing) There are only twenty-four hours in a day!

MN: I know. You know, it's amazing the amount of abuse I've taken over those rules that I gave.

LGB: Really?

MN: I never meant this in a very literal way. I meant this in a way that reading is really important. You just can't write all the time. You have to fill up. That's all that I meant. I did *not* mean that one should have a schedule posted on the door, and that you can't get up.

LGB: (laughing) When I read that I said, "My God, this woman never sleeps!" Do you still take yourself out to lunch without the answer to a question? With no paper?

MN: I do. I still do that. And I still write myself questions. That business of the yellow pad with the questions. I have this big one that says, "Where was Aimee Semple McPherson during those three weeks?" I still find that's really useful. You know

I'm not required by the world to say what really, honestly happened. I'm just required to say what I feel probably happened. What seems right to me.

LGB: Well, that sort of goes back to what you said about Lillian Hellman, that you weren't interested in her telling the literal truth.

MN: Right. Right. I mean, the "truth" clearly is a word that's been overrated. Truth is not just one thing at all. What two people could even agree's the truth is not. Even yourself, the experience that you've had, you will say, "Well, that's what happened." A month later or a year later, or five years later, you realize that that wasn't what happened at all. This other thing happened. Do you know what I mean? This idea of truth is very slippery. That's what I mean about this business of truth, the whole truth, and nothing but the truth. This is like patriarchal sun worship, kind of worship of the known. In fact, who on earth is capable of telling the truth, the whole truth, and nothing but the truth? Nobody. You what I mean? You don't even know what it is.

LGB: Yes.

MN: So why not say, "Here's what I think now is what happened then." It's all so subjective. We just do not live in a world of the known.

LGB: True.

MN: We live in a world of guesses and instincts, and coincidence and accidents, and that. We live in a constantly unfolding mystery. This is the good news. It's not a ride at Disneyland that we're on, where you know you can safely get off at the end, and you know that nothing will happen except what has been thought of to happen.

LGB: Hmmmm.

MN: All kind of randomness is one of the best things about the earth.

LGB: But I always think of you as a very positive writer in your work. You don't see us looking over the void, do you? You're not one of these Beckettians. You see the possibilities, don't you?

MN: Right. I see the possibilities instead of the doom. Again, because he looked over the abyss and couldn't see what was there, couldn't know what was there, he thought, "Well, it's empty." This is crazy. Again, this is a worship of the known. Only the known is valuable and useful. In fact, who knows what kinds of things are down in that abyss? Right?

LGB: There might just be some very good things down there.

MN: Oh, all kinds of good things, crawling up the side as you're looking. Right? About to get flung out at you.

LGB: I agree. Now, about that yellow legal pad, do you still use it? Have you thrown the word processor out?

MN: Oh, no, I still have it. I still have it. It's essential for communicating with stage managers.

LGB: (loud laugh) Hah!

MN: I still like both, you know. There's a legal pad in the pocket of my coat over there, along with a copy of the computer-generated script pages that we were talking about today. So those two things are very important to me. I still like, best of all, the feeling of my hand on the side of the paper. That's absolutely my favorite.

LGB: I do, too.

MN: Clearly, we can't do without word processors, but I think it's very important not to become enslaved by them so that you forget about this other sort of handwritten, handmade thing. It's very important to remember that writing is a craft; it's a way of making something by hand.

LGB: Physically.

MN: Right, that's the part that thrills me.

MN: That reminds me of where you talk about your father giving you the legal pads for Christmas, and how much that meant to you.

MN: Best present I ever had.

LGB: You still feel that way?

MN: Absolutely.

LGB: I could sit here all night and talk. This is so wonderful, Marsha. But I do want to wrap it up here. Just a couple of questions. When you went to Martha's Vineyard that day with Robert Brustein to talk with Lillian Hellman, in the article you wrote afterward you said that working in the theater is an act of faith and that it requires regular communion with those who are older in faith. You were referring to Hellman then. Now that she's gone, is there someone older in the faith for you? Someone in the theater that you can talk to? Even though you hadn't met Hellman, you had her writings—her memoirs.

MN: There are no women. Wendy [Wasserstein] and I are pretty much it. We're as old as you can get (laughing) in the theater.

LGB: (laughing) Well, there's a recent article that talks about the second tier, the new generation of women playwrights.

MN: Well, it's very good to know that they're there. In fact, what has happened is that I am now the sort of older generation in the theater. That's hard for me to believe, but Heidi

[Landesman] and I were saying the other day, "Well, we've really flown up now." You know that old Girl Scout saying, "Fly up." You know that Girl Scout saying? You're not Brownies. You're really *it*.

LGB: Yes. You're not a Brownie anymore, then?

MN: No, I'm not a Brownie anymore. After this *Red Shoes* experience, it's just been so difficult. There is a kind of pleasure in accepting that that's who I am now, and a kind of mystery about it. You know, who would've thought? But I know that's where I am. Now I have to manage to stay here because I think it's very important to keep the door open. If Wendy or I, or Tina [Howe], or any of the other people, should let the door close, then it's a problem because it's a very difficult door to get open again. So Wendy does what she does, Tina does what she does, I do what I do, so we're all out there. I don't mean to suggest that there are only four or five of us.

LGB: I know what you mean.

MN: But there aren't very many.

LGB: No, and there aren't that many women playwrights in the anthologies either.

MN: Right.

LGB: I think the university faculty have to start demanding more inclusion of women playwrights in these texts. We can't just do O'Neill, or Pinter, or Beckett, or Shaw. We have to expose our students to these possibilities. For years we only had Lorraine Hansberry and Lillian Hellman—well, Susan Glaspell, too. There were only two or three that you ever read when you were studying drama.

MN: Right, and I think that if you don't keep my memory from being erased, it will be. We have lots of history to show that this is true. I live because you, women like you, continue to insist that my work is important.

LGB: Well, this kind of goes back to the issue of sexism in theater. I wish we could work this out. I think I remember that you said that fifty percent of the producers need to be women. It's the same thing all over the country. It's not just in the theater. It's in the university, the people who have tenure. You know female professors are not in the majority. I think it's in all kinds of professions. What can we do about that? How can we make sure that we don't go back, that the doors don't close? Twenty years down the road when Katherine's in college, we don't want to be starting again. You know, like Charlotte Perkins Gilman was blasting the patriarchy around the turn of the century. What's the answer to that as far as the theater's concerned?

MN: Well, I think it's kind of easy to say it. The answer is that we all have to be aware that every moment we are in a battle for our survival, every single instant. We can't ever take it for granted that we will continue to have the positions that we have—that we will continue to be listened to or be allowed to speak or that we will be heard. It is *still* the case that since *'night, Mother* I have not had a play produced on Broadway in New York. Now, you would think that was inconceivable, that having won the Pulitzer Prize you would not. But, in fact, *Sarah and Abraham, Boone,* no one wants to do those plays.

LGB: But aren't they coming to New York?

MN: Both are supposed to, but I'm just enough of a realist to say that until we actually see them hanging the marquee. . . .

LGB: Is Cybill Shepherd going to play Sarah?

MN: She's going to play Sarah.

LGB: (giggles) I love it.

MN: She's very smart.

LGB: Yes, I know. I have a contingent from Ohio that wants to come see it. That's why I wanted to know.

MN: Good.

LGB: OK, one last question, Marsha? Can you say anything about *Red Shoes*, what you're currently working on?

MN: What I can say about *Red Shoes* is that it's been a real interesting journey in terms of the threat that was posed to me personally by this whole experience.

LGB: What do you mean threat?

MN: Well, they've basically been threatening to fire me since day one. I have just, so far, survived.

LGB: Well, Susan [Schulman] and the actress didn't. I read they were recently fired.

MN: Susan was fired. For a director to come into a cast that he didn't pick is very difficult.

LGB: I would imagine.

MN: So it's not surprising that of all the people that Susan cast, Stanley didn't want two of them. He should've done it earlier, however. He shouldn't continue to hold out for surprises—for people that he didn't think were right for the roles. But Susan and I had a view of the story that was more about the life of the ballet, that was about more people. However, when the decision was made by the producer that the production was going to pursue the vision of the film, not anything new, I felt that that was something I could do for a purpose that was my own, which was to make it very clear that a woman of great talent is in grave danger in this world. It was quite true in the twenties, and it is really true in the nineties. So this portrait of Victoria Paige that I have made here in this musical is for the purpose of demonstrating that we are not safe. She was not safe; we are not safe.

LGB: What do you mean by that?

MN: I mean that we need to be constantly on guard about the people who want to use us for their own purposes. I think the piece is also a lot about how quickly the creative force turns destructive.

LGB: Which creative force are you talking about?

MN: In Lermontov, he has this major element out of this girl. When it seems that she's not going to belong exclusively to him, he tries to destroy her. After you see it, we'll talk. There are so many scenes in this piece that we lived through in rehearsal. In that final scene where Lermontov and Julian are fighting over what Vicky will do and she's just standing there as though she were watching a tennis match, I mean this seems like a rather ludicrous scene. But in rehearsal that day, Stanley [Donen] and Laura [Lubovitch] were fighting over what Margaret [Illmann], who plays Vicky, is going to do . She's standing there as if it's an *exact* duplicate of the scene.

LGB: Well, I know I read where you had said it wasn't going to be an ending where she says, "OK now, which man shall I pick? Here I am, who do I go with?" I know you're not going to give away the ending, but this whole experience seems incredibly tense.

MN: It's just been hideous. It's been an environment of threat.

LGB: Not like *The Secret Garden* at all.

MN: No.

LGB: I have one last question before we call it quits. Do you think
      you'll ever write another play about a mother/daughter rela-
      tionship?

MN: I don't know. I think that being a mother and having a daugh-
      ter makes it a lot more complicated to write about.

LGB: Well, I'm thinking that maybe your viewpoint may change—
      that you'll have something different to share now that you
      have Katherine. When you wrote 'night, Mother you didn't
      have any children. Now you have a little girl. That's quite a
      different experience than having a little boy, don't you think?

MN: Yes, quite different. My goal is now to make the world safe
      for Katherine. This is hard to do. We'll just have to wait and
      see. I don't know what I'm going to write about. I think it's
      not even a very good idea for me to think about that because
      then I begin to watch myself work and watch myself think.

LGB: And that impedes the process?

MN: Yes. Yes. I still think it's very good to preserve the unknown
      even in my own mind, to have those folks in the back room
      up here (taps head) think about whatever they want.

LGB: I see. You know you told Lois Rosenthal [of Writer's Digest]
      you had this omen about not having all the time in the world.
      You said you had about ten plays in you. You've already writ-
      ten eight, so certainly you have more than ten, don't you
      think?

MN: I just don't know. I would love to think that. Sometimes I
      think about what it would be like to have a life like Brian
      [Friel, the playwright] lives. He lives in his house in Ireland.
      He has his little theater down the road, and he does a play
      every couple of years. That's his life. He isn't writing for the

movies; he isn't doing musicals. He's reading and drinking at pub and playing darts and walking across the moors—and whatever else that he does. That's not the life that I have. I fantasize about things like that. I think about what if I had grown up in the west. I'm really sad that I can't just live some of the lives I might have lived had I turned off in some of the directions I could have. But I like this life a lot. I'm absolutely crazy about it. If I thought I had to live without being a writer, I would be really upset. As much as I think it would've been fun to be a pediatrician in Sante Fe. . . .

LGB: (interrupting) No, No. I can't see you as a pediatrician. You know you said you had that pull between music and writing. This way you've been able to satisfy both those longings.

MN: Right. I have.

LGB: Marsha, I said that was my last question, and it was. It's been great talking to you in person. It's been a wonderful experience. Thank you.

MN: Thank you.

More with Marsha Norman

Linda Ginter Brown

Editor's Note When I informed Marsha Norman that I'd finished the casebook for Garland Publishing on her work, she asked if I would include her latest work, *Trudy Blue,* a play about a middle-aged playwright who experiences what can best be called mid-life angst. The play, which had not yet been mounted, was scheduled for its premier at Actor's Theatre in Louisville, the "birthing place" for many of Norman's pieces. I drove to Louisville for the premier and interviewed Norman the day after, a cold, rainy, depressing afternoon in late March 1995. Here is the resulting interview.

LGB: Well, when you and I talked a little over a year ago it was right before *Red Shoes* was opening so you had that experience that you went through; oh, and by the way one of my friends taped the KET special and mailed me the tape, so I was able to see you when you entered the Gershwin with your long gown.

MN: Oh, good!

LGB: Maybe this is comparing apples and oranges, so maybe it's not a fair question, but how are you feeling today, the day after *Trudy Blue* as opposed to how you were feeling the day after *Shoes?*

MN: Well, yes, it's wildly different. The *Red Shoes* was a disaster of unheralded proportions. It was painful every minute of the journey. It ended up being finally humiliating and, really, quite upsetting, not because of the nature of the reviews, but because what we ultimately had in *Red Shoes* was a show which would've run. After we had the "Code Blue," to save the patient, and we did, then he went home from the hospital and was killed by a train on the way home. Do you know what I mean?

LGB: Yes, I do. I could not believe how quickly they closed it. They really didn't give it a chance, did they? Did they just want to cut their losses?

MN: I suppose so, but I think it was embarassing to Marty Starver to have the piece be there, to know he had to take responsibility for what was there because he had *literally* forced everyone to do his bidding. I think he was just actually ashamed.

LGB: Yes.

MN: You know this is quite a different feeling from that. I love this play. I think the work in this play is quite wonderful, and I'm quite pleased with the voice and the whole approach to the task of writing for the theater that's here. I think it's a real departure for me.

LGB: Well, as I was sitting in the audience last night, I was so impressed with how well the jokes were done—and not overdone, you know? I can't think of the exact word I want, but it was really good writing. I was reading some of the preliminary publicity about it, about it being comic, and sexy, and funny—and I think it was all of those.

But let me ask you this. Sitting there last night I was thinking, when we last talked you had said, "We all do these plays, we do a marriage play, we do this kind of play, that kind of play." Is this Marsha Norman's mid-life crisis play?

MN: No, I don't think so. I don't think so at all—at least not in the traditional sense of the term "mid-life crisis." But you know, I was quite sick after *Red Shoes* last year.

LGB: No, I didn't know that. I do know that you told me you'd be working on the Aimee Semple McPherson piece, and we didn't discuss any of this going on. So it seemed new to me; I wondered if it were some kind of reaction to *Shoes*.

MN: Well, no. I think it was a reaction to being sick. Being sick was probably a reaction to *Red Shoes*.

LGB: All the stress?

MN: Yes. I became deathly, deathly ill, and I went to my doctor. He ordered me to go get x-rays and a CAT scan and an MRI. The results came back, and they said, "This is aggressive lung cancer, and you have two years to live."

LGB: Oh, my God! I didn't know that!

MN: Then he said, "I want you to go get a CAT scan and talk to Nate Serrif, who is this pulmonary surgeon. So I did that. Then this next doctor said to me, after a pretty long series of more tests, "Well, actually I don't know what it is. It may be aggressive lung cancer. It may not. Take this medication for two weeks, and then we'll see. I don't think we should biopsy it today."

So for two weeks I lived not only with this real debilitating sickness but also with a death sentence.

LGB: How horrible!

MN: It was also two weeks of, "Well, maybe you're gonna die." It absolutely changed my life forever. I decided I wanted to write about pleasure. I'd been thinking about it a lot. I realized when I was under the MRI that I didn't care—I wasn't nearly attached enough to life. And that I ought to try to get that way.

LGB: You were or were not?

MN: Were not.

LGB: So before this diagnosis, you didn't really feel you were attached that much to life. What do you mean by that?

MN: Well, by that I mean that when I was in the CAT scan, there were only two things that I really wanted to know the outcome of. (Pauses) You know, you have those moments when you think, "Oh, Lord, if I only want to know the answer to two things then, this is not enough, and I'd better see what's the matter."

LGB: What were the two things?

MN: The two things were: I would not get to see Angus, get to see what he looked like as a man, and I would not know the outcome of the Madeline project—which outcome I know. They fired me.

LGB: What was the Madeline project?

MN: Madeline movie.

LGB: Sort of in *The Secret Garden* vein?

MN: Yes, a children's work. So, the play's about that. But you know, it's not just about me. This piece is certainly not autobiographical in a restricted way. I mean, it's about looking at that question of happiness and saying, "Well, how happy do I have to be?"

LGB: Right, but you know in the KET production, or it might've been in one of the publicity reviews you're quoted as saying, and I'm paraphrasing here, "I'm going to write about myself. I'm darn good enough to write about. I'm not a boring person, and I think it'll be interesting to explore.

     Certainly, we've got Ginger/Marsha in some instances, wouldn't you agree?

MN: (emphatically) Oh, absolutely! Absolutely! I think the fact that

my friends and I have a lot in common means that whether the
husband is a fisherman or a diver, it's not all that different. But
what I think what we are all coming up against, what we all feel
is. . . Oh, well, Julie Krutcher talks about it as the big, "Huh?"

LGB: Well, what was it Peggy Lee said, "Is that all there is?" You
know, in that song a number of years ago? So we're in our
forties, fifties; this is pretty much it.

MN: Yes, so I think I'm quite unwilling to accept that, and I also
think that it seems to be very difficult for women to approach
pleasure as a goal. We don't ever see women doing this. The
women who do this are sort of. . . .

LGB: (continuing) They're the bad women!

MN: Yes, the bad women.

LGB: As my husband said last night at the play, "You know that
Trudy Blue is a slut." (laughing)

MN: Is that what he said?

LGB: Well, when she came out, you know? I told him, But, she's
the woman in the novel though; she's in this fantasy. He was
just reacting to the portrayal, you know. I just thought it was
funny that he said that.

MN: Yes, it is. I just wish I could listen to the conversations going
home from this play. It's a shame that I don't get to hear them.

LGB: I know I was talking to the man in the seat next to me last
night, and he liked it very much.

MN: Oh, the audience was crazy about it.

LGB: They were. They were. This one woman was insisting upon a
standing ovation; she was standing and kept clapping and

clapping. There really was a good response to it. And PLEASE, PLEASE, tell Ann Pitoniak—I didn't know she was in it before I came—her portrayal of the mother was just outstanding. Will you tell her for me?

MN: Yes, yes I will.

LGB: (voice rising) I thought, "My God, now I've got to do another Marsha Norman paper; we've got another mother/daughter deal here."

I saw a little bit, certainly not much, but I did see a little bit of Thelma and Jessie. Here's another mother/daughter. (pauses) I don't know what exactly I was experiencing, but (pauses again), sometimes, I didn't like Ginger.

MN: But when?

LGB: Well, frankly, I thought she was kind of selfish. You know she triumphs in the end. Here she is in her hot-tub out there in Montana, but it seemed to me, if we can just bring 'night, Mother in for a minute, that was a painful experience too. Jessie was having all of these bad experiences, and she wanted to opt out, "to get off the bus," as she said.

But it seemed to me that Jessie, even though she killed herself—and you and I agree that there is a triumph in that play, and it's a very positive ending—took more pains to care about Thelma's feelings. I was mulling this over as I sat in the theater last night. Jessie took a lot more time and made more effort to explain her decision. Can you talk a little bit more about Ginger? It seemed to me that she was determined. . . (trails off) Maybe I'm responding to the pleasure part; in my life experience, as with many women, I've been trained to nurture my family and put myself last. You were probably taught that little "JOY" verse at Bible school.

MN: (nods) Yes, yes.

LGB: Jesus first, others second, yourself last. You're always last as a woman. So you're taking care of your husband; you're taking care of your children. But it just seemed that (emphatically) nothing was enough for Ginger! On one hand I was feeling for her and trying to understand her thoughts. On the other hand, part of me thought she was really being selfish. Sometimes I didn't like her.

Remember what Sue said? "Do you have to be happy, too?" So is Ginger/Marsha saying, "Yeah, yeah dammit, I have to have happiness, too, besides being everything else that I am and having what I have. I have two wonderful children; I have Tim, and I have this wonderful career. But yeah, I want more. Is that what you're saying?

MN: (pauses). I don't know. I'll have to think about it. I think that I'm saying that the things that we've been taught will make us happy don't always end up making us happy. We, as women, I think, have been sold a real bill of goods about what a good life is. I think this version of the good life is based upon what the species needs us to do and what society needs us to do.

LGB: To keep going?

MN: Yes, it has very little to do with us as individuals. I think that once we know that, if that's where we want to live, that's fine. But I think that what I was concerned about is this idea that the needs of the society and the needs of the species are quite separate from your needs. You have to recognize that. It goes a long way toward explaining why you feel used. I think for women to feel victimized is probably the most natural thing in the world.

Yet, we *are* used by society—to calm the men down and take care of the children—you know, breed the children and take care of the children we breed.

LGB: We keep it all going. We juggle all the balls.

MN: We do. We keep it all going, and some people might want to say that that actually makes them happy, and it feels good, and it's a lot of fun. I'm just not able to say that.

LGB: OK.

MN: That does not mean that I do not love my children.

LGB: Sure.

MN: That doesn't mean anything other than just that we need to understand that we are not, so long as there is a particle of hormone left in the world, we are not free and independent creatures. We are part of a society that has its own needs. We will quite often feel victimized and quite often be exactly right about it. That's not to say men aren't victimized too.

LGB: Right.

MN: This is only the part that I know.

LGB: Yes, I've always felt that men were victims of patriarchy, too, in many respects.

MN: Right. You know what's really interesting is this work by Dorothy Dinnerstein.

LGB: Yes, *The Mermaid and the Minotaur.*

MN: Yes, you know she says there's a problem in everybody being raised by women. If people are raised by both men and women, then there would be a lot more opportunities to approach women as. . . .

LGB: Well, Nancy Chodorow says the same thing—that men need to participate more in the nurturing and the bringing up of the children. There has to be more of a partnership.

Can you talk a little more about the mother/daughter relationship in this play? Do Annie and Ginger love each other?
How do you feel about them as a mother and daughter?

MN: I think they love each other. I don't think they've ever gotten
     along. I don't think that they probably feel the kind of arbi-
     trariness that Jessie felt about Thelma. And yet, I don't think
     Ginger is really angry at her mother in the same way. I don't
     think that she's trying to escape from her.

LGB: Do you think it's just more a generation thing? You know,
     Ginger broke all the rules; she didn't listen.

MN: Ummm.

LGB: So you didn't think much about the mother/daughter rela-
     tionship in this play?

MN: No, I'm much more interested in—well, clearly this is mother
     as projection. This is mother as introjection. Here she is—
     she's dead, and she doesn't go away. She's there still judging
     and holding her standards. The line that has the central pur-
     pose/identifying thing is James' line where he says, "Ginny,
     the things in your mind are as real as anything else."

LGB: Right.

MN: This is what I was really trying to look at—the effects of
     trying to make a decision. What shall I do now? I realize that
     I'm unhappy. This sort of discussion begins to go on among
     all of the voices.

LGB: Right. The voices in your head.

MN: And this is simply a way of giving shape, a form to those voices.

LGB: OK. You know, I thought that Don was an interesting char-
     acter in the play, although the critic in the *Courier Journal*

didn't seem to think he was developed. I thought he was certainly developed enough.

MN: Well, yes. I think that what they're complaining about is that it wasn't about them.

LGB: (smiles) Probably so. Probably so. But you know, this relationship between Don and Ginger, I thought it was typical of all of our relationships with our husbands in many ways. Don't you think it's kind of a male/female communication thing? Have you read Deborah Tannen's book?

MN: I have.

LGB: We really don't hear. You know, she has the "ear problem," and that was a metaphor for the fact that we're not listening to one another. We may be talking to one another, but we're not hearing what the other one is saying. Was that where you were coming from in developing the character of Don? How do you feel about Don as a character? Is he kind of an "everyhusband"? Or most husbands?

MN: (reflects) I don't know. He's certainly every husband I've had.

LGB: Even the present one?

MN: Yes, sure. And every husband I know of among my friends. But this is what I think. I'm not willing to live in a situation where there is a language barrier so extreme that it begins to be treated as a physical symptom. "Oh, well, she's sick." No, you're just not listening.

And I think that for too long, there's been real complacence about relationships—like it was good to have one, regardless of what it was.

LGB: Right. So as long as you get a husband, you're somehow legitimized.

MN: Yes. See, I think this is all part of that same bill of goods. Get the husband. (indignantly) This has nothing to do with company, conversation, pleasure, enjoyment, growth—anything. This has to do with making children.

LGB: Or the old story of my generation at least, it legitimizes you as a woman. There's something wrong with you if you can't get a husband, God forbid.

MN: Well, I would find that so offensive.

LGB: Oh, I would, too, now, but I can remember my cousin—this seems ludicrous to me now—but she was 24, and the whole family was worried that she wasn't going to be able to get a husband and get married. Actually, it *is* ludicrous! But I think we've improved, and we've come some distance, anyway.

MN: Um, hum.

LGB: Well, back to Don. I really felt for him in that scene before she leaves. It seemed to me that they were really trying to communicate and still weren't getting through to each other. He says, "Don't try to tell me how I feel. I know whether or not I love you." And she says, "Well, if I don't feel it, then it isn't so." Or something to that effect.

MN: Right.

LGB: Can you talk about that scene a little bit? Because I felt for both of them there. They clearly still were not getting through to one another.

MN: Yelling didn't help.

LGB: Right, but it seemed to me that he was hurting, too. I thought the actor brought that out really well.

MN: Yes. Well, I don't know how it is that you resolve this issue.

It's not really my business to suggest, you know. This is what therapists are for. I really dare to say this central problem exists between men and women. Men assume that if they've ever said, "I love you," that they still love you.

LGB: That's enough.

MN: This is just not the case. This is why relationships fall apart, ebb away. People mistakenly assume that the other person is some kind of "just different by gender" version of them.

LGB: And that it can't ever be any different, so you just might as well accept it.

MN: Right.

LGB: OK, what would you say about the dialogue in the play about the bottomless pit? You and I talked about the void last time. I remember quite well that you were very positive that we might be looking into the void, and there might be something wonderful down there. We don't know.

MN: Yes.

LGB: But it seems to me, Marsha, that you've looked in this past year, and, perhaps, you've seen something that wasn't so wonderful. Could you talk a bit about that?

MN: (pauses) Well. . .

LGB: Or is it just maybe not so wonderful for these two characters? I think that conversation is between Sue and Ginger, if I remember correctly. But they're talking about the bottomless pit.

MN: (firmly) No, it's when she's writing. She's just had the conversation with Don, and she goes back to the typewriter, and says, "Don turned away and . . .

LGB: Oh, right. Right.

MN: . . . fell into the bottomless pit."

LGB: (laughing) And then she chuckles to herself as she types that into the laptop.

MN: Right. That's about, you know, a level of barely covered violence. I think this is exactly the point where most marriages end. Whether they actually get divorced or not, that's a different story. But the idea of marriage ends here where two people obviously feel some kind of love for each other but cannot communicate that consistently enough to make the other person believe it. So it becomes empty.

And (emphatically), I think Ginger's point is right. You shouldn't live and sleep and celebrate Christmas with people you don't love.

LGB: But I mean, we all go through . . . I've been married 34 years now. Some of it's been up; some of it's been down. But we're still hanging together. Don't you think any relationship has these ups and downs?

MN: They do, but I just think that to feel that what you have to do is stay. . . .

LGB: When you think you've exhausted all the possibilities?

MN: Yes. When you allow yourself to go, you can go. That's exactly the same sort of *'night, Mother* message.

LGB: When I've had enough, I've had enough.

MN: When you want to get off the bus, you can get off. There is no reason to pour your entire life down the drain. I think that because this thought is so contrary to our instruction, it's hard for us to hear it. My mother, for example, felt abso-

lutely that if she gave up her life for us, that we would someday repay her by coming back and all being there together
with our grandkids. We'd all be this happy band.

LGB: (incredulous) Did she actually verbalize that to you?

MN: No. You know what happened was, we couldn't stand to be
around each other because she had really driven big wedges
between us all, and when she died it was the first time in
twenty years that all four of us had been in the same room.

LGB: Really? Is that because all of you took such different paths in
life, or that you just simply didn't want to be around each
other?

MN: Well, we certainly weren't that way as kids. (It's apparent that
this line of questioning is finished.)

LGB: OK, before we call it quits, I'd like to get some of your views
about the scene with the salesman and the lie detector.

MN: Yes.

LGB: It's not just Ginger's friends who are lying to her, but isn't she
lying to herself?

MN: (emphatically) Oh, absolutely! Absolutely! I had written a
scene where she calls back home, and she speaks to Ginger.
So Trudy calls Ginger to try and find out if Ginger is lying.
But it was just too tough. It was hard for the audience to get
their minds around the idea of what was happening.

I think the lie detector scene was about how do I know I'm
not being lied to. I'm basing my life on these decisions, and
I'm making my decisions on these lies I've been told. I think
this is a dangerous thing.

LGB: Um, hum.

MN: She wins. she wins. . . .

LGB: Because she's honest with herself. Aren't you saying here, though, when it comes right down to it, we only have ourselves?

MN: That's right.

LGB: And even though that might be scary, that's what we have to deal with.

MN: I think that's exactly it.

LGB: Well, what about the significance of the moon in the last scene, where she's in the hot tub?

MN: How did you feel about that scene?

LGB: Well, I *loved* that scene! Especially from the technical standpoint. When I first read the play, I wondered how they would stage it. I thought they did a brilliant job of it.

You know, when my husband and I were discussing this scene, he said, "Well, there you go. Right there. That's the rebirth of Ginger—the water. . . ."

MN: Exactly.

LGB: (laughing) Maybe I should have my husband in here interviewing you.

MN: No, that's exactly what it is—rebirth.

LGB: OK then. What about the moon?

MN: Well, I think that what she has discovered about happiness is that happiness as it's defined in the new life, is going to be different. It's going to be a "not constant," "not definable," "not always around, but always coming back."

LGB: But it's going to be on Ginger's terms.

MN: Yes. And I think that she's become unafraid to make mistakes, and I think that this is critical, you know? There are real clues to obtaining your freedom. It's a kind of guide.

LGB: What are some of the clues to obtaining your freedom?

MN: Obviously, there's the "stop lying to yourself." Stop inviting other people to lie to you. Don't try to obey any codes of any kind because they're ultimately restrictive.

LGB: All codes?

MN: Well, no. The codes like "the code of perfect," for example. When she says, "There's no such thing as perfect."

LGB: Oh, to James.

MN: No, she says it to Annie, the mother.

LGB: But wasn't there something there with James?

MN: Oh, yes. (smiling) That's when he says he's perfect, and that's when we find out that he's not real.

LGB: Right. He's only in her mind. (pausing) Well, I really can't imagine that all of this came forward from your mind in such a short time.

MN: I wrote most of it from September until now.

LGB: Did you really? Amazing.

MN: I wrote three scenes in March, April, and May. Then over the summer I was just working on Aimee full time. Then, really, between October and now, I wrote the rest of it.

LGB: That's amazing. I really don't want to pry here; that's not my intention, but since you brought up the issue of your health earlier, was that almost similiar to the situation where you wrote 'night, Mother in such a short time?

You remember. You went to New York. Nobody was calling you for lunch, and you said, "By God, I'm going to write this play, and I'm going to do it exactly the way I want. I don't care if anybody ever sees it. This is what I'm going to do." Was this kind of a similiar situation?

MN: Yes. exactly. I'm going to sit down and write this and say all the things I'm not supposed to say. I'm going to tell about how marriage rarely makes one happy, that basically we outgrow our men and then have to figure out what the hell to do.

We've been so schooled in our lack of entitlement to pleasure that we are living half lives.

LGB: But you're not necessarily just talking about sexual pleasure, are you?

MN: No. No. Not at all. I'm talking about everything that there is. You know two years ago, I woke up one morning. I was talking to Kate Medina on the phone and I said, "Oh, every morning when I wake up I think, "Oh, good, only 10 1/2 more hours, and then they'll all be asleep again, and I can read."

LGB: You've got to be kidding! Why? Because you feel you have to go in and sit in front of your word processor and write? Or just your life? I mean, I really find that hard to believe.

MN: No, this is how I feel.

LGB: Why?

MN: Because at that moment I was sort of in a state of feeling "anhedonic." Is that the phrase? I was really feeling that pleasure had all but evaporated from my life.

LGB: You mean because of all your responsibilities with the children, your husband, your writing career? Those kinds of things?

MN: (nods) Yes.

LGB: So you had these responsibilities where you had to check in every day, and maybe you would like just to go off and chuck it for a while.

MN: Right. Exactly.

LGB: But you can do that, can't you?

MN: Well, I can do that now, but at that time I was not allowing myself to do that. At that time, I was living a perfect life.

LGB: So you were being the perfect writer/mother/wife—doing it all.

MN: Right.

LGB: Well, that's a bag of goods we've all been sold. I don't think we can have it all. Do you?

MN: No. I think, well, for example in the intervening time, with this play coming in, Tim took the kids to Aspen with his mother and father and the nanny and did that vacation by himself with them. I've stayed down here a lot more than I normally would have. I usually would rush back up.

So I'm feeling that there is a point where this mother/artist balance begins to swing the other way. For me, that's certainly what's happening.

LGB: So we want more of the artist part of our lives. Well, Tim's an artist, isn't he?

MN: Yes. He understands.

LGB: He's much more understanding than, say, the character, Don, in the play.

MN: Oh, absolutely. (smiling) Don is much more like other friends' husbands.

LGB: (laughing) I understand. OK, so back to what we were discussing about your health and the impetus for this play. You finally found out that it wasn't lung cancer.

MN: Yes, it was pneumonia. I went in, got a new x-ray, and found out that it was gone. But it was very frightening. I stopped smoking, got a lot of hynopsis, and acupuncture.

LGB: Do you feel that acupuncture helps?

MN: The only thing that helped me.

LGB: Really. I had a similiar experience about three years ago. Thankfully, it turned out to be a misdiagnosis, but it puts everything in perspective and forces you to ask yourself, "What's really important here? What do I really want if I'm going to check out of here fairly soon? What do I need to take care of?"

I think it's just about time to wrap this up, Marsha, but before we do, could we just talk a little bit more about the moon motif in the play?

MN: One of the problems about this whole question of the happily ever after thing is that happily ever indicates some kind of stasis—that you would arrive at some place where you were happy and you would never be unhappy again. You would be about the same level of happy every day, you know? Sort of like getting to your ideal weight.

LGB: (laughs) Yeah, right.

MN: We all know that with ideal weight you get there, and then it goes up and then it goes down; it's more like a mean rather than anything that's true of any given moment. I think that's what I ended up feeling about all of these ideas about pleasure and happiness. There wasn't some kind of cure-all; there wasn't a prescription. There wasn't a definition that you could say, "When I have a million dollars in the bank, and homes on both coasts, and have the kids through college, and I win the Pulitzer Prize again, then I will be happy." That's not how it works. That's not what it is.

I really wanted to look at that. Certainly, for Ginger, she needed to see, feel, and taste her personal freedom. Now what she does from here, we don't know.

LGB: But she might go back.

MN: She might go back. But what she absolutely had to know was that she was not in any kind of jail—that life was not a jail.

LGB: So she had to know that she could exercise her options. She might go back to Don; she might not.

MN: Right. And she has her kids with her. I think she did the undoable, she's thought the unthinkable thought—that you could actually go to a place where you were deeply happy. I think there's a widespread fear of this in our culture. That's when you really begin to get into trouble—when you begin to think about what will make you happy. I think that this is so so wrong.

People ought to think about their happiness more and more. As it is, it's a kind of non-subject. It's like death. They don't think about death, and they don't think about being happy either. Well, this is major denial.

LGB: Okay, but wait a minute. I agree with you, but this business about living happily ever after, that's the last line of a fairy tale!

MN: No, I'm saying that we don't want to live happily ever after. That's what I'm trying to throw out that idea in favor of another notion of happiness. Instead of being like the air, which is around you all the time, it's more like the moon which comes and goes. It's a startling object, a kind of strange, celestial force. Sometimes you feel it; sometimes you don't.

LGB: But you don't have to beat yourself up looking for it. Just because maybe a species is in charge.

MN: But no. What I think you can't do is be afraid of it, either. You can't be like that's the road to perdition. I think this is what we have been told—all for the purpose of keeping us in line as women. Don't go looking for happiness.

LGB: But that's part of our puritanical heritage, as well as our religious heritage. You know, God forbid that we should be happy.

MN: Self-sacrifice, all these other things are put above happiness. You know what I think, if we don't know anything about our own happiness, we can't begin to contribute to anyone else's. We don't know anything about it. It's just like the death thing. Because we never talk about death, we never know what to say to somebody when someone they love has died.

LGB: That's true.

MN: I think that our lack of familiarity in this whole subject of happiness is just obscene. What are we doing here? Are we trying to work ourselves to death, fill up the time? People adopt these systems.

LGB: Career goals and such.

MN: Yes, strategies. Strategies for living. What I feel is is that if you've not had that physical sensation of happiness, if you don't know what you enjoy and you don't do a lot of it, then you've missed the point.

LGB: Well, what makes Marsha Norman happy?

MN: Well, I'm in this process. I like to read. I like to drive this convertible. I like hot water.

LGB: What kind of convertible do you have?

MN: It's my friend's Miata.

LGB: Red?

MN: White. I like making up poems with children. I love conversation at a real high level. I like encountering people who have passion for things. I love relationships that develop over a long period of time with real smart women. You know, there are lots of things, but you only begin to recognize those things when you pull away this artificially painted-on "happily ever after" idea.

When you say, "Okay, I realize that there are certain things that have gone from my marriage. Is there enough there to keep me there? If there is, where else am I going to find this happiness? Am I going to find it in the garden?" I think there's a certain sensitivity to our own happiness. It's like when you're sick, and you need to sleep. I think there's a whole society of people who don't know what makes them happy. So it's easy for Madison Avenue or the movies or T.V. to come in and say, "I'll take care of that. I'll make you happy. Just spray this on your hair. Wear these shoes." People have no idea.

It may be changing. I just had lunch with Bill Samuels, who owns Maker's Mark. This is the thing that people just don't do—decide there's someone they'd like to meet and track them down and meet them.

LGB: Is that what you decided? That you wanted to meet Bill Samuels?

MN: Yes.

LGB: Why?

MN: I think Maker's Mark is an extraordinary bourbon. It's my favorite thing to drink. I had heard a lot of stories about him that I found real intriguing. You know, kind of a rocket scientist type—eccentric. I thought he was great.

You know as long as you are willing to let your pleasures be dictated by consumer products, then you're just sunk. My therapist says that in her practice, sex became almost non-existent. People seemed to lose interest in it. She said it was because it was free. It didn't cost them anything—in marriage at least. So it was of no value.

LGB: OK, well, Ginger's taking a look inside herself and being truthful, and it costs her something. At least at that point, it costs her relationship with Don. We don't know if they'll go back together or not. She summons that strength, and she does say, "Okay, I'm going off here. I'm going to pursue this and see where it takes me."

MN I'm just asking, "What does it mean when so many people would like not to be in their marriages? So many people are living in marriages that are a lie. Why is that?" I grew up in one of those marriages.

LGB: You mean your mother and father?

MN: Absolutely! They had a deal, they had an arrangement. Not that either one of them was out doing anything, but just that they didn't have any contact with each other. I think we're raising generations of kids that don't know anything about contact—that don't get it. They don't see it. They see parental energy. They don't see male/female energy. It's really troubling to me—this lack of real contact. That's what I want. That's the pleasure in my life.

LGB: That's really at a spiritual level that you're talking about. It's not things. It's not pursuit of career. It's relationships.

MN: It's kind of a weaving of the fabric of love. I feel like I'm just kind of a shuttle (laughs).

LGB: (laughing) Maybe they'll take you in at Berea and have you do workshops.

MN: Wouldn't that be nice? I could eat spoonbread to my heart's content.

LGB: Gosh, yes. Well, this has been fun, Marsha. I love *Trudy Blue*. Do you think it has a chance of going to New York?

MN: Yes, oh, yes.

LGB: Good, I'll watch for it. Thanks again for talking to me.

MN: Thank you.

A Marsha Norman Bibliography

Robert Conklin

Primary Bibliography of Works of Marsha Norman

Plays

Getting Out. In *The Best Plays of 1978–1979.* Abridged. Edited by Otis L. Guernsey. New York: Dodd, Mead, 1979; Garden City, N.Y.: Doubleday, 1979; New York: Dramatists Play Service, 1979; New York: Avon Books, 1980; in *Four Plays.* New York: Theatre Communications Group, 1988. 1–56.

'night, Mother. In *The Best Plays of 1982–1983.* Abridged. Edited by Otis L. Guernsey. New York: Dodd, Mead, 1983; New York: Dramatists Play Service, 1983; New York: Hill and Wang, 1983; London: Faber, 1984.

Third and Oak: The Laundromat. New York: Dramatists Play Service, 1980; in *Four Plays.* New York: Theatre Communications Group, 1988. 60–81.

Third and Oak: The Pool Hall. New York: Dramatists Play Service, 1985.

Traveler in the Dark. In *Four Plays.* New York: Theatre Communications Group, 1988.

The Secret Garden. New York: Theatre Communications Group, 1992.

Performances

Getting Out. Louisville, Kentucky, The Actors Theatre of Louisville, 1977; Los Angeles, Mark Taper Forum, 1978; New York, Phoenix Theatre, 1978; London, 1988.

Third and Oak: The Laundromat. Louisville, Kentucky, The Actors Theatre of Louisville, 1978.

Third and Oak: The Pool Hall. Louisville, Kentucky, The Actors Theatre of Louisville, 1978.

Circus Valentine in *Holidays.* Louisville, Kentucky, The Actors Theatre of Louisville, 1979.

The Holdup. San Francisco, The American Conservatory Theatre, 1983.

'night, Mother. Cambridge, Massachusetts, The American Repertory Theatre, 1983; New York, John Golden Theatre, 1983; London, Hampstead Theatre, 1985.

Traveler in the Dark. Cambridge, Massachusetts, The American Repertory Theatre, 1984; revised version, Los Angeles, Mark Taper Forum, 1985; Louisville, The Actors Theatre of Louisville, 1985; New York, York Theater Company, 1990.

Sarah and Abraham. Louisville, Kentucky, The Actors Theatre of Louisville, 1988.

The Secret Garden. Norfolk, Virginia, Virginia Stage Company, 1990; New York, Saint James Theater, 1991.

D. Boone. Louisville, Kentucky, The Actors Theatre of Louisville, 1992.

Red Shoes. New York, Gershwin Theater, 1993.

Trudy Blue. Louisville, Kentucky, The Actors Theatre of Louisville, 1995.

Interviews

Beard, Sherilyn. "An Interview With Marsha Norman." *Southern California Anthology* 3 (1985): 11–17.

Betsko, Kathleen, and Rachel Koenig. *Interviews with Contemporary Women Playwrights.* New York: Beech Tree Books, 1987.

Brustein, Robert. "Conversations with . . . Marsha Norman." *Dramatists Guild Quarterly* 21 (September 1984): 9–21. Reprinted in Otis Guernsey, ed., *Broadway Song and Story.* New York: Dodd, Mead, 1985.

Guernsey, Otis R. "Five Dramatists Discuss the Value of Criticism." *Dramatists Guild Quarterly* 21 (March 1984): 11–25. Reprinted in Otis Guernsey, ed., *Broadway Song and Story.* New York: Dodd, Mead, 1985.

Selected Articles and Novel

"Articles of Faith: A Conversation with Lillian Hellman." *American Theatre* 1 (May 1984): 10–15.

The Fortune Teller. New York: Random House, 1987; London: Collins, 1988.

"How Can One Man Do So Much? And Look So Good? A Meditation on a Mystery." *Vogue* (February 1984): 356–358.

"Ten Golden Rules for Playwrights." *Writer* (September 1985): 13, 45.

"Why Do We Need New Plays? And Other Difficult Questions." *Dramatists Guild Quarterly* 24 (Winter 1987): 18, 31–33.

Television

In Trouble at Fifteen. Skag series, 1980.

It's the Willingness. Visions series, 1978.

Annotated Bibliography of Critical Works

The following bibliography of critical works of Marsha Norman's plays includes entries found to June 1, 1993, in *MLA International Bibliography*; "Modern Drama Studies: An Annual Bibliography" in *Modern Drama*; *Annual Bibliography of English Language and Literature*; "Marsha Norman: A Classified Bibliography" by Irmgard H. Wolfe in *Studies in American Drama: 1945–Present* 3 (1988): 148–175; and "Marsha Norman," by Irmgard H. Wolfe, in Philip C. Kolin, ed., *American Playwrights Since 1945: A Guide to Scholarship, Criticism, and Performance* (New York: Greenwood Press, 1989), 339–348. Linda L. Hubert also discusses a selected number of reviews and critical articles in a bibliographical essay, "Marsha Norman," in Matthew C. Roudane, ed., *American Dramatists* (Detroit: Gale, 1989), 271–287. Although dissertations and biographical articles are listed, only essays and chapters appearing in scholarly journals and books are annotated. Each annotation summarizes rather than evaluates the chief critical argument.

Bigsby, C.W.E. "Women's Theatre." In *A Critical Introduction to Twentieth Century American Drama: Beyond Broadway.* Vol. 3. Cambridge, England: Cambridge UP, 1985. 420–440.
In his history of women's theater, set in the context of the American women's movement of the 1960s and 1970s, Bigsby calls attention to *'night, Mother*, the Broadway production of which initiated a debate concerning the status of women's drama within the male theater establishment. Bigsby finds it interesting that a debate of this nature would surface in the 1980s, a debate focusing on the role of the woman dramatist, the problem of "male praise" of plays by women, and feminist suspicion of commercial success and "individual achievement." Yet he recognizes that "women have found it difficult to create sufficient space within the American theatre for their own concerns."

Browder, Sally. "'I Thought You Were Mine': Marsha Norman's *'night, Mother*." In *Mother Puzzles: Daughters and Mothers in Contemporary American Literature.* Edited by Mickey Pearlman. New York: Greenwood Press, 1989. 109–113.
Browder's discussion of the mother-daughter conflict in *'night, Mother* is informed by Nancy Chodorow's theory of "early socialization experience of females," a theory suggesting that daughters experience more difficulty than sons in separating themselves from their mothers. Jessie experiences a "tragic realization" of her failure to achieve an identity apart from the role initially provided her by her mother, and her suicide becomes an extreme measure of drawing "the boundaries between mother and daughter." This avenue of analysis excuses Thelma's role in Jessie's suicide: "If Thelma is at fault, it is

only in believing she could provide everything for this daughter, that
she alone could be enough."

Brown, Janet. "*Getting Out/'night, Mother.*" In *Taking Center
    Stage: Feminism in Contemporary U.S. Drama*. Metuchen, NJ:
    Scarecrow, 1991. 60–77.
Brown discusses *Getting Out* and *'night, Mother* as feminist plays
that emphasize the issues of autonomy and of connection, the ways
in which each protagonist must assert her independence and define
her boundaries while establishing a caring relationship with significant others. Because Arlene and Jessie "struggle within the patriarchal society to define themselves as autonomous beings," each play
"can rightly be termed an example of feminist drama." More specifically, Brown examines the way Arlene learns to assert herself through
speech, the relationship of each protagonist to "domestic interior
settings redolent of women's material culture," and psychological
concepts of self-division and separation from the mother.

Brown, Linda Ginter. "Toward a More Cohesive Self: Women in the
    Works of Lillian Hellman and Marsha Norman." Ph.D. diss.,
    Ohio State University, 1991.

Burkman, Katherine H. "The Demeter Myth and Doubling in
    Marsha Norman's *'night, Mother.*" In *Modern American
    Drama: The Female Canon*. Edited by June Schlueter.
    Rutherford, N.J.: Fairleigh Dickinson UP, 1990. 254–263.
Drawing upon Otto Rank's conception of doubling and Jung's and
Kerenyi's interpretations of the Demeter-Kore myth, Burkman identifies "rhythms and resonance" of that myth unforeseen by Norman.
Burkman views Thelma as a modern Demeter figure "trying to res-
cue her child from death" and Jessie as part Kore (Persephone), "who
feels used or raped," and also part Demeter, who "has lost the zest
for life." She demonstrates a unity between mother and daughter
prefigured by the mythical oneness of Demeter and Kore in order to
show that the play is not only about loss but renewal, Mama's "quick-
ened sense of life" through Jessie's suicide.

Carlson, Susan L. "Women in Comedy: Problem, Promise, Para-
    dox." In *Drama, Sex and Politics: Themes in Drama*. Vol. 7.
    Edited by James Redmond. Cambridge, England: Cambridge
    UP, 1985. 159–171.
"Is comedy sexist?" Carlson asks, and looks to W. Somerset
Maugham's *The Constant Wife* for her answer. In traditional comedy,
women characters are caught in a paradox. Although comedy prom-
ises them equality with men, comedy's happy ending returns them to
their traditional roles. Carlson looks briefly at Gems' *Piaf* and Norman's

Getting Out as examples of feminist dramas seeking replacement forms that attempt "to relegate to the past the assumptions and structures that stymie the promise of comedies like *The Constant Wife*." Her analysis of *Getting Out* is brief but suggests a method of analyzing comic structures and women characters in Norman's plays in terms of a feminist theater.

Chinoy, Helen Krich. "Here Are the Women Playwrights." In *Women in American Theatre*. 2nd ed. Edited by Helen Krich Chinoy and Linda Walsh Jenkins. New York: Theatre Communications Group, 1988. 341–353.

Drawing upon a number of quotations by contemporary American women playwrights, Chinoy discusses a variety of issues that women dramatists in the 1970s and early 1980s have faced, issues such as the usefulness of the label "woman playwright," the negative influence of male critics, and the difficulty of producing work in male-dominated mainstream theaters. She also addresses the challenge of beginning a career as a playwright, the importance of women role models in the theater, the problem of a "female aesthetic," and the degree to which plays by women should be feminist or political. She briefly quotes Marsha Norman's view on "the importance of the female character" in women's drama.

Cline, Gretchen Sarah. "The Psychodrama of the 'Dysfunctional' Family: Desire, Subjectivity, and Regression in Twentieth-Century American Drama." Ph.D. diss. Ohio State University, 1991.

Demastes, William W. "New Voices Using New Realism: Fuller, Henley, and Norman." In *Beyond Naturalism: A New Realism in American Theatre*. New York: Greenwood Press, 1988. 125–154.

As Norman attempts in *'night, Mother* to give voice to the marginally voiceless, she is subject to the criticism that her play is unrealistic because she alters the speech of her protagonists to suit her artistic ends. Yet Norman employs a "modified" or "new realism" to provide access to "under-represented elements of our society." Instead of presenting a naturalistic transcription of middle-class voices, Norman conveys the "dignity" of Thelma and Jessie "by fusing the realistic . . . rhythms of common speech with the heightened thought that she wishes to introduce."

Dolan, Jill. "Feminism and the Canon: The Question of Universality." In *The Feminist Spectator as Critic*. Ann Arbor: UMI, 1988. 19–40.

Using *'night, Mother* as a case study, Dolan assesses the various ways the male-dominated theater establishment, including its male reviewers and critics, shapes the audience's reception of a play by a woman. She questions whether *'night, Mother* is mainly a "contender for membership in the canon because it so closely follows the male precedent the canon has already set." Whereas Norman's aim was a "transcendent universality," the Broadway production of the play allowed a majority of male critics to categorize it as domestic melodrama. Dolan herself considers *'night, Mother* as "typical of liberal and cultural feminist drama" and demonstrates how the liberal feminist press ironically defused Norman's imposition on the male theatrical sphere by highlighting the woman rather than the play. In essence, Dolan's discussion reveals the gender issues that surface as "women playwrights continue to assert their voices in the traditional male forum."

Erben, Rudolph. "The Western Holdup Play: The Pilgrimage Continues." *Western American Literature* 23 (1989): 311–322.
Erben uses the title of Norman's play *The Holdup* to designate a new genre: "The western holdup play presents the American West in dramatic tension" as "the old and the new West meet," usually in an isolated way station of the rural southwest. He argues that *The Holdup* "combines all the characteristics" of earlier plays constituting the genre, namely, Sherwood's *Petrified Forest*, Inge's *Bus Stop*, Medoff's *When You Comin' Back, Red Ryder?* and Lanford Wilson's *Angels Fall*. With an old outlaw and a would-be gunslinger symbolizing the dying frontier, and a woman hotel owner and an educated youth representing the dynamic present of the West, Norman's play, like the others, "recalls the West's formative frontier period in a post-frontier setting," dramatizing its transformation.

Forman, Robert J. "Marsha Norman." *Critical Survey of Drama: Supplement.* Edited by Frank N. Magill. Pasadena, CA: Salem, 1987. 288–293.

Forte, Jeanie. "Realism, Narrative, and the Feminist Playwright: A Problem of Reception." *Modern Drama* 32 (1989): 115–127.
Forte questions whether the dramatic form of classic realism, its narrative animated by Oedipal desire toward closure, would be "useful for feminists interested in the subversion of a patriarchal social structure." In comparison with more subversive or plural texts such as Carolyn Meyer's *Dos Lesbos* and Adrienne Kennedy's *The Owl Answers*, *'night, Mother* is an example of a "realist text," whose cathartic closure caters to the demands of a patriarchal playwriting practice. Yet in terms of an incipient feminist theory of reception, *'night, Mother*'s impact on its audience is subversive, challenging "on some material level the reality of male power."

Greiff, Louis K. "Fathers, Daughters, and Spiritual Sisters: Marsha
    Norman's 'night, Mother and Tennessee Williams's The Glass
    Menagerie." Text and Performance Quarterly 9 (1989): 224–
    228.
Jessie Cates and Laura Wingfield are viewed as "sisters in disguise."
Realizing he is risking a patrocentric reading, Greiff builds his comparison on the influence of the absent father on each daughter in
'night, Mother and The Glass Menagerie. Each father is represented
as an escapist, while both "Laura and Jessie prove to be faithful daughters who keep alive their fathers' memory." Whereas Laura's imagi-
native escapism, modeled on her father's, leads to a confrontation
with reality, Jessie's unhappiness with reality leads to her "artful or-
chestration of her own death," a creative act allowing Jessie to reunite with her father, "the informing figure of her imagination." What
these parallels convey is "a creative kinship between Tennessee Williams and Marsha Norman."

Harriott, Esther. "Marsha Norman: Getting Out." In American
    Voices: Five Contemporary Playwrights in Essays and Inter-
    views. Jefferson, NC: McFarland, 1988. 129–147.
Harriott cites as Norman's chief concern characters "on the verge of
cutting ties" and suggests what drives Norman's characters is "their
passion . . . to escape from situations in which they feel trapped,"
primarily situations defined by the parent-child relationship. She focuses at length on four plays, praising "the economy of language"
and humor of Getting Out, the "pungent and authentic dialogue" of
The Laundromat, and the "complex pattern of relationships and emotions, actions and reactions" of 'night, Mother. In contrast to these
plays' strengths of characterization and language is the dramatic
weakness of Traveler in the Dark, a play that stresses philosophy
over human interaction: "The argument—faith versus reason—comes
first, and the characters dramatize it. The result is less a drama than
a debate."

Hart, Lynda. "Doing Time: Hunger for Power in Marsha Norman's
    Plays." Southern Quarterly 25, no.3 (1987): 67–79.
Hart extensively analyzes the way hunger operates as a metaphor in
Getting Out and 'night, Mother. She investigates the issue of food as
a source of conflict in the mother-daughter relationship and examines how hunger plays an essential role in each protagonist's struggle
for autonomy. Arlene's "figurative starvation" represents a "hunger
for power, freedom and control" as she strives for "sovereignty over
her body." Like Arlene, Jessie "rejects food and yearns for
nurturance"; her "hunger for honest dialogue and truth about her
past must be satisfied." In addition, Hart relates Arlie/Arlene's split
self to the issue of women's eating disorders and connects each

protagonist's quest to a feminist paradigm of growth, from "self-negation," through spiritual "awakening," to an "affirmation through community." Arlie/Arlene moves successfully through each phase, but Jessie is unable to see beyond her "confrontation with non-being."

Herman, William. "Marsha Norman." In *Understanding Contemporary American Drama*. Columbia: U of South Carolina P, 1987. 246–249.

Herman briefly discusses *Getting Out* and *'night, Mother* in a section devoted to "other voices" of the American theater from 1964 to 1984, including those of Jack Gelber, Amiri Baraka, Arthur Kopit, Adrienne Kennedy, and Jean-Claude Van Itallie. He suggests that *'night, Mother* dramatizes themes "ancillary" to those of *Getting Out*. He also postulates an affinity of Norman's "blue-collar world" with the "fictional worlds of Bobbie Ann Mason, Jayne Anne Phillips, and Raymond Carver."

Kachur, Barbara. "Women Playwrights on Broadway: Henley, Howe, Norman and Wasserstein." In *Contemporary American Theatre*. Edited by Bruce King. Basingstoke, England: Macmillan, 1991. 15–39.

Kachur attempts to free critical discussion of the work of commercially successful women playwrights from the double bind of male critics who tend to fault it "for a lack of universal vision" and feminist critics who find that the mainstream "forum precludes deployment of the more preferred subversive modes and themes found in contemporary experimental drama and performance art by women." By highlighting the "dramaturgical and thematic variety" within the work of four contemporary women dramatists, she also encourages a break from "the assumption that women's plays are identical thematically . . . and that women playwrights are a segregated group." She focuses on *Getting Out, Third and Oak: The Laundromat, 'night, Mother*, and *Traveler in the Dark*, demonstrating that the first three plays deal both with women's issues and more "global verities."

Kane, Leslie. "The Way Out, The Way In: Paths to Self in the Plays of Marsha Norman." In *Feminine Focus: The New Women Playwrights*. Edited by Enoch Brater. New York: Oxford UP, 1989. 255–274.

Kane discusses four of Norman's plays—*Getting Out, Third and Oak: The Laundromat, 'night, Mother*, and *Traveler in the Dark*—in relation to the problems of autonomy, "people struggling to have a self," and of "mothering" and "Norman's continuing concern with mother-child relationships." Kane demonstrates that "mothers in Norman's early plays provide neither protection nor guidance; they do not nourish with food or love." With *Traveler in the Dark*, Norman breaks new ground by creating a psychologically complex male protagonist and presenting "for the first time loving and supportive wives who are warm, affectionate mothers."

Keyssar, Helene. "Success and Its Limits: Mary O'Malley, Wendy Wasserstein, Nell Dunn, Beth Henley, Catherine Hayes, Marsha Norman." In *Feminist Theatre: An Introduction to Plays of Contemporary British and American Women*. New York: St. Martin's, 1984. 148–166.

Despite certain strengths of plays by the women in Keyssar's title, their main weakness is that "no matter how serious the topic, they are all comedies of manners, revelations of the surfaces of sexual identity and sexism." As mainstream plays, they take "fewer theatrical risks" than more feminist dramas. Keyssar praises *Getting Out* for forcing its audience to "rethink" the nature of the dramatic protagonist as double rather than "singular." On the other hand, she criticizes *'night, Mother* for dwelling on the "sheltered space of the family room" while neglecting "the real constraints outside." In addition, the commercial success of *'night, Mother* suggests that the "most appealing role for the audience continues to be that of the voyeur."

Kintz, Linda. "The Dramaturgy of the Subject(s): Refining the Deconstruction and
Construction of the Subject to Include Gender and Materiality." Ph.D. diss., U of Oregon, 1986.

McDonnell, Lisa J. "Diverse Similitude: Beth Henley and Marsha Norman." *Southern Quarterly* 25, no. 3 (1987): 95–104.

Claiming that Henley's plays are "theatrical" whereas Norman's are "literary," McDonnell compares the two playwrights' use of narrative, humor, and the family. She highlights Norman's "narrative gift of a very high order," illustrating how storytelling within her plays provides comic relief, creates horror, propels the plot, and reveals character. Each playwright views "stories as crucial purveyors of truth in an individual's quest for self-determination." Although each playwright relies on southern gothic humor, Henley's is "wild and outrageous" whereas Norman's is "dry and sardonic." Finally, Henley's vision of the family is more optimistic than Norman's, suggesting that self-actualization can occur within the family as a source of support. Norman expresses the opposite view, that personal identity can be obtained only outside the family circle.

McKenna, Suzanne. "*Getting Out*: The Impact of Female Consciousness on Dramaturgy." Ph.D. diss., U of Utah, 1986.

Miner, Madonne. "'What's These B'ars Doin' Here?'—The Impossi-
    bility of *Getting Out.*" *Theatre Annual* 40 (1985): 115–134.
In distancing herself from "the theatrics and fictionalizing" of Arlie,
Arlene adheres to an ideology of "self-determination," an ideology
that the play challenges. *Getting Out* reveals the ways Arlene is still a
prisoner on the "outside," her identity as Arlene assigned to her by
an Other, the prison chaplain, and her decision to go "straight" the
product of "authority's desires." Ironically, as the audience approves
of Arlene's rejection of Arlie, what is revealed is the audience's unconscious preference of the safety of autonomous selfhood rather
than the more uncomfortable condition of multiple selves: "We find
ourselves cheering for Arlene, because as she kills off Arlie, she
checks our own impulses to Arlie-behavior." Thus, *Getting Out*
"breaks from more mainstream twentieth-century drama, which valo-
rizes and protects tenaciously-held assumptions about the self."

Moore, Honor. "Woman Alone, Women Together." In *Women in
    American Theatre: Careers, Images, Movements.* Edited by
    Helen Krich Chinoy and Linda Walsh Jenkins. New York:
    Crown, 1981. 184–190. Reprinted in *Women in American The-
    atre.* 2nd ed. Edited by Helen Krich Chinoy and Linda Walsh
    Jenkins. New York: Theatre Communications Group, 1988.
    186–191.
Moore divides plays by women playwrights into two categories: "autonomous woman plays," which depict "one female protagonist, a
fragment of whose journey toward autonomy we share"; and "cho-
ral plays," which dramatize a group of women "seeking integration
by attempting community." Norman's *Getting Out* represents a type
of autonomous woman play whose protagonist is divided, indicating
a "conflict . . . between a self acceptable to (male) society and a savage self who cannot conform." Moore suggests that women identify
with both Arlie and Arlene, both the breaker of rules and the "other
who keeps that rule breaker in line."

Morrow, Laura. "Orality and Identity in *'night, Mother* and *Crimes
    of the Heart.*" *Studies in American Drama, 1945–Present* 3
    (1988): 23–39.
Morrow extensively analyzes food imagery and speech patterns as a
key to understanding the respectively tragic and comic outcomes of
'night, Mother and Beth Henley's *Crimes of the Heart,* which dramatizes the opposite scenario of three daughters coping with their
mother's suicide. She focuses on orality as a common denominator
in Norman's and Henley's works. In Thelma's case, her fixation on
sweets reveals her emotional immaturity and dependency on Jessie,
whereas her "counterfeiting obtuseness" through ceaseless chatter
makes her a "figure of tragic intensity" who consciously refuses to

"acknowledge unpleasant truth." In contrast, Jessie uses silence to "restrict others' access to her innermost self," and her oral fixation on cigarettes, the symbolic equivalent of suicide, provides her with a negative means of achieving control of her life.

Murray, Timothy. "Patriarchal Panopticism, or The Seduction of a
    Bad Joke: *Getting Out* in Theory." *Theatre Journal* 35 (1983):
    376–388.
Murray examines the ways *Getting Out* demonstrates a disruption between the panoptic, macho gaze of the institutional world of confinement and the creative, liberating force of Arlie's jokes. He equates the prison and its authority figures with the theater and its patrons; in each case, a voyeurism is at work in which the spectators judge Arlie's transformation into Arlene: "Does the audience experiment vicariously in a visual laboratory of power, control, and sadistic pleasure?" Murray suggests that the audience is caught in a double bind of desiring the promise of renewal affected by the system in its handling of Arlie/Arlene and realizing the need of Arlene "to be free of the macho world of control" as she indulges in mental replays of Arlie's cruel jokes.

Natalle, Elizabeth. "Feminist Theatre and the Women's Move-
    ment." In *Feminist Theatre: A Study in Persuasion*. Metuchen,
    NJ: Scarecrow, 1985. 113–129.
Natalle briefly mentions Marsha Norman and other mainstream women playwrights with a "feminist vision" in contrast with feminist playwrights working within purely feminist theaters. "The drama," she says, "written by individual playwrights who have no connections with a particular feminist group is intended as a very different kind of statement than the drama associated with a group of individuals who write, produce, and act in that drama." In this chapter, however, Natalle is chiefly concerned with the messages of feminist theater, along with its transition from radicalism toward a more inclusive humanism.

Nischik, Reingard M. "'Look Back in Gender': Beziehungskonstella-
    tionen in Dramen von Beth Henley und Marsha Norman—
    Einige Grundzuge des zeitgenossischen feministischen The-
    aters in den USA." *Anglistik & Englischunterricht* 35 (1988):
    61–89.
If one considers as a goal of feminist writing the abolition of the patriarchal social structure, then *'night, Mother* may barely be considered a feminist play. Nischik conducts a thematic analysis of *'night, Mother* and Henley's *Crimes of the Heart*, an analysis that considers the following questions: What picture of woman is sketched in these two successful plays by American women dramatists in the 1980s? In

what constellation of roles do women characters appear? To what extent are they impaired because of these roles? Which characteristics of these works are typical of contemporary feminist theater in the United States? He concludes that *Crimes of the Heart* may better be defended as a feminist play than *'night, Mother.*

Patraka, Vivian M. "Staging Memory: Contemporary Plays by
    Women." *Michigan Quarterly Review* 26 (1987): 285–292.
Patraka reviews two groups of contemporary plays by women dramatists, one group "linking women's memory to women's history— be it emotional, economic, political, or mythic," the second group focusing on "women's collective memory" or "the history of women's expectations." She considers *'night, Mother* as a member of this second group, seeing that the play presents "in part the struggle of memories between a mother and a daughter concerning their concept of and relationship to the deceased father." She relates Norman's drama to Joanna Glass' *Play Memory*, which also dramatizes a daughter's memory of her deceased father.

Pevitts, Beverly Byers. "Feminist Thematic Trends in Plays Written
    by Women for the American Theatre: 1970–1979." Ph.D. diss.
    Southern Illinois U at Carbondale, 1980.

Piazza, Roberta. "A Conversational Analysis of Theatrical Dis-
    course: Repair Procedures as the Expression of Dramatic Inter-
    action." Ph.D. diss. Columbia Teachers College, 1987.

Porter, Laurin R. "Women Re-Conceived: Changing Perceptions of
    Women in Contemporary American Drama." *Conference of
    College Teachers of English Studies* 54 (1989): 53–59.
Porter focuses on Henley's *Crimes of the Heart*, John Pielmeier's *Agnes of God*, and *'night, Mother* as indicators of the ways contemporary dramas depicting women reflect cultural concerns. She identifies two primary characteristics of these plays: the presentation of all-female families and the concentration on the mother-daughter relationship. These plays represent a positive change in the culture inasmuch as they dramatize women who "do not need to define themselves in terms of men" and insist upon "the importance and value of the mother-daughter nexus and its centrality in our lives."

Scharine, Richard G. "Caste Iron Bars: Marsha Norman's *Getting
    Out* as Political Theatre." In *Women in Theatre: Themes in
    Drama*. Vol. 11. Edited by James Redmond. Cambridge,
    England: Cambridge UP, 1989. 185–198.
Describing women as "the true invisible caste," Scharine draws on studies of the oppression of women in America to illuminate the po-

litical content of *Getting Out*. The play is an example of "political theatre," a genre that "shows public policy, laws, or unquestioned social codes impinging unfairly and destructively upon private lives," for example, the life of Arlene Holsclaw. As a political drama, *Getting Out* blames the "system": "The factors that mitigate against Arlene taking charge of her life must be seen as flaws in the social system and not as purely personal problems." In Arlie/Arlene's case, these factors include child abuse and "a sexually discriminating legal system." Scharine labels *Getting Out* "an economic primer for American women," who may see their concerns as lower-caste U.S. citizens reflected in the condition of Arlie/Arlene.

———. "Getting Out." *From Class to Caste in American Drama: Political and Social Themes Since the 1930s*. New York: Greenwood Press, 1991. 219–227.
The above argument is couched in a chapter concerning issues of gender in American drama, including African-American feminism and gay civil rights.

Schroeder, Patricia R. "Locked Behind the Proscenium: Feminist Strategies in *Getting Out* and *My Sister in This House*." *Modern Drama* 32 (1989): 104–114.
When a feminist theater, in opposition to male-dominated theater, restricts itself to nonlinear, nontraditional forms, the result is self-defeating: "an undeviating separatism of dramatic forms can only mean that fewer feminist concerns will be dramatised, fewer audiences will be reached, and feminist playwrights . . . will be left unheard." Norman's *Getting Out* and Wendy Kesselman's *My Sister in This House* provide Schroeder with examples of "flexible realism" by women playwrights, dramas that address feminist concerns while appealing to mainstream audiences. Although *Getting Out* follows a "chronological plot" and contains "conventional dialogue," the play addresses the feminist problem of a woman's "imprisonment in limited and limiting social roles." The device of the split character illustrates a "fragmentation of personality that is the result of [Arlie/Arlene's] oppression," and the play promotes women's experience as Arlene discovers "the importance of female bonding."

Simon, John. "Theatre Chronicle: Kopit, Norman, and Shepard." *Hudson Review* 32 (1979): 77–88.
Simon provides a scene analysis of the initial New York production of *Getting Out*, which along with Kopit's *Wings* and Shepard's *Buried Child* he considers as one of "the three best plays of the season so far." He calls attention to the dramatic effectiveness of Norman's language, her use of "evasions, understatements, and silences. Miss Norman has that essential dramatist's gift of letting the unsaid speak

for itself." He also describes Norman's humor as "not a writer's wit that is superimposed on the characters; it is an earthy humor that stays very much in character." Assessing all three plays, Simon sees that "language is the least important element," that each play is meant to be performed rather than read. In addition, all three deal with "split personalities," prompting Simon to ask: "has the recession of the word caused the loss of a sense of full, unified selfhood? Or is it the other way round?"

Smith, Raynette Halvorsen. " 'night, Mother and True West: Mirror
    Images of Violence and Gender." In Violence in Drama:
    Themes in Drama. Vol. 13. Edited by James Redmond.
    Cambridge, England: Cambridge UP, 1991. 277–289.
Responding to feminist critics who see no feminism in Shepard's work and only "stereotypical feminine masochism" in Norman's, Smith concentrates on the issue of gender definition in each play as a feminist concern: "violence is seen as the agent for the transformation out of . . . . [Mama's or Mom's] domesticity to freedom, autonomy, and individualism." Drawing upon Freudian theories of gender in relation to the mother, Smith considers how separation from the mother for the female is psychologically "more complicated" than for the male. Jessie's suicide becomes a tragedy representative of women in American culture who suffer anorexia and agoraphobia as extreme means of gaining control over the self.

Spencer, Jenny S. "Marsha Norman's She-tragedies." In Making a
    Spectacle: Feminist Essays on Contemporary Women's The-
    atre. Edited by Lynda Hart. Ann Arbor: Michigan UP, 1989.
    147–165.
Resurrecting the eighteenth-century generic term "she-tragedy," Spencer applies it to three of Norman's plays that "focus on female characters, address a female audience, and foreground issues of female identity": Getting Out, Third and Oak: The Laundromat, and 'night, Mother. She considers the ways Norman develops a modern form of "she-tragedy," focusing on the importance of conversation as action in Norman's work, the dialogue between women underscoring the "problem of female autonomy." Just as in eighteenth-century "she-tragedies," whichæ dramatize "the character's potentially pathetic situation," Norman's dramas indicate the extent to which women in society are still manipulated and controlled within a patriarchal system: "We are asked to consider the ways in which male misrecognition itself shapes and determines female subjectivity."

————. "Norman's 'night, Mother: Psycho-drama of the Female
    Identity." Modern Drama 30 (1987): 364–375.
Spencer assesses audience response to 'night, Mother along gen-

der lines, determining that males may view the play in a detached manner as "relatively predictable," whereas female viewers will be caught up in the "representation of repressed infantile complexes" peculiar to the mother-daughter relationship, with its issues of "feminine identity and female autonomy." Exploring the Freudian psychodynamics of Jessie's relationship to Mama, she concludes that these dynamics make the play "aesthetically over-distanced for men (producing indifference) and aesthetically under-distanced for women (producing pain)."

Steadman, Susan M. "Marsha Norman." In *Notable Women in the American Theatre: A Biographical Dictionary.* Edited by Vera Mowry Roberts, Milly S. Barranger, and Alice M. Robinson. Fredericksburg, VA: U Publications of America, 1988. 691–695.

Wattenberg, Richard. "Feminizing the Frontier Myth: Marsha Norman's *The Holdup.*" *Modern Drama* 33 (1990): 507–517.
In *The Holdup,* Norman creates a feminist version of the traditional American myth of the frontier, a version that promotes maturation over adolescent violence. Her play avoids the "synthesis" of "Eastern civilization and Western savagery" typical of late nineteenth- and early twentieth- century dramas set in the West. Instead, "Norman presents Western savage violence as a self-destructive delusion that can and must be transcended." She resolves a tension that Shepard leaves open-ended at the end of *True West,* whose two brothers, one representing the civilized east and the other the primitive West, anticipate Norman's structural use of two similar brothers in *The Holdup.*

Wertheim, Albert. "Eugene O'Neill's *Days without End* and the Tradition of the Split Character in Modern American and British Drama." *Eugene O'Neill Newsletter* 6 (Winter 1982): 5–9.
O'Neill's *Days without End* is a progenitor of contemporary American and British dramas, including *Getting Out,* dramatizing the "inner voice" through use of a second actor. Whereas the doubling device in *Days without End* was unjustly criticized in its day as "a gimmick," the same device has been praised by critics of Adrienne Kennedy's *Funnyhouse of a Negro,* Hugh Leonard's *Da* and *A Life,* and Peter Nichols' *Forget-Me-Not-Lane.* Wertheim suggests that *Getting Out* "marries the psychological, spiritual and philosophical divisions explored by . . . O'Neill and Kennedy with the chronological divisions presented by Leonard and Nichols." *Getting Out* is unusual because the Arlene/Arlie split is both one of time (with a current self engaging a former self) and one of dialectic (as each self represents a conflicting impulse). Although Wertheim identifies echoes of *Days without End* within *Getting Out,* a claim for direct influence would require further evidence.

Contributors

Marya Bednerik is a stage director and professor of theater at Kent State University. She directed David Cohen's *Baby Grand* for the Charleston Premiere Theatre at the Piccolo Spoleto Festival and Don Nigro's *The Girlhood of Shakespeare's Heroines* for the Circle Repertory Lab in New York. Her recent article, "Some Particular Pursuits: The Double Fiction of Simon Gray," appears in *Simon Gray: A Casebook*, edited by Katherine H. Burkman.

Linda Ginter Brown is an assistant professor of humanities at the University of Cincinnati, where she teaches writing and literature. Her interests include biblical images of women in literature and mother/daughter relationships in contemporary literature. Her doctoral dissertation focused upon women in the works of Marsha Norman and Lillian Hellman.

Robert Brustein is a professor of English at Harvard University. An established drama critic, Professor Brustein is also associated with Actors' Repertory Theater.

Katherine H. Burkman is a professor of English at Ohio State University. A Pinter scholar, she has published *Simon Gray: A Casebook* as well as numerous articles. She is the creator of Women at Play, a dramatic workshop group.

Gretchen Cline teaches literature and writing at Ohio University at Lancaster. She also conducts workshops on creative journal writing, art appreciation, and women's issues at Ohio University at Lancaster and the Cultural Arts Center in Columbus. Her writing examines the "dysfunctional" family in selected modern plays from feminist and psychoanalytic frameworks.

Robert Conklin is a tutor at Yavapai Community College in Prescott, Arizona. He has published articles on drama and American literature in *West Virginia University Philological Papers* and the *Pinter Review*.

Robert Cooperman is a doctoral student in English at Ohio State University, where he is a modern drama specialist. He has been represented in the *Eugene O'Neill Review* as well as the *Bulletin of Bibliography*, and his essay on Lanford Wilson's Talley trilogy appears in *Lanford Wilson: A Casebook* (Garland). He has also published *Clifford Odets: An Annotated Bibliography, 1935-1989*. He is working on an article concerning the plays of David Henry Hwang for *Staging Difference: Cultural Pluralism in American Theatre and Drama*. Mr. Cooperman's own plays have been produced in New York City and Columbus, Ohio.

Anne Marie Drew is an associate professor of the English Department at the United States Naval Academy. She is the editor of *Past Crimson, Past Woe: The Shakespeare-Beckett Connection* (Garland, 1993). Her work has appeared in *Comparative Literature Studies*, *Theatre Journal*, and *Theatre Studies*. She has published a children's novel, *Rainbows in the Twelfth Row* (Trillium Press, 1991), and a volume of dramatic readings, *The Innkeeper's Wife and Four Other Dramatic Readings for Christmas* (Abingdon, 1990). She is the scriptwriter for *Legends and Letters*, a radio program funded by the National Endowment for the Humanities. She has served as dramaturge for the Indianapolis Shakespeare Festival and is presently director of Masqueraders, the USNA theatre group.

Grace Epstein is an assistant professor at Stephens College, where she teaches literature and composition. Her manuscript *Textual Hysteria: Female Desire, Narrative and Resistance in the Feminist Novel,* which deals with the work of Toni Morrison, Margaret Atwood, Doris Lessing, and Marguerite Duras is under consideration by Northern Illinois University Press. Dr. Epstein has also published on the work of Harold Pinter.

Claire R. Fried received her master's degree from Ohio State University and is currently studying law at Duke University.

Scott Hinson is a visiting assistant professor of English at Wittenberg University; where he teaches literature and writing. His scholarly interests focus upon twentieth-century American literature as well as contemporary drama.

John Kundert-Gibbs' doctoral work uses his earlier studies in science and philosophy as a means to probe the inner workings of representative Beckett plays. Publications include "Power Play in Kafka's *The Trial* and Pinter's *Victoria Station,*" appearing in *Pinter at 60,* which he coedited with Katherine Burkman; and "Ohio Impromptu a Zen Koan," in *Comparative Drama.* A practicing playwright, he has had several plays produced at Ohio State.

Lisa Tyler is an assistant professor of English at Sinclair Community College in Dayton, Ohio. She received her Ph.D. from Ohio State University, where she wrote a dissertation on mother-daughter relationships and myth in twentieth-century British literature by women. Her essays have appeared in *Hemingway Review, Doris Lessing Newsletter, Children's Literature Association Quarterly,* and *Studies in Short Fiction.*

Index

Series List

Casebooks on Modern Dramatists

Kimball King, General Editor

Sam Shepard
A Casebook
edited by Kimball King

David Storey
A Casebook
edited by William Hutchings

Caryl Churchill
A Casebook
edited by Phyllis R. Randall

Peter Shaffer
A Casebook
edited by C.J. Gianakaras

Christopher Hampton
A Casebook
edited by Robert Gross

David Mamet
A Casebook
edited by Leslie Kane

Harold Pinter
A Casebook
edited by Lois Gordon

Simon Gray
A Casebook
edited by Katherine H. Burkman

Lanford Wilson
A Casebook
edited by Jackson R. Bryer

David Hare
A Casebook
edited by Hersh Zeifman

Howard Brenton
A Casebook
edited by Ann Wilson

August Wilson
A Casebook
edited by Marilyn Elkins